AF675237

CLASSIC TEXTS SERIES

THE ELEMENTS OF STATICS AND DYNAMICS

PART 2 DYNAMICS

SL LONEY

arihant

SUCCESS AND NOTHING LESS

arihant
SUCCESS AND NOTHING LESS

ARIHANT PRAKASHAN (Series), MEERUT

卐 **Administrative & Production Offices**

Regd. Office

'Ramchhaya' 4577/15, Agarwal Road, Darya Ganj, New Delhi -110002
Tele: 011- 47630600, 43518550

卐 **Head Office**

Kalindi, TP Nagar, Meerut (UP) - 250002
Tel: 0121-7156203, 7156204

卐 **Sales & Support Offices**

Agra, Ahmedabad, Bengaluru, Bareilly, Chennai, Delhi, Guwahati, Hyderabad, Jaipur, Jhansi, Kolkata, Lucknow, Nagpur & Pune.

卐 **PRICE** ₹140.00

卐 **PO No :** TXT-59-T064080-03-25

Published by Arihant Publications (India) Ltd.

For further information about the books published by Arihant, log on to www.arihantbooks.com or e-mail at info@arihantbooks.com

Follow us on

PREFACE

The present book forms Part II. of The Elements of Statics and Dynamics, of which Part I. (statics) has Already been published.

It aims at being useful for schools and the less advanced students of Colleges; the examples are, in consequence, large in number, and generally of a numerical and easy character. Except in two articles and a few examples at the end of the Chapter on Projectiles, it is only presumed that the student has a knowledge of Elementary Geometry and Algebra, and of the Elements of Trigonometry.

It is suggested that, on a first reading of the subjects, all articles marked with an asterisk should be omitted.

Part I. and part II. are, as far as is possible, independent of one another; hence, any teacher, who wishes his pupils to commence with Dynamics, may take Part II. before Part I., by omitting an occasional article which refers to statics.

Any corrections of mistakes, or hints for improvement will be gratefully received.

SL LONEY

BARNES, SW

PREFACE

To The Third Edition...

It having become desirable to re-set the type for a new Edition, I have taken the opportunity of thoroughly over-hauling the whole book. Its general scope is unaltered, but I have introduced more graphical and experimental work; I have, however, confined myself to experiments that Van be arranged by a teacher with the simplest of apparatus in an ordinary class-room

For two new figures on Pages 106 and 133 I am indebted to the kindness of Dr R.T. Glazebrook, who allowed me to make use of blocks prepared for his mechanics.

I hope that the additions that have been made will add to the usefulness of the book.

SL LONEY

Royal Holloway College,
Englefield Green, Surrey.

To The Fourth Edition...

This standard work is widely used throughout India and since it was last revised in 1906 considerable changes have been made in the courses of studies in Mathematics in the Indian universities. The Decimal currency and the metric System of Weights and Measures have been adopted and it turns out that the major portion of the courses in Mathematics should cover problems and exercises in the new units. Accordingly this revised edition is brought out introducing the problems in M.K.S. system. Ex.2. on page 79 has been retained intentionally as an example in FPS units and for conventional working with Horsepower as a unit.

In addition some materials from the authors An Elementary treatise on the Dynamics of a Particle and Rigid Bodies involving elementary use of Calculus are included in the new edition. A short introductory chapter on Vectors is also added. These are incorporated in order to cover the requirements to the students.

THE EDITOR

CONTENTS

1

Velocity

1. If at any instant the position of a moving point be P, and at any subsequent instant it be Q, then PQ is the change in its position in the intervening time.

A point is said to be in motion when it changes its position. The path of a moving point is the curve drawn through all the successive positions of the point.

2. Speed. Def. *The speed of a moving point is the rate at which it describes its path.*

A point is said to be moving with uniform speed when it moves through equal lengths of its path in equal times, however small these times may be.

Suppose a train describes 60 km in each of several consecutive hours. We are not justified in saying that its speed is uniform unless we know that it describes one kilometre in *each* minute, $16\frac{2}{3}$ m in *each* second one-millionth of 60 km in *each* one-millionth of an hour, and so on.

When uniform, the speed of a point is measured by the distance passed over by it in a unit of time; when variable, by the distance which would be passed over by the point in a unit of time, if it continued to move during that unit of time with the speed which it has at the instant under consideration.

By saying that a train is moving with a speed of 64 km an hour, we do not mean that it has gone 64 km in the last hour, or that it will go 64 km in the next hour, but that, if its speed remained constant for one hour, then it would describe 64 km in that hour.

When the speed of a point is not uniform, it may be measured at any instant as follows; take the distance s that it describes in the next tenth of a second; then the quantity $\frac{s}{\frac{1}{10}}$, i.e., $\frac{\text{space described}}{\text{time taken}}$, is an approximation to the speed required.

For a nearer approximation, let s_1 be the distance described by it in the one-hundredth of a second which follows the moment considered; then $\frac{s_1}{\frac{1}{100}}$, i.e., $\frac{\text{space described}}{\text{time taken}}$, is a nearer approximation. A still nearer approximation is $\frac{s_2}{\frac{1}{1000}}$, where s_2 is the distance described in the one-thousandth of a second which follows the moment under consideration; and so on, the time being taken smaller and smaller. By this means we obtain a definite notion of the varying velocity at any instant.

In mathematical language this conception amounts to the following : *Let s be the length of the portion of the path described by a moving point in the small time t following the instant under consideration; then the ultimate value of* $\frac{s}{t}$, *as the time t is taken smaller and smaller, is the measure of the speed of the moving point at the instant under consideration.*

In a similar way the **rate of change** of any quantity (be it money, population of a country, or speed or anything else whose change can be measured) is the ratio of the change in that quantity to the small time in which the change occurs.

3. The units of length and time usually employed in England are a foot and a second.

A foot is the third part of a yard. A yard is defined to be the distance between the centres of two small gold plugs inserted in a solid brass bar which is kept at West-minster.

*A day, i.e., the time taken by the Earth to rotate once on its axis, is divided into 24 hours, each hour into 60 minutes and each minute into 60 seconds. Hence the definition of a second.

In scientific measurements the unit of length generally used is the centimetre, which is the one hundredth part of a metre. A metre was meant to be defined as one ten-millionth part of a quadrant of the Earth's surface, i.e., of the distance from the North Pole to the Equator. In practice it is the length of a certain platinum bar kept in Paris.

One metre = 39.37 inches approximately, and therefore a foot

= 30.48 centimetres nearly.

A decimetre is $\frac{1}{10}$th, and a millimetre $\frac{1}{1000}$ th of a metre.

4. The unit of speed is the speed of a point which moves uniformly over a unit of length in a unit of time. Hence the unit of speed depends on these two units, and if either, or both of them, be altered, the unit of speed will also, in general, be altered.

5. If a point be moving with speed *u*, then in each unit of time the point moves over *u* units of length.

Hence in *t* units of time the point passes over $u.\,t$ units of length.

Hence the distance *s* passed over by a point which moves with speed *u* for time *t* is given by $s = u.t$.

It is easy to change a velocity expressed in one set of units to other units. For instance a velocity of 60 km per hour is equivalent to

1 km per minute,

or $\frac{1}{60}$ km per second,

*The day referred to is a sidereal day. In practice the system of mean solar day (civil day) is used.

or $\frac{1000}{60}$ m per second,

i.e., $16\frac{2}{3}$ m per second.

Ex. 1. Show that the speed of the centre of the earth is about 29.6 km per second, assuming that it describes a circle of radius 1.488×10^8 km in 365 days.

Ex. 2. Show that the speed of light is about 310,400 km per second assuming that it takes 8 minutes to describe the distance from the sun to the earth.

6. Displacement. The displacement of a moving point is its change of position. To know the displacement of a moving point, we must know both the length and the direction of the line joining the two positions of the moving point. Hence the displacement of a point involves both magnitude and direction.

Ex. 1. A man walks 6 km due east and then 8 km due north; show that his displacement is 10 km at an angle $\tan^{-1}\frac{4}{3}$ north of east.

Ex. 2. A ship sails 2 km due south and then 2 km west; show that its displacement is 2 km in a direction $\tan^{-1}\frac{1}{2}$ west of south.

Ex. 3. A vessel proceeded as follows, all the angles being reckoned from the north towards the east; 10 km at 225°, 12 north, 2 at 90°, 6 at 135°, 8 at 300°. The time taken was 2 hours, and the tide was flowing from east to west at the rate of 6 km per hour. Show graphically that the true distance between the initial and final positions of the vessel is about 18.36 km and that it had moved towards the west a distance of 17.76 km approximately.

7. Velocity. Def. *The velocity of a moving point is the rate of its displacement.*

A velocity therefore possesses both magnitude and direction.

A point is said to be moving with uniform velocity, when it is moving in a constant direction and passes over equal lengths in equal times, however small these times may be.

When uniform, the velocity of a moving point is measured by its displacement per unit of time; when variable, it is measured, at any instant, by the displacement that the moving point would have in a unit of time, if it moved during that unit of time with the velocity which it has at the instant under consideration.

As in Art. 2, the velocity of a moving point, when not uniform, may be obtained by finding its displacements in the next $\frac{1}{10}, \frac{1}{100}, \frac{1}{1000}$ ... of a second after the moment considered, and we thus obtain approximations gradually getting nearer and nearer and nearer to the measure required.

Mathematically, *if d be the displacement of the point in the small time t following the instant under consideration, then the ultimate value of* $\frac{d}{t}$, *as t is taken smaller and smaller, is the velocity at the instant under consideration.*

8. It will be noted that when the moving point is moving in a straight line, the velocity is the same as the speed.

If the motion be not in a straight line the velocity is not the same as the speed. For example, suppose a point to be describing a circle uniformly, so that it passes over equal lengths of the arc in equal times however small; then its direction of motion (viz., the tangent to the circle) is different at different points of the circumference; hence in this case the *velocity* of the point (strictly so called) is variable, whilst its *speed* is constant.

9. The magnitude of the unit of velocity is the velocity of a point which undergoes a displacement equal to a unit of length in a unit of time.

When we say that a moving point has velocity v, we mean that it possesses v units of velocity, i.e., that it would undergo a displacement, equal to v units of length, in the unit of time.

If the velocity of a moving point in one direction be denoted by v, an equal velocity in an opposite direction is necessarily denoted by $-v$.

The expression m/sec. is by some writers used to denote a velocity of one metre per second. Thus "a velocity of 3 m/sec." means "a velocity of 3 m per second." So "a velocity of 10 cm/sec." means "a velocity of 10 centimetres per second." 10 cm/sec. is also written 10 $cm.s^{-1}$.

10. Since the velocity of a point is known when its direction and magnitude are both known, we can conveniently represent the velocity of a moving point by a straight line AB; thus, when we say that the velocities of two moving points are represented in magnitude and direction by the straight lines AB and CD, we mean that they move in directions parallel to the lines drawn from A to B, and C to D respectively, and with velocities which are proportional to the lengths AB and CD.

11. A body may have simultaneously velocities in two, or more, different directions. One of the simplest examples of this is when a person walks on the deck of a moving ship from one point of the deck to another. He has one motion with the ship, and another along the deck of the ship, and his motion in space is clearly different from what it would have been had either the ship remained at rest, or had the man stayed at his original position on the deck.

Again, consider the case of a ship steaming with its bow pointing in a constant direction, say due north, whilst a current carries it in a different direction, say south-east, and suppose a sailor is climbing a vertical mast of the ship. The actual change of position and the velocity of the sailor clearly depend on three quantities, viz., the rate and direction of the ship's sailing, the rate and direction of the current, and the rate at which he climbs the mast. His actual velocity is said to be "compounded" of these three velocities.

In the following article we show how to find the velocity which is equivalent to or compounded of, two velocities given in magnitude and direction.

12. Theorem. Parallelogram of Velocities. *If a moving point possess simultaneously velocities which are represented in magnitude and direction by the* *two sides of a parallelogram drawn from a point, they are equivalent to a velocity which is represented in magnitude and direction by the diagonal of the parallelogram passing through the point.*

Let the two simultaneous velocities be represented by the lines *AB* and *AC*, and let their magnitudes be *u* and *v*.

Complete the parallelogram *BACD*.

Then we may imagine the motion of the point to be along the line *AB* with the velocity *u*, whilst the line *AB* moves parallel to the foot of the page so that its end *A* describes the line *AC* with velocity *v*. In the unit of time the moving point will have moved through a distance *AB* along the line *AB*, and the line *AB* will have in the same time moved into the position *CD*, so that at the end of the unit of time the moving point will be at *D*.

Now, since the two coexistent velocities are constant in magnitude and direction, the velocity of the point from *A* to *D* must also be constant in magnitude and direction; hence *AD* is the path described by the moving point in the unit of time.

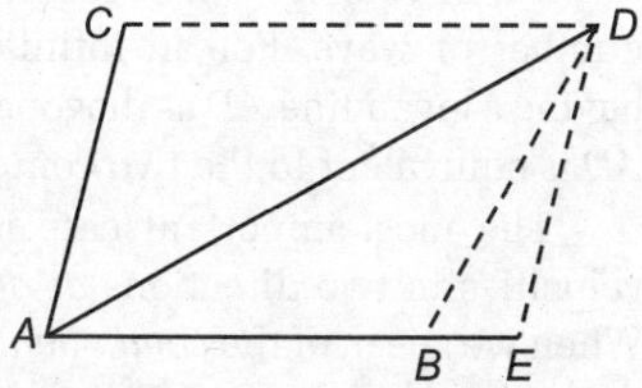

Hence *AD* represents in magnitude and direction the velocity which is equivalent to the velocities represented by *AB* and *AC*.

To facilitate his understanding of the previous article the student may look on *AC* as the direction of motion of a steamer, whilst *AB* is a chalked line, drawn along the deck of the ship, along which a man is walking at a uniform rate.

13. Def. *The velocity which is equivalent to two or more velocities is called their* **resultant**, *and these velocities are called the* **components** *of this resultant.*

The resultant of two velocities *u* and *v* in directions which are inclined to one another at a given angle α may be easily obtained.

In the figure of Art. 12, let *AB* and *AC* represent the velocities *u* and *v*, so that the angle *BAC* is α.

Then we have, by Trigonometry,

$$AD^2 = AB^2 + BD^2 - 2AB \cdot BD \cos ABD.$$

Hence, if we represent the resultant velocity *AD* by *w*, we have

$$w^2 = u^2 + v^2 + 2uv\cos\alpha, \text{ since } \angle ABD = \pi - \alpha.$$

Also, if we denote the angle *BAD* by θ, we have

$$\frac{AB}{BD} = \frac{\sin ADB}{\sin BAD} = \frac{\sin DAC}{\sin BAD};$$

$$\therefore \qquad \frac{u}{v} = \frac{\sin(\alpha - \theta)}{\sin\theta} = \frac{\sin\alpha\cos\theta - \cos\alpha\sin\theta}{\sin\theta}$$

$$= \sin\alpha\cot\theta - \cos\alpha$$

$$\therefore \qquad \cot\theta = \frac{u + v\cos\alpha}{v\sin\alpha},$$

so that

$$\tan\theta = \frac{v\sin\alpha}{u + v\cos\alpha}.$$

Hence the resultant of two velocities u and v inclined to one another at an angle α, is a velocity $\sqrt{u^2 + v^2 + 2uv\cos\alpha}$ *inclined at an angle* $\tan^{-1}\dfrac{v\sin\alpha}{u + v\cos\alpha}$ *to the direction of the velocity u.*

The direction of the resultant velocity may also be obtained as follows; draw *DE* perpendicular to *AB* to meet it, produced if necessary, in *E*; we then have

$$\tan DAB = \frac{ED}{AE} = \frac{BD\sin EBD}{AB + BD\cos EBD}$$

$$= \frac{v\sin\alpha}{u + v\cos\alpha}.$$

14. A velocity can be resolved into two component velocities in an infinite number of ways. For an infinite number of parallelograms can be described having a given line *AD* as diagonal; and, if *ABDC* by *any* one of these, the velocity *AD* is equivalent to the two component velocities *AB* and *AC*.

The most important case is when a velocity is to be resolved into two velocities in two directions *at right angles,* one of these directions being given. When we speak of the *component of a velocity in a given direction* it is understood that the other direction in which the given velocity is to be resolved is perpendicular to this given direction.

Thus, suppose we wish to resolve a velocity *u*, represented by *AD*, into two components at right angles to one another, one of these components being along a line *AB* making an angle θ with *AD*.

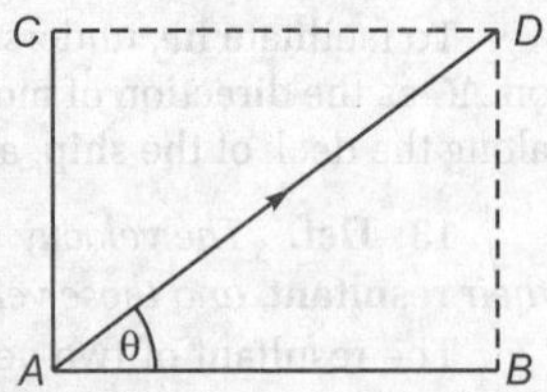

Draw *DB* perpendicular to *AB*, and complete the rectangle *ABDC*.

Then the velocity *AD* is equivalent to the two component velocities *AB* and *AC*.

Also $$AB = AD\cos\theta = u\cos\theta,$$

and $$AC = BD = AD\sin\theta = u\sin\theta.$$

We thus have the following important

Theorem. *A velocity u is equivalent to a velocity u cos θ along a line making an angle θ with its own direction together with a velocity u sin θ perpendicular to the direction of the first component.*

The case in which the angle θ is greater than a right angle may be considered as in Statics, Art. 30.

Ex. 1. A man is walking in a north-easterly direction with a velocity of 8 km per hour; find the components of his velocity in directions due north and due east respectively.

Ans. Each is $4\sqrt{2}$ km per hour.

Ex. 2. A point is moving in a straight line with a velocity of 10 m per second; find the component of its velocity in a direction inclined at an angle of 30° to its direction of motion.

Ans. $5\sqrt{3}$ m per second.

Ex. 3. A body is sliding down an inclined plane whose inclination to the horizontal is 60°; find the components of its velocity in the horizontal and vertical directions.

Ans. $\frac{u}{2}$ and $u\frac{\sqrt{3}}{2}$, where u is the velocity of the body.

15. *Components of a velocity in two given directions.*

If we wish to find the components of a velocity u in two given directions making angles α and β with it, we proceed as follows.

Let AD represent u in magnitude and direction. Draw AB and AC making angles α and β with it, and through D draw parallels to complete the parallelogram $ABDC$ as in Art. 12. Since the sides of a triangle are proportional to the sines of the opposite angles, we have

$$\frac{AB}{\sin ADB} = \frac{BD}{\sin BAD} = \frac{AD}{\sin ABD},$$

i.e.,
$$\frac{AB}{\sin\beta} = \frac{BD}{\sin\alpha} = \frac{AD}{\sin(\alpha+\beta)},$$

$$\therefore \quad AB = AD\frac{\sin\beta}{\sin(\alpha+\beta)}, \text{ and } BD = AD\frac{\sin\alpha}{\sin(\alpha+\beta)}.$$

Hence the component velocities in these two directions are

$$u\frac{\sin\beta}{\sin(\alpha+\beta)} \text{ and } u\frac{\sin\alpha}{\sin(\alpha+\beta)}.$$

16. Triangle of Velocities. *If a moving point possesses simultaneously velocities represented by the two sides AB and BC of a triangle taken in order, they are equivalent to a velocity represented by AC.*

For, completing the parallelogram $ABCD$, the lines AB and BC represent the same velocities as AB and AD and hence have as their resultant the velocity represented by AC.

Cor. 1. If there be simultaneously impressed on a point three velocities represented by the sides of a triangle taken in order, the point will be at rest.

Cor. 2. If a moving point possesses velocities represented by $\lambda \cdot OA$ and $\mu \cdot OB$, they are equivalent to a velocity $(\lambda+\mu).OG$, where G is a point on AB such that

$$\lambda \cdot AG = \mu \cdot GB.$$

For, by the triangle of velocities, the velocity $\lambda \cdot OA$ is equivalent to velocities $\lambda \cdot OG$ and $\lambda \cdot GA$; also the velocity $\mu \cdot OB$ is equivalent to $\mu \cdot OG$ and $\mu \cdot GB$; but the velocities $\lambda \cdot GA$ and $\mu \cdot GB$ destroy one another; hence the resultant velocity is $(\lambda+\mu)\cdot OG$.

17. Parallelopiped of Velocities. By a proof similar to that for the parallelogram of velocities, it may be shown that the resultant of three velocities represented by the three edges of a parallelopiped meeting in a point, is a velocity represented by the diagonal of the parallelopiped passing through that angular point. Conversely, a velocity may be resolved into three others.

18. Polygon of Velocities. If a moving point possess simultaneously velocities represented by the sides, $AB, BC, CD, \ldots KL$ of a polygon (whether the sides of the polygon are, or are not, in one plane), the resultant velocity is represented by AL.

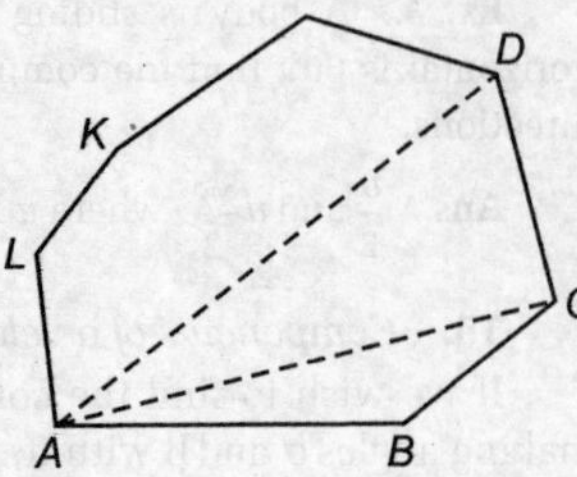

For, by Art. 16, the velocities AB and BC are equivalent to that represented by AC; and again the velocities AC and CD to AD, and so on; so that the final velocity is represented by AL.

Cor. If the point L coincides with A (so that the polygon is a closed figure) the resultant velocity vanishes, and the point is at rest.

19. When a point possesses simultaneously velocities in several different directions in the same plane, their resultant may be found by resolving the velocities along two fixed directions at right angles, and then compounding the resultant velocities in these directions.

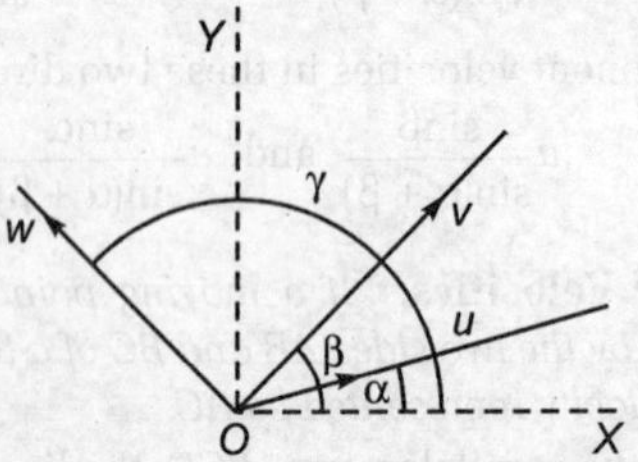

Suppose a point possesses velocities $u, v, w, \ldots$ in directions inclined at angles $\alpha, \beta, \gamma, \ldots$ to a fixed line OX, and let OY be perpendicular to OX. The components of u along OX and OY are respectively $u\cos\alpha$ and $u\sin\alpha$; the components of v are $v\cos\beta$ and $v\sin\beta$; and so for the others.

Hence the velocities are equivalent to

$$u\cos\alpha + v\cos\beta + w\cos\gamma \ldots \text{ parallel to } OX$$

and $$u\sin\alpha + v\sin\beta + w\sin\gamma \ldots \text{ parallel to } OY.$$

If their resultant be a velocity V at an angle θ to OX, we must have

$$V\cos\theta = u\cos\alpha + v\cos\beta + w\cos\gamma + \ldots,$$

and $$V\sin\theta = u\sin\alpha + v\sin\beta + w\sin\gamma + \ldots$$

Hence, by squaring and adding,

$$V^2 = (u\cos\alpha + v\cos\beta + \ldots)^2 + (u\sin\alpha + v\sin\beta + \ldots)^2;$$

and, by division, $\tan\theta = \dfrac{u\sin\alpha + v\sin\beta + \ldots}{u\cos\alpha + v\cos\beta + \ldots}$

These two equations give V and θ.

Examples. I.

1. *A vessel steams with its bow pointed due north with a velocity of* 15 *km an hour, and is carried by a current which flows in a south-easterly direction at the rate of* $3\sqrt{2}$ *km per hour. At the end of an hour find its distance and bearing from the point from which it started.*

The ship has two velocities, one being 15 km per hour northwards, and the other $3\sqrt{2}$ km per hour south-east.

Now the latter velocity is equivalent to

$3\sqrt{2}\cos 45°$, that is, 3 km per hour eastward,

and $3\sqrt{2}\sin 45°$, that is 3 km per hour southward.

Hence the total velocity of the ship is 12 km per hour northwards and 3 km per hour eastward.

Hence its resultant velocity is $\sqrt{12^2 + 3^2}$, i.e., $\sqrt{153}$ km per hour in a direction inclined at an angle $\tan^{-1}\frac{1}{4}$ to the north, i.e., 12.37 km per hour at 14°2′ east of north.

2. *A point possesses simultaneously velocities whose measures are* 4, 3, 2 *and* 1; *the angle between the first and second is* 30°, *between the second and third* 90°, *and between the third and fourth* 120°; *find their resultant.*

Take OX along the direction of the first velocity and OY perpendicular to it.

The angles which the velocities make with OX are respectively 0°, 30°, 120°, and 240°.

Hence, if V be the resultant velocity inclined at an angle θ to OX, we have

$$V\cos\theta = 4 + 3\cos 30° + 2\cos 120° + 1.\cos 240°;$$

and $$V\sin\theta = 3\sin 30° + 2\sin 120° + 1.\sin 240°.$$

We therefore have

$$V\cos\theta = 4 + 3\cdot\frac{\sqrt{3}}{2} + 2\left(-\frac{1}{2}\right) + 1\left(-\frac{1}{2}\right) = \frac{5+3\sqrt{3}}{2},$$

and $$V\sin\theta = 3\cdot\frac{1}{2} + 2\cdot\frac{\sqrt{3}}{2} - 1\cdot\frac{\sqrt{3}}{2} = \frac{3+\sqrt{3}}{2}.$$

Hence, by squaring and adding,

$$V^2 = 16 + 9\sqrt{3} = 31.5885, \text{ so that } V = 5.62,$$

and, by division, $$\tan\theta = \frac{3+\sqrt{3}}{5+3\sqrt{3}} = 2\sqrt{3} - 3 = 0.4641 = \tan 24°54'.$$

Hence the resultant is a velocity equal to 5.62 inclined at an angle 24°54′ to the direction of the first velocity.

Graphically, this result may also be obtained by drawing; mark off OA on OX equal to 4 cm and draw AB, making AB equal to 3 cm and XAB equal to 30°.

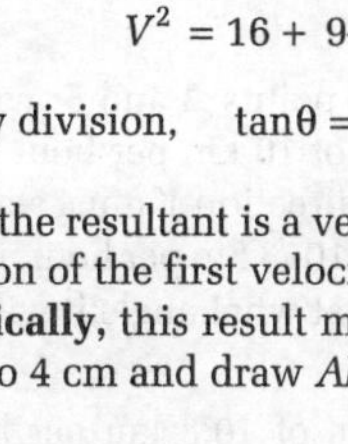

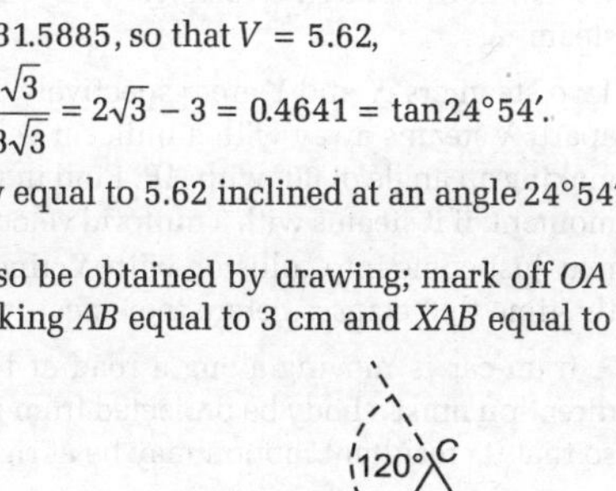

Draw BC perpendicular to AB and equal to 2 cm and then CD at an angle of 120° with BC produced and equal to 1 cm.
Join OD.
On measurement, OD = 5.62 cm, and the $\angle AOD$ = 25° nearly.

3. The velocity of a ship is $13\frac{1}{11}$ km per hour, and a ball is bowled across the ship perpendicular to the direction of the ship with a velocity of $2\frac{3}{11}$ m per second; describe the path of the ball in space and show that it passes over $13\frac{1}{11}$ m in 3 seconds.
4. A boat is rowed with a velocity of 6 km per hour straight across a river which flows at the rate of 2 km per hour. If its breadth be 300 metres, find how far down the river the boat will reach the opposite bank below the point at which it was originally directed.
5. A man wishes to cross a river to an exactly opposite point on the other bank; if he can pull his boat with twice the velocity of the current, find at what inclination to the current he must keep the boat pointed.
6. A boat is rowed on a river so that its speed in still water would be 6 km per hour. If the river flows at the rate of 4 km per hour, draw a figure to show the direction in which the head of the boat must point so that the motion of the boat may be at right angles to the current.
7. A stream runs with a velocity of $1\frac{1}{2}$ km per hour; find in what direction, a swimmer, whose velocity is $2\frac{1}{2}$ km per hour, should start in order to cross the stream perpendicularly.
What direction should be taken in order to cross in the shortest *time*?
8. A ship is steaming in a direction due north across a current running due west. At the end of one hour it is found that the ship has made $8\sqrt{3}$ km in a direction 30° west of north. Find the velocity of the current, and the rate at which the ship is steaming.
9. Two steamers X and Y are respectively at two points A and B, which are 5 km apart. X steams away with a uniform velocity of 10 km per hour in a direction making an angle of 60° with AB. Find in what direction Y must start at the same moment, if it steams with a uniform velocity of $10\sqrt{3}$ km per hour, in order that it may just come into collision with X; find also at what angle it will strike X and the time that elapses before they meet.
10. A tram-car is moving along a road at the rate of 10.8 km per hour; in what direction must a body be projected from it with a velocity of 500 cm per second, so that its resultant motion may be at right angles to the tram-car?
11. A ship is sailing north at the rate of 4 metres per second; the current is taking it east at the rate of 3 metres per second, and a sailor is climbing a vertical pole at the rate of 2 metres per second; find the velocity and direction of the sailor in space.
12. Find the components of a velocity u resolved along two lines inclined at angles of 30° and 45° respectively to its direction.

13. A point which possesses velocities represented by 7, 8, and 13 is at rest; find the angle between the direction of the two smaller velocities.

14. A point possesses velocities represented by 3, 19, and 9 inclined at angles of 120° to one another; find by drawing and by calculation their resultant.

15. A point possesses simultaneously velocities represented by $u, 2u, 3\sqrt{3}\,u,$ and $4u$; the angles between the first and second, the second and third, and the third and fourth, are respectively 60°, 90°, and 150°; show, by drawing and by calculation, that the resultant is u in a direction inclined at an angle of 120° to that of the first velocity.

16. A point has equal velocities in two given directions; if one of these velocities be halved, the angle which the resultant makes with the other is halved also. Show that the angle between the velocities is 120°.

17. A point possesses velocities represented in magnitude and direction by the lines joining any point on a circle to the ends of a diameter; show that their resultant is represented by the diameter through the point.

18. A point possesses simultaneously four velocities: the first is 24 metres per sec.; the second is 36 metres per sec. at 40° to the first; the third is 45 metres per sec. at 50° to the second; and the fourth is 60 metres per sec. at 35° with the third; show, by a drawing, that the resultant velocity is about 118.5 metres per sec. at about 82° with the direction of the first component velocity.

20. Average Speed and Velocity. The average speed of a point in a given period of time is the same as the speed of a moving point which moves with uniform speed, and describes the same path as the given point in the given time. Thus, the average speed of a moving point in a given period of time is the whole distance described by the point in the given time divided by the whole time. The average speed of an athlete who runs 100 m in $10\frac{2}{5}$ seconds is $100 \div 10\frac{2}{5}$ or $9\frac{8}{13}$ m per second.

Again suppose a train describes 2 km in the first 5 minutes after leaving a station, then runs 15 min. at the rate of 40 km per hour, and finally takes 6 min. over the last 2 km before coming to rest.

The total space described $= 2 + \frac{40}{4} + 2 = 14$ km.

The time taken $= 5 + 15 + 6 = 26$ minutes.

Its average speed $= \frac{14}{26}$ km per minute $= \frac{7}{13} \times 60$ km per hour $= 32.3$ km per hour nearly.

The average velocity of a given point in any direction (strictly so called) is the whole displacement in the given direction in the given time divided by the given time.

21. Relative Motion. Rest and motion are relative terms; we do not know what absolute motion is; all motion that we become acquainted with is relative.

For example, when we say that a train is travelling northward at the rate of 40 miles an hour, we mean that is its velocity relative to the earth, i.e., it is the velocity that a person standing at rest on the earth would observe in the train. Beside this motion along the surface it partakes with the rest of the earth in the diurnal motion about the axis of the earth; it also moves with the earth round the sun; and in addition has, in common with the whole solar system, any velocity that system may have.

22. Consider the case of two trains moving on parallel rails in the same direction with equal velocities and let A and B be two points, one on each train; a person at one of them, A say, would, if he kept his attention fixed on B and if he were unconscious of his own motion, consider B to be at rest. The line AB would remain constant in magnitude and direction, and the velocity of B relative to A would be zero.

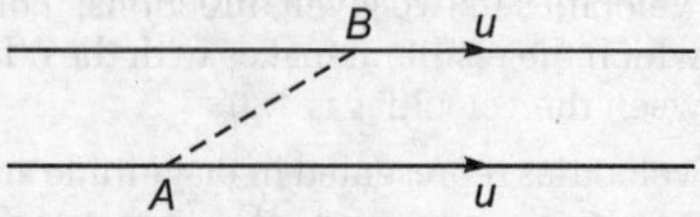

Next, let the first train be moving at the rate of 20 km per hour, and let the second train B be moving in the same direction at the rate of 25 km per hour. In this case the line joining A to B would (if we neglect the distance between the rails) be increasing at the rate of 5 km per hour, and this would be the velocity of B relative to A.

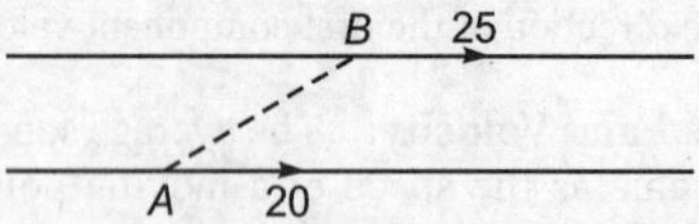

Thirdly, let the second train be moving with a velocity of 25 km per hour in the opposite direction to that of the first; the line joining A to B would now be increasing at the rate of 45 km per hour in a direction opposite to that of A's motion, and the relative velocity of B with respect to A would be –45 km per hour.

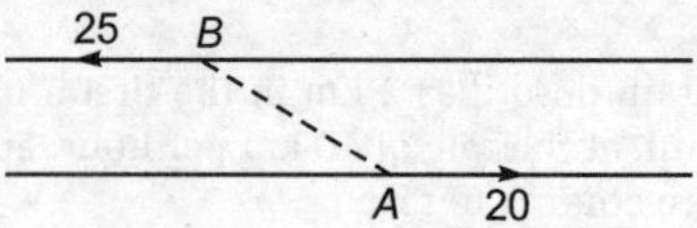

In each of these cases it will be noticed that the relative velocity of the second train with respect to the first is obtained by compounding with its own velocity a velocity equal and opposite to that of the first.

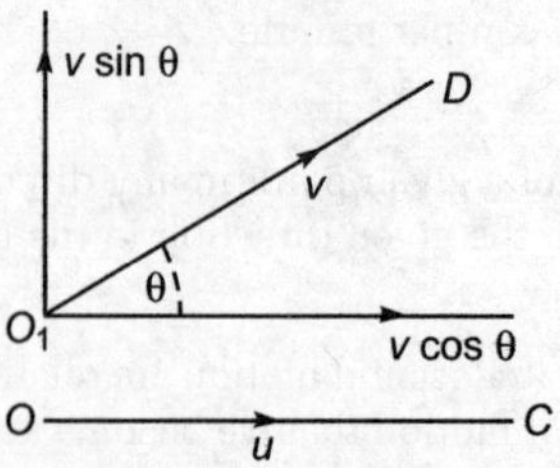

Lastly, let the first train be moving along the line OC with velocity u, whilst the second train is moving with velocity v along a line O_1D inclined at an angle θ to OC.

Resolve the velocity v into two components, viz., $v\cos\theta$ parallel to OC and sinθ in the perpendicular direction.

As before, the velocity of B relative to A, parallel to OC, is $v\cos\theta - u$; also, ince the point A has no velocity perpendicular to OC, the velocity of B relative to in that direction is $v\sin\theta$.

Hence the velocity of B relative to A consists of two components, viz., cos $\theta - u$ parallel to OC, and $v\sin\theta$ perpendicular to OC. These two components re equivalent to the original velocity v of the train B combined with a velocity qual and opposite to that of A.

Hence we have the following important result :

Relative Velocity. *When the distance between two points is altering, either ı direction or in magnitude or in both, then either point is said to have a velocity elative to the other; also the relative velocity of one point B with respect to a second oint A is obtained by compounding with the velocity of B a velocity which is equal nd opposite to that of A.*

23. It may be advisable for the student to consider relative motion in a ightly different manner. Suppose the velocities of the two points A and B to be epresented by the lines AP and BQ, so that in one second the positions of the oints change from A and B to P and Q. Complete the parallelogram $APRB$ and oin RQ.

By Art. 16 the velocity BQ is equivalent to two velocities represented by BR nd RQ; also BR is equal and parallel to AP.

Hence the velocity of B is equivalent to two velocities, one, BR, equal and arallel to that of A, and the other by RQ.

The velocity of B relative to A is therefore represented by RQ.

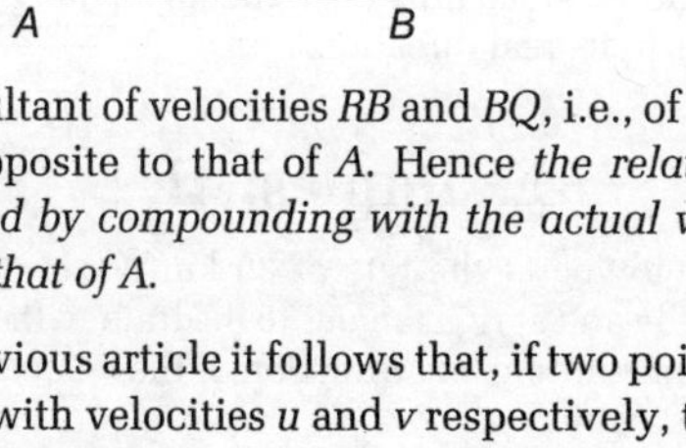

But RQ is the resultant of velocities RB and BQ, i.e., of the velocity of B and a elocity equal and opposite to that of A. Hence *the relative velocity of B with espect to A is obtained by compounding with the actual velocity of B a velocity qual and opposite to that of A.*

24. From the previous article it follows that, if two points A and B be moving ı the same direction with velocities u and v respectively, the relative velocity of with respect to A in that direction is $v - u$, and that of A with respect to B is $- v$.

If they be moving in different directions the relative velocity is found by ompounding velocities by means of the parallelogram of velocities.

Ex. *A train is travelling along a horizontal rail at the rate of* 60 *km per hour, and ain is driven by the wind, which is in the same direction as the motion of the train, so* *that it falls with a velocity of $8\frac{1}{3}$ m per second and at an angle of 30° with the vertical. Find the apparent direction of the rain to a person travelling with the train.*

Ans. The velocity of the train is $16\frac{2}{3}$ m per second.

Let *AB* represent the actual velocity of the rain so that, if *AE* be a vertical line, the angle *EAB* is 30°.

Draw *AC* horizontal and opposite to the direction of the train and let it represent in magnitude the velocity, $16\frac{2}{3}$ m per second, of the train.

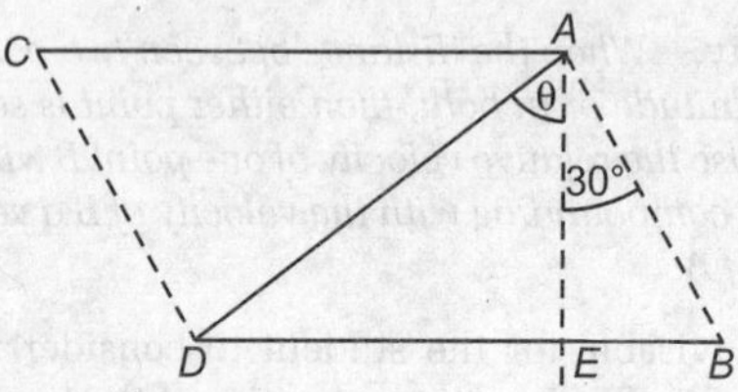

Complete the parallelogram *ABDC*.

Join *AD*, and let the angle *EAD* be θ.

AD is the apparent direction of the rain.

From the triangle *BAD*, we have

$$\frac{BD}{AB} = \frac{\sin DAB}{\sin BDA} = \frac{\sin(\theta + 30°)}{\cos\theta}.$$

$$\therefore \quad \frac{16\frac{2}{3}}{8\frac{1}{3}} = \frac{\sin\theta\cos 30° + \cos\theta\sin 30°}{\cos\theta} = \tan\theta\cos 30° + \sin 30°.$$

$$\therefore \quad 2 = \tan\theta\cdot\frac{\sqrt{3}}{2} + \frac{1}{2}.$$

$$\therefore \quad \tan\theta = \sqrt{3} = \tan 60°.$$

Hence θ is 60°. It follows, since *BAD* is a right angle, that the apparent direction of the rain is at right angles to its real direction.

Examples. II.

1. A railway train, moving at the rate of 36 km per hour, is struck by a stone moving horizontally and at right angles to the train with a velocity of 500 cm per second. Find the magnitude and direction of the velocity with which the stone appears to meet the train.
2. One ship is sailing due east at the rate of 12 km per hour, and another ship is sailing due north at the rate of 16 km per hour; find the relative velocity of the second ship with respect to the first.
3. One ship is sailing south with a velocity of $15\sqrt{2}$ km per hour and another south-east at the rate of 15 km per hour. Find the apparent velocity and direction of motion of the second vessel to an observer on the first vessel.

4. A ship is sailing north-east with a velocity of 10 km per hour, and to a passenger on board the wind appears to blow from the north with a velocity of $10\sqrt{2}$ km per hour. Find the true velocity and direction of the wind.

5. A ship steams due west at the rate of 15 km per hour relative to the current which is flowing at the rate of 6 km per hour due south. What is the velocity relative to the ship of a train going due north at the rate of 30 km per hour ?

6. In a tunnel, drops of water which are falling from the roof are noticed to pass the carriage window of a train in a direction making an angle $\tan^{-1}\frac{1}{2}$ with the horizon, and they are known to have a velocity of 730 cm per second. Neglecting the resistance of the air, find the velocity of the train.

7. To a man walking at the rate of 2 km an hour the rain appears to fall vertically; when he increases his speed to 4 km per hour it appears to meet him at an angle of 45°; find the real direction and speed of the rain.

8. A steamer is going due west at 14 km hour, and the wind appears from the drift of the clouds to be blowing at 7 km per hour from the north-west. Find its actual velocity and make a geometrical construction for its direction.

9. A railway train is moving at the rate of 45 km per hour, when a pistol shot strikes it in a direction making an angle $\sin^{-1}\frac{3}{5}$ with the train. The shot enters one compartment at the corner furthest from the engine and passes out at the diagonally opposite corner; the compartment being 2.44 metres wide and 1.83 metres long, show that the shot is moving at the rate of 128 km per hour, and traverses the carriage in 0.114 second.

10. Two trains, each 61 metres long, are moving towards each other on parallel lines with velocities of 32 and 48 km per hour respectively. Find the time that elapses from the instant when they first meet until they have cleared each other.

11. The wind blowing exactly along a line of railway, two trains, moving with the same speed in opposite directions, have the steam track of the one double that of the other; show that the speed of each train is three times that of the wind.

12. *One ship, sailing east with a speed of* 15 *km per hour, passes a certain point at noon; and a second ship, sailing north at the same speed, passes the same point at* 1.30 *p.m.; at what time are they closest together, and what is the distance then ?*

Let O be the fixed point, A the position of the second ship at 12.00 noon, so that $OA = 22\frac{1}{2}$ km.

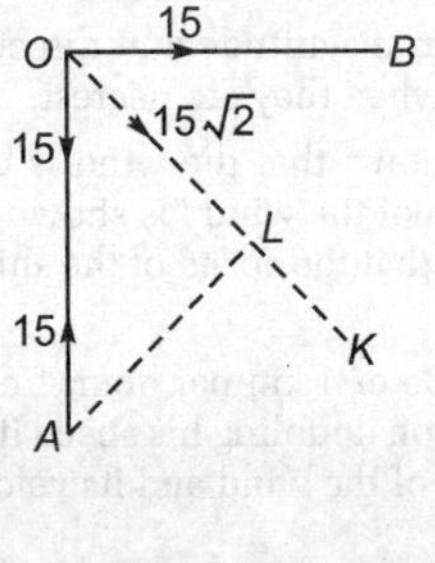

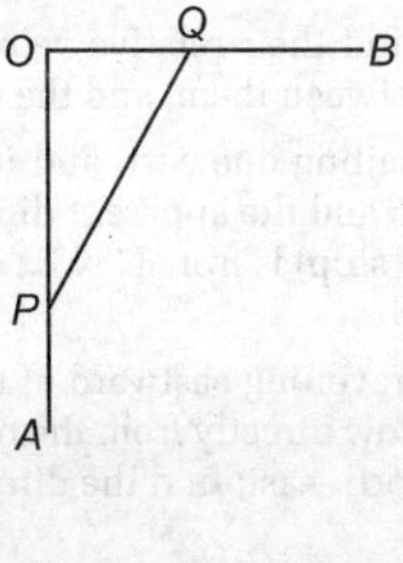

The relative velocity of the first ship with respect to the second is obtained by compounding with its velocity of 15 a velocity equal and opposite to that of the second ship, i.e., a velocity of 15 southwards. Hence this relative velocity is $15\sqrt{2}$ in the direction *OK*, i.e., south-east.

Draw *AL* perpendicular to *OK*. Then *AL* is clearly the shortest distance required. It

$$= OA \sin AOL = 22\frac{1}{2} \times \frac{1}{\sqrt{2}} = \frac{45}{4}\sqrt{2} = 15.9 \text{ km nearly.}$$

Also the time after 12.00 noon.
= the time in which *OL* is described with the relative velocity $15\sqrt{2}$

$$= \frac{OL}{15\sqrt{2}} = \frac{22\frac{1}{2} \times \frac{1}{\sqrt{2}}}{15\sqrt{2}} = \frac{3}{4} \text{ hour.}$$

Otherwise thus : Let *P* and *Q* be the actual positions of the ships at the end of time *t*, and let $PQ = x$.

Then $\quad OP = OA - 15t = 15\left[\frac{3}{2} - t\right],$

and $\quad OQ = 15t.$

Hence $\quad x^2 = 15^2\left[\left(\frac{3}{2} - t\right)^2 + t^2\right] = 15^2 \times 2\left[t^2 - \frac{3}{2}t + \frac{9}{8}\right]$

$$= 2 \times 15^2 \times \left[\left(t - \frac{3}{4}\right)^2 + \frac{9}{16}\right]$$

Now a square can never be negative, so that its least value is zero.
Hence the least value of *x* is when $t = \frac{3}{4}$, and then

$$x = \sqrt{2} \times 15 \times \sqrt{\frac{9}{16}} = \frac{45}{4}\sqrt{2} = 15.9 \text{ nearly.}$$

13. A ship steaming north at the rate of 12 km per hour observes a ship, due east of itself and distant 10 km, which is steaming due west at the rate of 16 km per hour; after what time are they at the least distance from one another and what is this least distance?

14. Two points are started simultaneously from points *A* and *B* which are 5 feet apart, one from *A* towards *B* with a velocity which would cause it to reach *B* in 3 seconds, and the other at right angles to the direction of the former with $\frac{3}{4}$ of its velocity. Find their relative velocity in magnitude and direction, the shortest distance between them, and the time when they are nearest.

15. A ship is sailing due east, and it is known that the wind is blowing from the north-west, and the apparent direction of the wind (as shown by a vane on the mast of the ship) is from N.N.E.; show that the speed of the ship is equal to that of the wind.

16. A person travelling eastward at the rate of 4 km per hour, finds that the wind seems to blow directly from the north; on doubling his speed it appears to come from the north-east; find the direction of the wind and its velocity.

17. A person travelling toward the north-east, finds that the wind appears to blow from the north, but when he doubles his speed it seems to come from a direction inclined at an angle $\cot^{-1} 2$ on the east of north. Find the true direction of the wind.

18. Two points move with velocities v and $2v$ respectively in opposite directions in the circumference of a circle. In what positions is their relative velocity greatest and least and what values has it then?

25. Angular Velocity. Def. *If a point P be in motion in a plane, and if O be a fixed point in the plane and OA a fixed straight line drawn through O, then the rate at which the angle AOP increases is called the angular velocity of the moving point P about O.*

When uniform, the angular velocity is measured by the number of radians in the angle which is turned through by *OP* in a unit of time.

When variable, it is measured at any instant by what would be the angle turned through by the line *OP* in a unit of time, if during that unit it continued to turn at the same rate as at the instant under consideration.

Exs. If the line *OP* turn through 4 right angles (i.e., 2π radians) in one second, the angular velocity is 2π.

If it turns through three-quarters of a right angle in one second, the angular velocity is $\frac{3}{4}.\frac{\pi}{2}$ or $\frac{3\pi}{8}$.

If *OP* makes 7 revolutions in one second, the angular velocity is $7 \times 2\pi$ or 14π.

26. The angular velocity can always be expressed in terms of the linear velocity when the path is known.

The only case that we shall consider is when the angular velocity is uniform, and the moving point *P* is describing a circle about the fixed point *O* as centre.

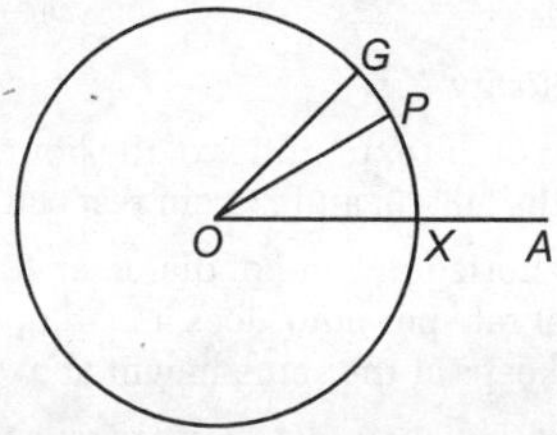

If a moving point describes a circle, its angular velocity about the centre of the circle is equal to its speed divided by the radius ot the circle.

Let *P* be the position of the moving point at any time, and in the unit of time let the point describe the arc *PQ*. In this time the line *OP* turns through the angle *POQ*.

Hence the angular velocity is equal to the number of radians in the angle *POQ*.

But the number of radians in $POQ = \frac{\text{arc } PQ}{OP}$.

Also, since the arc *PQ* is described in one second, it is equal to the speed v.

Hence, if ω be the angular velocity and r the radius of the circle, we have

$$\omega = \frac{v}{r},$$

i.e., $$v = r\omega$$

Exs. (1) If the moving point describes a circle of 3 m radius with uni angular velocity, the speed is given by $v = 3.1 = 3$ m per second.

(2) If the moving point describes a circle of 5 m radius with speed 8 m pe second, its angular velocity ω is given by $\omega = \frac{6}{5}$ radian per second.

(3) The earth makes a complete revolution about its own axis in 24 hours. The angular velocity of any point on its surface therefore

$$= \frac{2\pi}{24 \times 60 \times 60} \text{ radians per second.}$$

Since the earth's radius is 4000 miles, the velocity of any point on the equator

$$= \frac{2\pi}{24 \times 60 \times 60} \times 4000 \text{ miles per second}$$

$$= 1047 \text{ miles per hour approximately.}$$

Examples. III.

1. A wheel turns about its centre, making 200 revolutions per minute; what is the angular velocity of any point on the wheel about the centre ?
2. A wheel turns about its centre, making 4 revolutions per second; what is the angular velocity of any point on the wheel about the centre and what is its linea velocity, if the radius of the wheel be 50 cm?
3. If the minute hand of a clock be 6 cm long, find the velocity of the end ir centimetre per second.

   What is its angular velocity ?
4. Compare the velocities of the extremities of the hour, minute, and second hand of a watch, their lengths .48, .8, and .24 cm respectively.
5. A treadmill, with axis horizontal and of diameter 40 feet, makes one revolutior in 40 seconds. At what rate per hour does a man upon it walk, over its surface supposing he always keeps at the same height above the ground?
6. From a train moving with velocity V a carriage on a road parallel to the line, at a distance d from it, is observed to move so as to appear always in a line with a more distant fixed object whose least distance from the railway is D. Find the velocity of the carriage.
7. A point moves in a circle with uniform speed; show that its angular velocity about any point on the circumference of the circle is constant.
8. A string has one end attached to the corner of a square board, fixed on a smooth horizontal table, and is wound round the square carrying a particle at its other end; the particle is projected with velocity u at right angles to the side of the square whose side is a; if the length of the string be $4a$, find the time that the string takes to unwrap itself from the square, assuming that the speed of the particle remains the same throughout the motion.

9. *A wheel rolls uniformly on the ground, without sliding, its centre describing a straight line; to find the velocities of different points of its rim.

Let O be the centre and r the radius of the wheel, and let v be the velocity with which the centre advances. Let A be the point of the wheel in contact with the ground at any instant.

Now the wheel turns uniformly round its centre whilst the centre moves forward in a straight line; also, since each point of the wheel in succession touches the ground, it follows that any point of the wheel describes the perimeter of the wheel relative to the centre, whilst the centre moves through a distance equal to the perimeter; hence the velocity of any of the wheel relative to the centre is equal in magnitude to the velocity v of the centre.

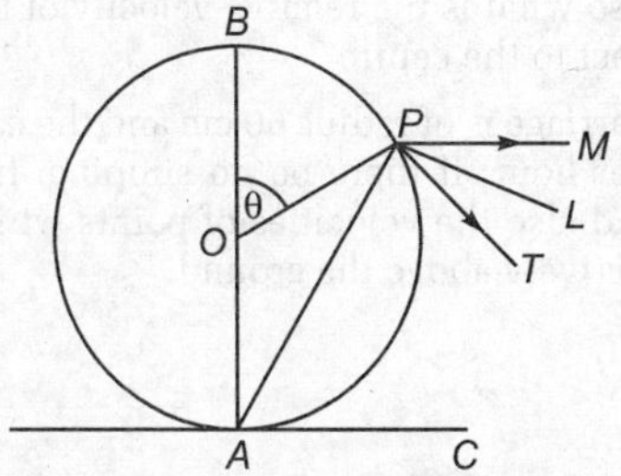

Hence any point P of the wheel possesses two velocities each equal to v, one along the tangent, PT, at P to the circle, and the other in the direction, PM, in which the centre O is moving.

Hence the velocity of $A = v - v = 0$, and so A is at rest for the instant.

So the velocity of $B = v + v = 2v$.

Consider the motion of any other point P. It has two velocities, each equal to v, along PM and PT respectively.

Now, since PM and PT are respectively perpendicular to OB and OP, the $\angle MPT = \angle POB = \theta$ (say).

The resultant of these two velocities v is a velocity $2v \cos \frac{\theta}{2}$ along PL, where

$$\angle LPT = \frac{1}{2} \angle MPT = \frac{\theta}{2} = \angle OPA.$$

Hence $\qquad \angle APL = \angle OPT =$ a right angle.

Hence the direction of motion of the point P is perpendicular to AP, and its angular velocity about A

$$= \frac{2v \cos \frac{\theta}{2}}{AP} = \frac{2v \cos \frac{\theta}{2}}{2r \cos \frac{\theta}{2}} = \frac{v}{r}$$

= the angular velocity of the wheel about O.

Hence each point of the wheel is turning about the point of contact of the wheel with the ground, with a constant angular velocity whose measure is the velocity of the centre of the wheel divided by the radius of the wheel.

10. An engine is travelling at the rate of 60 km per hour and its wheel is $1\frac{1}{2}$ m i diameter; find the velocity and direction of motion of each of the tw points of the wheel which are at a height of $1\frac{1}{2}$ m above the ground.

11. If a railway carriage be moving at the rate of 36 km per hour and th diameter of its wheel be 90 cm, what is the angular velocity of the whee when there is no sliding ? Find also the relative velocity of the highest poin of the wheel with respect to the centre.

12. If a railway carriage be moving at the rate of 36 km per hour and the radiu of the wheel be 60 cm, what is the angular velocity of the wheel when ther is no sliding? Also what is the relative velocity of the highest point of th wheel with respect to the centre ?

13. The wheel of a carriage is of radius 60 cm and the carriage is moving at th rate of 16 km per hour; if there be no slipping, find the velocity of th highest point, and also the velocities of points which are at heights of 3 and 90 cm respectively above the ground.

2

Acceleration

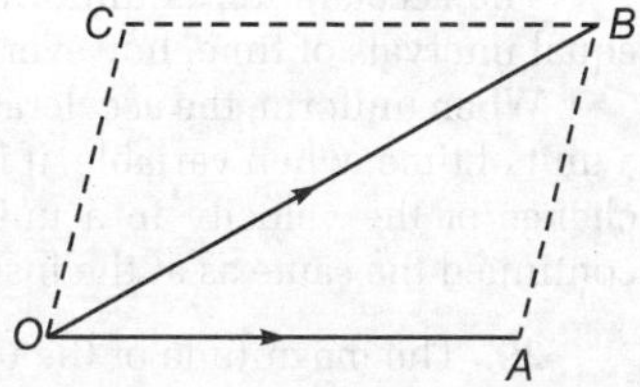

27. Change of Velocity. Suppose a point at any instant to be moving with a velocity represented by *OA*, and that at some subsequent time its velocity is represented by *OB*.

Join *AB*, and complete the parallelogram *OABC*.

Then the velocities represented by *OA* and *OC* are equivalent to the velocity *OB*. Hence the velocity *OC* is the velocity which must be compounded with *OA* to produce the velocity *OB*. The velocity *OC* is therefore the change of velocity in the given time.

Thus the change of velocity is not, in general, the difference in magnitude between the magnitudes of the two velocities, but is that velocity which compounded with the original velocity gives the final velocity.

The change of velocity is not constant unless the change is consant both in magnitude and direction.

Examples. IV.

1. *A point is moving with a velocity of* 10 *metres per second, and at a subsequent instant it is moving at the same rate in a direction inclined at* 30° *to the former direction; find the change of velocity.*

On drawing the figure, as in the last article, we have $OA = OB = 10$, and the angle $AOB = 30°$.

Since $OA = OB$, we have $\angle OAB = 75°$, and therefore $\angle AOC = 105°$.

$$\text{Also } AB = 2OA \sin 15° = 20 \cdot \frac{\sqrt{3}-1}{2\sqrt{2}} = 5(\sqrt{6}-\sqrt{2}) = 5.176.$$

Hence the change in the velocity, i.e., *OC*, is 5.176 metres per second in a direction inclined at 105° to the original direction of motion.

2. A ship is observed to be moving eastward with a velocity of 3 km per hour, and at a subsequent instant it is found to be moving northward at the rate of 4 km per hour; find the change of velocity.

3. A point is moving with a velocity of 5 metres per second, and at a subsequent instant it is moving at the same rate in a direction inclined at 60° to its former direction; find the change of velocity.

4. A point is moving eastward with a velocity of 20 metres per second, and one hour afterwards it is moving north-east with the same speed; find the change of velocity.
5. A point is describing with uniform speed a circle, of radius 7 metres in 11 seconds, starting from the end of a fixed diameter; find the change in its velocity after it has described one-sixth of the circumference.

28. Acceleration. Def. *The acceleration of a moving point is the rate of change of its velocity.*

Note that the acceleration of a moving point has both magnitude and direction.

The acceleration is uniform when equal changes of velocity take place in equal intervals of time, however small these intervals may be.

When uniform, the acceleration is measured by the change in the velocity in a unit of time; when variable, it is measured at any instant by what would be the change of the velocity in a unit of time, if during that time the acceleration continued the same as at the instant under consideration.

29. The magnitude of the unit of acceleration is the acceleration of a point which moves so that its velocity is changed by the unit of velocity in each unit of time.

Hence a point is moving with *n* units of acceleration when its velocity is changed by *n* units of velocity in each unit of time.

Thus a point is moving with 10 centimetre-second units of acceleration when its change of velocity is 10 cm per second in each second. This acceleration is called an acceleration of 10 cm/sec^2 also written as 10 cm. s^{-2}.

30. Theorem. Parallelogram of Accelerations. *If a moving point have simultaneously two accelerations represented in magnitude and direction by two sides of a parallelogram drawn from a point, they are equivalent to an acceleration represented by the diagonal of the parallelogram passing through that angular point.*

Let the accelerations be represented by the sides *AB* and *AC* of the parallelogram *ABCD*, i.e., let *AB* and *AC* represent the velocities added to the velocity of the point in a unit of time. On the same scale let *EF* represent the velocity which the particle has at any instant.

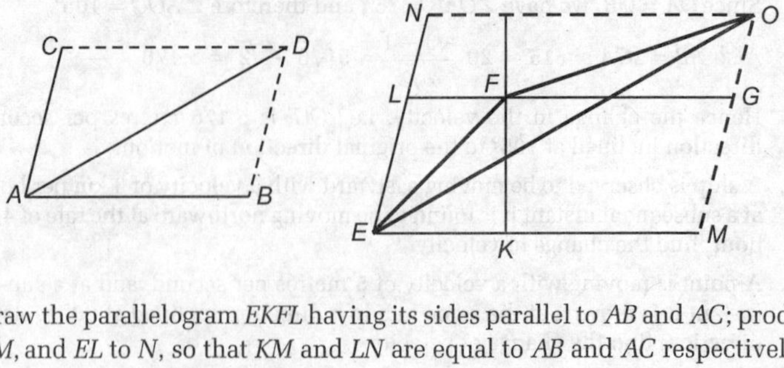

Draw the parallelogram *EKFL* having its sides parallel to *AB* and *AC*; produce *EK* to *M*, and *EL* to *N*, so that *KM* and *LN* are equal to *AB* and *AC* respectively.

Complete the parallelogram as in the above figure.

Then the velocity *EF* is equivalent to velocities *EK* and *EL*. But in the unit of time the velocities *KM* and *LN* are the changes of velocity.

Therefore at the end of a unit of time the component velocities are equivalent to *EM* and *EN*, which are equivalent to *EO*, and this latter velocity is equivalent to velocities *EF* and *FO*. (Art. 16.)

Hence in the unit of time *FO* is the change of velocity of the moving point, i.e., *FO* is the resultant acceleration of the point.

But *FO* is equal and parallel to *AD*.

Hence *AD* represents the acceleration which is equivalent to the accelerations *AB* and *AC*, i.e., *AD* is the resultant of the accelerations *AB* and *AC*.

31. It follows from the preceding Article that accelerations are resolved and compounded in the same way as velocities, and propositions similar to those of Arts. 13-19 will be true when we substitute "acceleration" for "velocity".

Velocities and accelerations, and also forces (Art. 72) are examples of an important class of Physical quantities which are called Vector quantities. The characteristic of a Vector quantity is that it has direction as well as magnitude, and is thus fitly represented by a straight line; in all cases Vector quantities are compounded by the parallelogrammic law.

In the language of Vectors Arts. 12 and 30 are examples of the Addition of Vectors, and it would be said that the addition of the Vectors *AB* and *BD* (or *AC*) gives the Vector *AD*.

In contradistinction to Vectors, quantities which only possess magnitude, and not direction, are called Scalars. Kinetic Energy, which will be defined later on, is an example of a physical quantity which is a Scalar; other examples are a ton of coal, a sum of money, etc. Scalar quantities are compounded by Simple Addition.

32. Theorem. *A point moves in a straight line, starting with velocity u, and moving with constant acceleration f in its direction of motion; if v be its velocity at the end of time t, and s be its distance at that instant from its starting point, then*

$$(1)\ v = u + ft,$$

$$(2)\ s = ut + \frac{1}{2} ft^2,$$

$$(3)\ v^2 = u^2 + 2fs.$$

(1) Since f denotes the acceleration, i.e., the change in the velocity per unit of time, ft denotes the change in the velocity in t units of time.

But, since the particle possessed u units of velocity initially, at the end of time t it must possess $u + ft$ units of velocity, i.e.,

$$v = u + ft.$$

(2) Let V be the velocity at the middle of the interval so that, by (1), $V = u + f \cdot \frac{t}{2}$.

Now the velocity changes uniformly throughout the interval t. Hence the velocity at any instant, preceding the middle of the interval by any time T, is as much less than V, as the velocity at the same time T after the middle of the interval is greater than V.

Hence, since the time t could be divided into pairs of such equal moments, the space described is the same as if the point moved for time t with velocity V.

$$\therefore \qquad s = V \cdot t = \left(u + f\frac{t}{2}\right)t = ut + \frac{1}{2}ft^2$$

(3) The third relation can be easily deduced from the first two by eliminating t between them.

For, from (1),
$$v^2 = (u + ft)^2$$
$$= u^2 + 2uft + f^2t^2$$
$$= u^2 + 2f\left(ut + \frac{1}{2}ft^2\right)$$

Hence, by (2),
$$v^2 = u^2 + 2fs.$$

32a. *Alternative proof of equation* (2).

Let the time t be divided into n equal intervals, each equal to τ so that $t = n\tau$. The velocities of the point at the beginning of these successive intervals are

$$u, u + f\tau, u + 2f\tau, \ldots u + (n-1)f\tau.$$

Hence the space s_1 which *would be* moved through by the point, if it moved during each of these intervals τ with the velocity which it has at the *beginning* of each, is

$$s_1 = u \cdot \tau + [u + f\tau] \cdot \tau + \ldots + [u + f(n-1)\tau] \cdot \tau$$
$$= n \cdot u\tau + f\tau^2 \cdot \{1 + 2 + 3 \ldots + (n-1)\}$$
$$= n \cdot u\tau + f\tau^2 \cdot \frac{n(n-1)}{1 \cdot 2}, \text{ on summing the A.P.,}$$
$$= ut + \frac{1}{2}ft^2 \cdot \left(1 - \frac{1}{n}\right), \text{ since } \tau = \frac{t}{n}.$$

Also the velocities at the ends of these successive intervals are

$$u + f\tau, u + 2f\tau, \ldots u + nf\tau.$$

Hence the space s_2 which *would be* moved through by the point, if it moved during each of these intervals τ with the velocity which it has at the *end* of each, is

$$s_2 = (u + f\tau) \cdot \tau + (u + 2f\tau) \cdot \tau + \ldots + (u - nf\tau) \cdot \tau$$
$$= nu\tau + f\tau^2(1 + 2 + 3 + \ldots + n)$$
$$= ut - \frac{1}{2}ft^2\left(1 + \frac{1}{n}\right), \text{ as before.}$$

Now the true space s is intermediate between s_1 and s_2; also the larger we make n and therefore the smaller the intervals τ become, the more nearly do the two hypotheses approach to coincidence.

If we make n infinitely large the values of s_1 and s_2 both become $ut + \frac{1}{2}ft^2$.

Hence
$$s = ut + \frac{1}{2}ft^2.$$

33. Equations. (1), (2) and (3) of Article 32 can also be established by use of calculus as follows :

A. Analytical expression for velocity and acceleration.

Let the distance of a moving point P from a fixed point O be x at any time t. Let its distance similarly at time $t + \Delta t$ be $x + \Delta x$, so that $PQ = \Delta x$.

The velocity of P at time

$$= \text{limit, when } \Delta t = 0, \text{ of } \frac{PQ}{\Delta t}$$

$$= \text{limit, when } \Delta t = 0, \text{ of } \frac{\Delta x}{\Delta t} = \frac{dx}{dt}$$

Hence the velocity $v = \dfrac{dx}{dt}$.

Let the velocity of the moving point at time $t + \Delta t$ be $\tau + \Delta\tau$

Then the acceleration of P at time

$$= \text{limit, when } \Delta t = 0, \text{ of } \frac{\Delta v}{\Delta t}$$

$$= \frac{dv}{dt}$$

$$= \frac{d^2 x}{dt^2}.$$

B. Motion in a straight line with constant acceleration f.

Let x be the distance of the moving point at time t from a fixed point in the straight line.

Then $$\frac{d^2 x}{dt^2} = f \quad \text{...(1),}$$

Hence, on integration, $$v = \frac{dx}{dt} = ft + A \quad \text{...(2),}$$

where A is an arbitrary constant.

Integrating again, we have

$$x = \frac{1}{2} ft^2 + At + B \quad \text{...(3),}$$

where B is an arbitrary constant.

Again, on multiplying (1) by $2\dfrac{dx}{dt}$, and integrating with respect to t, we have

$$v^2 = \left(\frac{dx}{dt}\right)^2 = 2fx + C \quad \text{...(4),}$$

where C is an arbitrary constant.

These three equations contain the solution of all questions on motion in a straight line with constant acceleration. The arbitrary constants A, B, C are determined from the initial conditions.

Suppose for example that the particle started from a fixed point O on the straight line with velocity u in a direction away from O, and suppose that the time t is reckoned from the instant of projection.

We then have when $t = 0$, then $v = u$ and $x = 0$. Hence the equations (2), (3) and (4) give

$$u = A, B = 0, \text{ and } u^2 = C.$$

Hence we have

$$v = u + ft,$$

$$x = ut + \frac{1}{2} ft^2,$$

and $$v^2 = u^2 + 2fx.$$

34. When the moving point starts from rest we have $u = 0$ and the formulae of Art. 32 take the simpler forms

$$v = ft,$$

$$s = \frac{1}{2} ft^2,$$

and $$v^2 = 2fs.$$

35. Graphic Method. Velocity-Time Curve. *To determine, by means of a graph, the distance described in a given time when the velocity of the moving point is varying.*

Take two straight lines OX and OY at right angles, and let times be represented by lengths drawn along OX, so that a unit of length in this direction represents a unit of time.

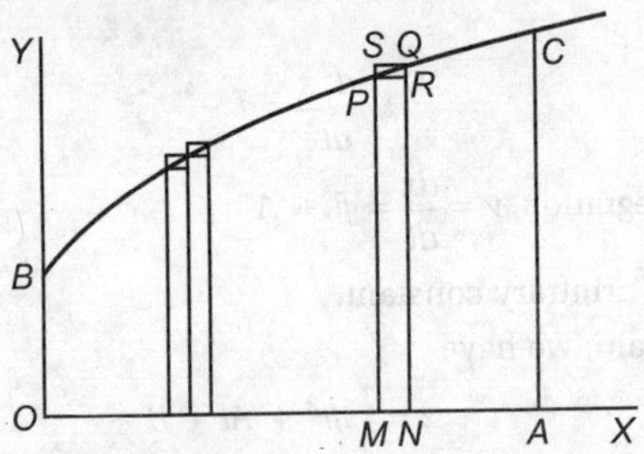

At *each* point M erect a perpendicular MP to represent the velocity of the moving point at the time represented by OM. The tops of all these ordinates will be found to lie on a line such as $BPQC$, which is curved or straight.

We shall show that the distance described in time OA by the moving point is represented by the area bounded by OB, OA, AC and the curved line BC.

Take an ordinate NQ close to MP. Then during the time MN the point moves with a veocity which is greater than MP and less than NQ. Hence, since the distance described with constant velocity = velocity × time, the distance described by it in time MN is $> MP . MN$ and is $< NQ . MN$, i.e., the number of units of space described in time MN is intermediate between the number of units of area in the rectangles *PN* and *QM*. Similarly, if we divide *OA* into any number of equal small parts and erect parallelograms on each.

Hence the number of units in the distance described in time *OA* is intermediate between the space represented by the sum of the inner rectangles and the sum of the outer rectangles.

Now let the number of portions of time into which the time *OA* is divided be made indefinitely large; then these two series of rectangles get nearer and nearer to one another and to the area of the curve. Hence the number of units of space described in time *OA* is ultimately equal to the number of units of area in the area *OACB*.

36. Case of uniform acceleration. Let u be the initial velocity and f the constant acceleration.

On *OY* mark off *OB* to represent the velocity u at time 0. Since the velocity at any time $t' = u - ft'$,

the coordinate MP at $M = OB + f.OM$ ...(1).

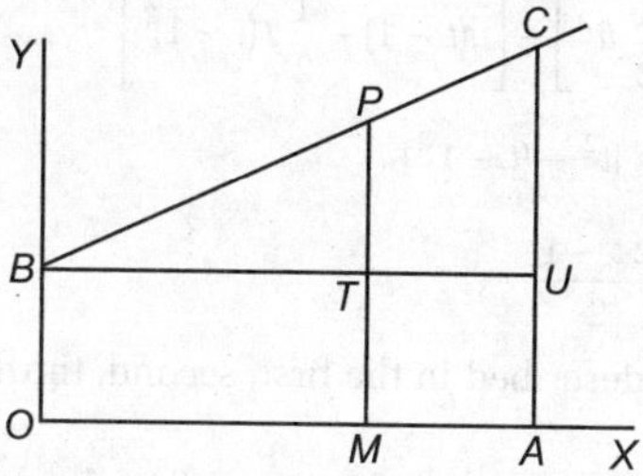

Draw *BTU* parallel to *OX* to meet *MP* in *T* and *AC* in *U*.

Then $TP = MP - OB = f.OM$, by (1),

so that $f = \dfrac{TP}{OM} = \dfrac{TP}{BT} = \tan PBT.$

Hence *TBP* is a constant angle, and therefore *P* lies on a straight line passing through *B*.

In this case, therefore, the velocity-time curve is the straight line *BC*, and $UC = BU.\tan CBU = f.t.$

Hence the number of units of space described in time t

$$= \text{the number of units of area in } OACB$$
$$= \text{area of } OBUA + \text{area } BUC$$
$$= OA.OB + \frac{1}{2}BU.UC$$
$$= OA\left[OB + \frac{1}{2}UC\right] = t\left[u + \frac{1}{2}ft\right]$$
$$= ut + \frac{1}{2}ft^2.$$

37. In the figure of Art. 35 since RQ is the increase of velocity in time MN the acceleration of the moving point at this instant = the value, when MN is made indefinitely small, of $\frac{RQ}{MN}$ [Art. 28]

$$= \text{the value of } \tan QPR.$$

But when MN is made indefinitely small the point Q moves up to P, PQ becomes the tangent at P, and tan QPR becomes the tangent of the angle that the tangent at P makes with OX.

Hence in the Velocity-Time graph the numerical value of the acceleration is the slope of the curve to the Time-Line.

38. *Space described in any particular second.*

[The student will notice carefully that the formula (2) of Art. 32 gives, not the space traversed in the tth second, but that traversed in t seconds.]

The space described in the tth second

$$= \text{space described in } t \text{ seconds} - \text{space described in } (t-1) \text{seconds}$$

$$= \left[ut + \frac{1}{2}ft^2\right] - \left[u(t-1) + \frac{1}{2}f(t-1)^2\right]$$

$$= u + \frac{1}{2}f\,[t^2 - (t-1)^2]$$

$$= u + f\,\frac{2t-1}{2}$$

Hence the spaces described in the first, second, third, ... nth seconds of the motion are

$$u + \frac{1}{2}f, u + \frac{3}{2}f, \ldots u + \frac{2n-1}{2}f.$$

These distances form an arithmetical progression whose common difference is f.

Hence, if a body move with a uniform acceleration, the distances described in successive seconds form an arithmetical progression, whose common difference is equal to the number of units in the acceleration.

The space described in any particular second may be otherwise found as follows. As in Art. 32, the space described in the tth second is the same as that which would be described if the point moved during that second with the velocity which it has at the middle of that second.

Now the velocity at the middle of the tth second

$$= \text{velocity at the end of time } \left(t - \frac{1}{2}\right)$$

$$= u + f\left(t - \frac{1}{2}\right)$$

Hence the space described in the tth second

$$= u + f\,\frac{2t-1}{2}$$

39. Ex. 1. *A train, which is moving at the rate of 60 km per hour, is brought to rest in 3 minutes with a uniform retardation; find this retardation, and also the distance that the train travels before coming to rest.*

$$60 \text{ km per hour} = \frac{60 \times 1000}{60 \times 60} = \frac{50}{3} \text{m per sec.}$$

Let f be the acceleration with which the train moves.

Since in 180 seconds a velocity of $\frac{50}{3}$ m per second is destroyed, we have (by formula (1), Art. 32)

$$0 = \frac{50}{3} + f(180)$$

$$\therefore \quad f = -\frac{5}{54} \text{ m/sec}^2$$

$$= -\frac{250}{27} \text{ cm/sec}^3$$

[N.B. f has a negative value because it is a retardation.]

Let x be the distance described. By formula (3), we have

$$0 = \left(\frac{50}{3}\right)^2 + 2\left(-\frac{5}{54}\right)x$$

$$\therefore \quad x = \left(\frac{50}{3}\right)^2 \times \frac{27}{5} = 1500 \text{ m}$$

Ex. 2. *A point is moving with uniform acceleration; in the eleventh and fifteenth seconds from the commencement it moves through 720 and 960 cm respectively; find its initial velocity, and the acceleration with which it moves.*

Let u be the initial velocity, and f the acceleration.

Then 720 = distance described in the eleventh second

$$= \left[u \cdot 11 + \frac{1}{2} f \cdot 11^2\right] - \left\{u \cdot 10 + \frac{1}{2} f \cdot 10^2\right\}$$

$$\therefore \quad 720 = u + \frac{21}{2} f \qquad \text{...(1).}$$

So

$$960 = \left[u \cdot 15 + \frac{1}{2} f \cdot 15^2\right] - \left\{u \cdot 14 + \frac{1}{2} f \cdot 14^2\right\}$$

$$\therefore \quad 960 = u + \frac{29}{2} f \qquad \text{...(2).}$$

Solving (1) and (2), we have $u = 90$, and $f = 60$.

Hence, the point started with a velocity of 90 cm/per second, and moved with an acceleration of 60 cm/sec. units.

Ex. 3. *A body starts from rest at A and moves with uniform acceleration in a straight line. T sec. later a second body starts from A and moves with uniform velocity u in the same line. If $u > 2f\,T$, prove that the second body will be ahead of the first for a time*

$$\frac{2}{f}\sqrt{u(u - 2\,f\,T)}$$

Let, the two bodies meet after t sec., the time being measured from the start of the first body.

Hence, we get,

$$\frac{1}{2} ft^2 = u(t - T) \quad ...(1),$$

Equation (1), being quadratic in t, shows that the bodies will meet twice with each other.

Solving (1), we have,

$$i = \frac{u}{f} \pm \frac{1}{f}\sqrt{u(u - 2fT)}$$

So, the required interval is

$$\left[\frac{u}{f} + \frac{1}{f}\sqrt{u(u-2fT)}\right] - \left[\frac{u}{f} - \frac{1}{f}\sqrt{u(u-2fT)}\right]$$

$= \frac{2}{f}\sqrt{u(u - 2fT)}$, which is real and non-zero only when $u - 2fT > 0$.

Ex. 4. *Two cars start off to race with velocities u_1 and u_2 and travel in a straight line with uniform accelerations f_1 and f_2. If the race ends in a dead heat, prove that the length of the course is*

$$\frac{2(u_1 - u_2)(u_1 f_2 - u_2 f_1)}{(f_1 - f_2)^2}$$

Let, the two cars reach the destination in time t and the distance travelled be s. Hence, we get

$$s = u_1 t + \frac{1}{2} f_1 t^2 \quad ...(1),$$

and

$$s = u_2 t + \frac{1}{2} f_2 t^2 \quad ...(2),$$

From (1) and (2), we get

$$t = \frac{2(u_1 - u_2)}{f_2 - f_1} \quad ...(3).$$

$\therefore \quad s = \frac{2(u_1 - u_2)(u_1 f_2 - u_2 f_1)}{(f_2 - f_1)^2}$ from (3) and (1) or (2).

Ex. 5. *If in the rectilinear motion of a point, the time t and position x satisfy the equation*

$$t = ax^2 + bx + c,$$

where a, b, c are given constants, prove that

(i) the velocity in the position x is $(2ax + b)^{-1}$;

(ii) the acceleration is inversely proportional to the cube of the distance from a certain fixed point in the line of motion, and find the coordinate of the fixed point.

Differentiating with respect to t,

$t = ax^2 + bx + c$, we get

$$\frac{dx}{dt} = \frac{1}{2ax + b} \quad ...(1),$$

Differentiating (1), we get

$$\frac{d^2x}{dt^2} = \frac{-2a}{(2ax + b)^2} \cdot \frac{dx}{dt}$$

$$= -\frac{1}{4a^2\left(x + \frac{b}{2a}\right)^3} \quad ...(2).$$

Equation (2) shows that the acceleration varies inversely as the cube of the distance of the moving point from a fixed point $-\frac{b}{2a}$ on the line of motion.

Ex. 6. *A particle moves towards a centre of attraction starting from rest at a distance a from the centre; if its velocity when at any distance x from the centre varies as* $\sqrt{\frac{a^2 - x^2}{x^2}}$*, find the law of force.*

Here $$\frac{dx}{dt} = \mu\sqrt{\frac{a^2 - x^2}{x^2}} \quad ...(1).$$

Differentiating (1) with respect to t, we get

$$\frac{d^2x}{dt^2} = \mu\left[\frac{1}{(a^2 - x^2)^{\frac{1}{2}}} + \frac{(a^2 - x^2)^{\frac{1}{2}}}{x^2}\right]\cdot\mu\sqrt{\frac{a^2 - x^2}{x^2}}$$

$$= \frac{-\mu^2 a^2}{x^3}$$

Thus, the force of attraction towards the fixed point varies inversely as x^3.

Examples. V.

1. The quantities u, f, v, s and t having the meanings assigned to them in Art. 32,

   (1) Given $u = 2$, $f = 3$, $t = 5$, find v and s;

   (2) Given $u = 7$, $f = -1$, $t = 7$, find v and s;

   (3) Given $u = 8$, $v = 3$, $s = 9$, find f and t;

   (4) Given $v = -6$, $s = -9$, $f = -\frac{3}{2}$, find u and t

   The units of length and time are a centimetre and a second.

2. A body, starting from rest, moves with an acceleration equal to 2 cm/sec. units; find the velocity at the end of 20 seconds, and the distance described in that time.

3. In what time would a body acquire a velocity of 36 km per hour, if it started with a velocity of 4 metres per second and moved with the cm/sec. unit of acceleration?

4. With what uniform acceleration does a body, starting from rest, describe 1000 cm in 10 seconds?

5. A body, starting from rest, moves with an acceleration of 3 centimetre-second units; in what time will it acquire a velocity of 30 centimetres per second, and what distance does it traverse in that time.

6. A point starts with a velocity of 100 cm per second and moves with −2 centimetre-second units of acceleration. When will its velocity be zero, and how far will it have gone?

7. A body, starting from rest and moving with uniform acceleration, describes 5130 cm in the tenth second; find its acceleration.

8. A particle is moving with uniform acceleration; in the eighth and thirteenth second after starting it moves through 255 and 225 cm respectively; find its initial velocity and its acceleration.

9. In two successive seconds a particle moves through 615 and 705 cm respectively; assuming that it was moving with uniform acceleration, finds its velocity at the commencement of the first of these two seconds and its acceleration. Find also how far it had moved from rest before the commencement of the first second.

10. A point, moving with uniform acceleration, describes in the last second of its motion $\frac{9}{25}$ths of the whole distance. If it started from rest, how long was it in motion and through what distance did it move, if it described 15 cm in the first second?

11. A point, moving with uniform acceleration, describes 25 cm in the half second which elapses after the first second of its motion, and 198 cm in the eleventh second of its motion; find the acceleration of the point and its initial velocity.

12. A body moves for 3 seconds with a constant acceleration during which time it describes 24 metres 30 cm the acceleration then ceases and during the next 3 seconds it describes 21 metres 60 cm; find its initial velocity and its acceleration.

13. The speed of a train is reduced from 36 km an hour to 9 km per hour whilst it travels a distance of 150 metres; if the retardation be uniform, find how much further it will travel before coming to rest?

14. A point starts from rest and moves with a uniform acceleration of 5 m/sec^2; find the time taken by it to traverse the first, second and third metre respectively.

15. A particle starts from a point O with a uniform velocity of 120 cm per second, and after 2 seconds another particle leaves O in the same direction with a velocity of 150 cm per second and with an acceleration equal to 90 cm per sec. Find when and where it will overtake the first particle.

16. A point moves over 7 metres in the first second during which it is observed, and over 11 and 17 metres in the third and sixth seconds respectively; is this consistent with the supposition that it is subject to a uniform acceleration?

17. A point is moving in a north-east direction with a velocity 6, and has acceleration 8 towards the north and 6 towards the east. Find its position after the lapse of one second. [The units are a centimetre and a second.]

18. A particle starts with a velocity of 200 cm per second and moves in a straight line with a retardation of 10 cm per sec.; find how long elapses before it has described 1500 cm and explain the double answer.

19. Two points move in the same straight line starting at the same moment from the same point in it; the first moves with constant velocity u and the second with constant acceleration f; during the time that elapses before the second catches the first, show that the greatest distance between the particles is $\frac{u^2}{2f}$ at the end of time $\frac{u}{f}$ from the start.

20. In a run of 12 minutes from rest to rest a train has the following speeds, in miles per hour, at the end of each minute; 25, 40, 50, 50, 45, 40, 40, 45, 45, 35, 20, 0. Draw a curve representing the relation between the speed at any instant and the time from the start, and estimate the average velocity during the run.

21. A point starts from rest, and its velocities at the end of each second up to the seventh are as follows : 5, 18, 38, 62, 78, 81 and 83 m per second. Sketch the velocity curve on a time base, and estimate the distance through which the point moves in the seven seconds. Estimate also the instant at which the acceleration is greatest and the value of the acceleration at that instant.

22. The velocities of a body are found to be 4, 8.8, 19, 22, 15.7 and 10 m per second at intervals of 5 seconds from rest. Plot the curve of velocities to a time base, and estimate the distance passed over in the 30 seconds. Find also the acceleration at 16 seconds from the start.

23. A train stopping at two stations 4 km apart takes 4 minutes on the journey from one of the stations to the other. Assuming that its motion is first that of uniform acceleration x and then that of uniform retardation, y, prove that $\frac{1}{x} + \frac{1}{y} = 2$.

24. If v_1, v_2, v_3 be the average velocities in three successive intervals of time t_1, t_2, t_3 of a point moving in a straight line with uniform acceleration, show that

$$\frac{v_1 - v_2}{v_2 - v_3} = \frac{t_1 + t_2}{t_2 + t_3}$$

25. Two trains on the same line are approaching one another with velocities u_1 and u_2 respectively. When there is a distance x between them each is seen from the other. prove that it is just possible to avoid a collision if

$$u_1^2 f_2 + u_2^2 f_1 = 2 f_1 f_2 x$$

where f_1 and f_2 are the greatest retardations which the brakes can produce in the respective trains.

26. If a point moving under uniform acceleration describes successive equal distances in time t_1, t_2, t_3, then

$$\frac{1}{t_1} - \frac{1}{t_2} + \frac{1}{t_3} = \frac{3}{t_1 + t_2 + t_3}$$

27. Prove that for a particle moving with uniform acceleration f in a straight line,

$$f = 2\left(\frac{s'}{t'} - \frac{s}{t}\right)\Big/(t + t')$$

where s is the space described in t seconds, s' during the next t' seconds.

28. A distance s is divided into n equal parts at the end of each of which the acceleration of a moving particle is increased by $\frac{f}{n}$; show that the velocity of the particle after describing the distance is $\sqrt{fs\left(3 - \frac{1}{n}\right)}$ where f is the initial acceleration of the particle starting from rest.

29. The velocity of a train increases at a constant rate f_1 from o at v, then remains constant for an interval, and finally decreases to 0 at the constant rate f_2. If x be the total distance described, prove that the total time taken is

$$\frac{x}{v} + \frac{v}{2}\left(\frac{1}{f_1} + \frac{1}{f_2}\right)$$

30. If a, b, c be the space described by a particle during the pth, q^{th}, r^{th}, seconds of its motion respectively, prove that

$$a(q - r) + b(q - p) + c(p - q) = 0$$

31. The law of motion of a body moving along a straight line is $x = \frac{1}{2}vt$, x being its distance from a fixed point on the line at time t, and v its velocity there; prove that it moves with a constant acceleration.

32. A particle moves from rest at a distance c from a fixed point o, with an acceleration $\frac{\mu}{x^2}$ away from o at a distance x. Find its velocity when it is at a distance $2c$ from o.

33. A particle moves in a straight line with an acceleration $n^2 x$ away from a fixed point o on the line, x being the distance of the particle from o and n being a constant.

If $x = a$ and $\frac{dx}{dt} = V$ at time $t = o$, show that at time t,

$$x = a\cosh nt + \frac{V}{n}\sinh nt$$

34. A particle moves along a straight line, and at a distance x from a fixed point o on the line its velocity is $\mu\sqrt{\frac{c - x}{x}}$. Prove that its acceleration is directed towards o and is inversely proportional to the square of the distance.

3

Motion Under Gravity

40. Acceleration of falling bodies. When a heavy body of any kind falls towards the earth, it is a matter of everyday experience that it goes quicker and quicker as it falls, or, in other words, that it moves with an *acceleration.* That is moves with a *constant* acceleration may be roughly shown by the following experiment first performed by Morin.

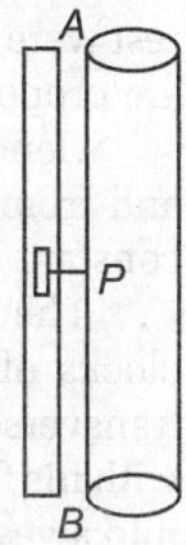

A circular cylinder covered with paper is connected with clock-work and made to rotate about its axis which is vertical. In front of the cylinder is an iron weight, carrying a pencil P, which is compelled by guides to fall in a vertical line and is so arranged that the tip of the pencil just touches the paper on the surface of the cylinder.

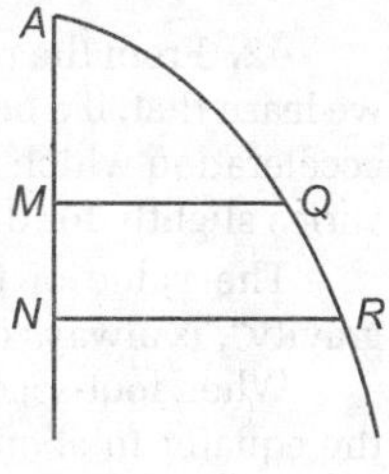

When the cylinder is revolving uniformly, the weight is allowed to drop and the pencil traces out a curve on the paper. When the weight has reached the ground the paper is unwrapped and stretched out on a flat surface. The curve marked out by the pencil is found to be such that the vertical distances described by the pencil from the beginning of the motion are always proportional to the squares of the horizontal distances described by it, so that, if Q, R be any two points on the curve, then

$$\frac{AM}{AN} = \frac{QM^2}{RN^2}.$$

Now since the cylinder revolved uniformly, these horizontal distances are proportional to times that have elapsed from the commencement of the motion. Hence the vertical distance described is proportional to the square of the time from the commencement of the motion.

But, from Art. 34, we know that, if a point moves from rest with a constant acceleration, the space described is proportional to the square of the time.

Hence we infer that a falling body moves with a constant acceleration.

41. Galileo's Experiment. That the acceleration of a falling body is constant was first shown by Galileo by some experiments conducted at Pisa about the year 1590. To avoid the difficulty of measuring the velocity of a freely falling body, which soon becomes very large, he considered the motion down an inclined plane instead, and assumed that the law of motion for a small sphere rolling down a groove in an inclined plane would be similar to that of a freely falling body.

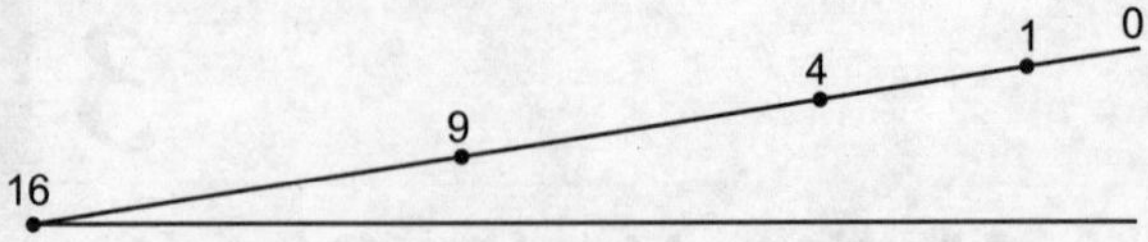

Commencing from the top of his groove, he measured off distances down it proportional to 1, 4, 9, 16, ..., i.e., proportional to $1^2, 2^2, 3^2, 4^2, \ldots$. He then let his small sphere start from the top, and verified that the times of its describing these distances were proportional to 1, 2, 3, 4, ... Hence the distances described from rest were proportional to the squares of the times. But, as in Art. 34, the distances are proportional to the squares of the times when the acceleration *f* is constant.

Hence it follows that the acceleration down the inclined plane is constant, and from that Galileo assumed that the acceleration of a freely falling body is constant also.

The great difficulty Galileo had was in measuring time accurately, as the clocks of his time were very inaccurate. He used a vessel of water of large transverse section which had in its bottom of small hole which he could close with his finger. When the ball started he removed his finger, and the water ran out into a vessel placed to receive it. When the ball had reached one of his marks he closed the hole; the water that had meantime run out was then weighed, and formed a fairly accurate measure of the time that had elapsed.

42. From the results of the foregoing, and other more accurate, experiments we learn that, if a body be let fall towards the earth *in vacuo*, it will move with an acceleration which is always the same at the same place on the earth, but which varies slightly for different places.

The value of this acceleration, which is called the "acceleration due to gravity", is always denoted by the letter "*g*".

When foot-second units are used, the value of *g* varies from about 32.091 at the equator to about 32.252 at the poles. In the latitude of London its value is about 32.19.

When centimetre-second units are used, the extreme limits are about 978 and 983 respectively, and in the latitude of London the value is about 981.17.

The best method of determining the value of "*g*" is by means of pendulum experiments; we shall return to the subject again in Chapter XI.

[*In all numerical examples, unless it is otherwise stated, the motion may be supposed to be* in vacuo, *and the value of g taken to be* 32 ft/sec^2 or ft.s^{-2}, and 981 cm/sec^2 or cm.s^{-2}.]

N.B. Where convenient, we assume $g = 980$ cm/sec^2 or 9.8 m/sec^2.

In the M.K.S. system, $g = 9.81$ m/sec^2.

43. Vertical motion under gravity. Suppose a body is projected vertically from a point on the earth's surface so that it starts with velocity *u*. The acceleration of the body is opposite to the initial direction of motion, and is therefore denoted by $-g$. Hence the velocity of the body continually gets less and less until it vanishes; the body is then for an instant at rest, but immediately begins to acquire a velocity in a downward direction, and retraces its steps.

Time to a given height. The height h at which a body has arrived in time t is given by substituting $-g$ for f in equation (2) of Art. 32, and is therefore given by

$$h = ut - \frac{1}{2}gt^2.$$

This is a quadratic equation with both roots positive; the lesser root gives the time at which the body is at the given height on the way up, and the greater the time at which it is at the same height on the way down.

Thus the time that elapses before a body, which starts with a velocity of 19.6 m per second, is at a height of 8.575 m is given by

$$857.5 = 1960t - 490t^2 \text{ whence}$$

$$t = \frac{1}{2} \text{ or } \frac{7}{2}$$

$$(\text{assume } g = 980\,\text{cm/sec}^2.)$$

Hence the particle is at the given height in half a second from the commencement of its motion, and again in 3 seconds afterwards.

44. *Velocity at a given height.*

The velocity v at a given height h is, by equation (3) of Art. 32, given by

$$v^2 = u^2 - 2gh.$$

Hence the velocity at a given height is independent of the time from the start, and is therefore the same at the same point whether the body be going upwards or downwards.

45. *Greatest height attained.*

At the highest point the velocity is just zero; hence, if x be the greatest height attained, we have

$$0 = u^2 - 2gx.$$

Hence, the greatest height attained $= \dfrac{u^2}{2g}$.

Also the time T to the greatest height is given by

$$0 = u - gT.$$

$$\therefore \quad T = \frac{u}{g}.$$

46. *Velocity due to a given vertical fall from rest.*

If a body be dropped from rest, its velocity after falling through a height h is obtained by substituting 0, g, and h for u, f and s in equation (3) of Art. 32;

$$\therefore \quad v = \sqrt{2gh}.$$

Examples. VI.

1. A body is projected from the earth vertically with a velocity of 1308 cm per second; find (1) how high it will go before coming to rest, (2) what times will elapse before it is at a height of 654 cm.
2. A particle is projected vertically upwards with a velocity of 1308 cm per second. Find (i) when its velocity will be 872 cm per second, and (ii) when it will be 872 cm above the point of projection.
3. A stone is thrown vertically upwards with a velocity of 3924 cm per second. After what times will its velocity be 1962 cm per second, and at what height will it then be?
4. Find (1) the distance fallen from rest by a body in 10 seconds, (2) the time of falling 327 cm, (3) the initial vertical velocity when the body describes 29430 cm downwards in 10 seconds.
5. A stone is thrown vertically into a mine-shaft with a velocity of 2943 cm per second, and reaches the bottom in 3 seconds; find the depth of the shaft.
6. A body is projected from the bottom of a mine, whose depth is $88g$ cm, with a velocity of $24g$ cm per second; find the time in which the body, after rising to its greatest height, will return to the surface of the earth again.
7. The greatest height attained by a particle projected vertically upwards is 5886 cm; find how soon after projection the particle will be at a height of 3270 cm.
8. A body moving in a vertical direction passes a point at a height of 54.5 centimetres with a velocity of 436 centimetres per second; with what initial velocity was it thrown up, and for how much longer will it rise?
9. A particle passes a given point moving downwards with a velocity of fifty metres per second; how long before this was it moving upwards at the same rate?
10. A body is projected vertically upwards with a velocity of 6540 centimetres per second; how high does it rise, and for how long is it moving upwards?
11. Given that a body falling freely passes through 5390 cm in the sixth second, find the value of g.
12. A falling particle in the last second of its fall passes through 5886 cm. Find the height from which it fell, and the time of its falling.
13. A body falls freely from the top of a tower, and during the last second of its flight falls $\frac{16}{25}$ths of the whole distance. Find the height of the tower.
14. A body falls freely from the top of a tower, and during the last second it falls $\frac{9}{25}$ths of the whole distance. Find the height of the tower.
15. A stone A is thrown vertically upwards with a velocity of 2943 cm per second; find how high it will rise. After 4 seconds from the projection of A, another stone B is let fall from the same point. Show that A will overtake B after 4 seconds more.
16. A body is projected upwards with a certain velocity, and it is found that when in its ascent it is 29430 cm from the ground it takes 4 seconds to return to the same point again; find the velocity of projection and the whole height ascended.

17. A body projected vertically downwards described $22072\frac{1}{2}$ cm in t seconds, and 68670 cm in $2t$ seconds; find t, and the velocity of projection.

18. A stone is dropped into a well, and the sound of the splash is heard in $7\frac{7}{10}$ seconds; if the velocity of sound be 343 m per second, find the depth of the well. Assume $g = 980 \text{ cm/sec}^2$.

19. A stone is dropped into a well and reaches the bottom with a velocity of 96 feet per second, and the sound of the splash on the water reaches the top of the well in $3\frac{9}{70}$ seconds from the time the stone starts; find the velocity of sound.

20. Assuming the acceleration of a falling body at the surface of the moon to be one-sixth of its value on the earth's surface, find the height to which a particle will rise if it be projected vertically upward from the surface of the moon with a velocity of 40 metres per second.

47. Motion down a smooth inclined plane.

Let AB be the vertical section of a smooth inclined plane inclined at a given angle α to the horizon, and let P be a body on the plane.

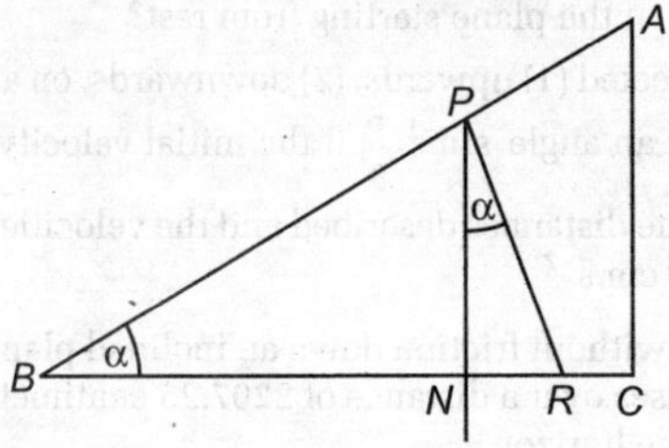

If there were no plane to stop its motion, the body would fall vertically with an acceleration g.

Now, by the parallelogram of accelerations, a vertical acceleration g is equivalent to

(1) an acceleration $g \cos \alpha$ perpendicular to the plane in the direction PR, and (2) an acceleration $g \sin \alpha$ down the plane.

The plane prevents any motion perpendicular to itself.

Hence the body moves down the plane with an acceleration $g \sin \alpha$, and the investigation of its motion is similar to that of a freely falling body, except that instead of g we have to substitute $g \sin \alpha$.

It follows at once that the velocity acquired in sliding from rest down a length l of the plane

$$= \sqrt{2g \sin \alpha \cdot l} = \sqrt{2g \cdot l \sin \alpha} = \sqrt{2g \cdot AC},$$

and is therefore the same as that acquired by a particle in falling freely through a vertical height equal to that of the plane. In other words the velocity acquired is independent of the inclination of the plane and depends only on the vertical height through which the particle has fallen.

48. If the body be projected up the plane with initial velocity u, an investigation similar to that of Arts. 43-45 will give the motion. The greatest distance attained, measured up the plane, is $\frac{u^2}{2g \sin \alpha}$; the time taken in traversing this distance is $\frac{u}{g \sin \alpha}$, and so on.

Examples. VII.

1. A body is projected with a velocity of 2943 cm per second up a smooth inclined plane, whose inclination is 30°; find the distance described, and the time that elapses, before it comes to rest.
2. A heavy particle slides from rest down a smooth inclined plane which is 1090 cm long and 218 cm high. What is its velocity when it reaches the ground, and how long does it take?
3. A particle sliding down a smooth plane, 1962 cm long, acquires a velocity of 981 $\sqrt{2}$ cm per second; find the inclination of the plane.
4. What is the ratio of the height to the length of a smooth inclined plane, so that a body may be four times as long in sliding down the plane as in falling freely down the height of the plane starting from rest?
5. A particle is projected (1) upwards, (2) downwards, on a plane which is inclined to the horizon at an angle $\sin^{-1} \frac{5}{3}$; if the initial velocity be 4.8 m per second in each case, find the distances described and the velocities acquired in 4 seconds. Assume $g = 980 \text{ cm.s}^{-2}$.
6. A particle slides without friction down an inclined plane, and in the 5th second after starting passes over a distance of 2207.25 centimetres; find the inclination of the plane to the horizon.
7. *AB* is a vertical diameter of a circle, whose plane is vertical, and *PQ* a diameter inclined at an angle θ to *AB*. Find θ so that the time of sliding down *PQ* may be twice that of sliding down *AB*.

49. Theorem. *The time that a body takes to slide down any smooth chord of a vertical circle, which is drawn from the highest point of the circle, is constant.*

Let *AB* be a diameter of a vertical circle, of which *A* is the highest point and *AD* any chord.

Let $\angle DAB = \theta$; put $AD = x$ and $AB = a$, so that

$$x = a \cos \theta.$$

As in the last article, the acceleration down *AD* is $g \cos \theta$. Let *T* be the time from *A* to *D*. Then *AD* is the distance described in time *T* by a particle starting from rest and moving with acceleration $g \cos \theta$.

$$\therefore \qquad x = \frac{1}{2} g \cos \theta \cdot T^2.$$

$$\therefore \qquad T = \sqrt{\frac{2x}{g \cos \theta}} = \sqrt{\frac{2a}{g}}.$$

This result is independent of θ, and is the same as the time of falling vertically through the distance AB.

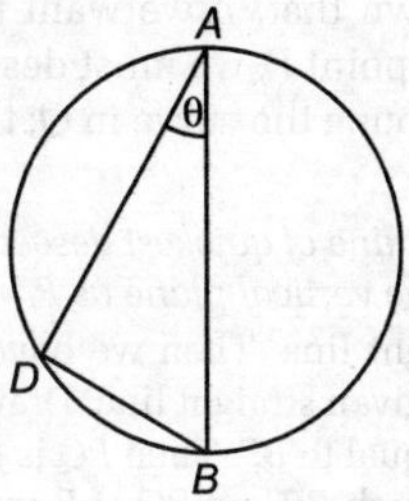

Hence the time of falling down all chords of this circle beginning at A is the same.

The same theorem will be found to be true for all chords of the same circle *ending* in the *lowest* point.

50. Lines of quickest descent. The line of quickest descent from a given point to a curve in the same vertical plane is the straight line down which a body would slide from the given point to the given curve in the shortest *time.*

It is not, in general, the same line as the geometrically shortest line that can be drawn from the given point to the curve. For example, the straight line down which the time from a given point to a given plane is least, is *not* the perpendicular from the given point upon the given plane, except in the case where the given plane is horizontal.

51. Theorem. *The chord of quickest descent from a given point P to a curve in the same vertical plane is PQ, where Q is a point on the curve such that a circle, having P at its highest point, touches the curve at Q.*

For let a circle be drawn, having its highest point at P, to touch the given curve externally in Q. Take *any* other point Q_1 on the curve, and let PQ_1 meet the circle again in R.

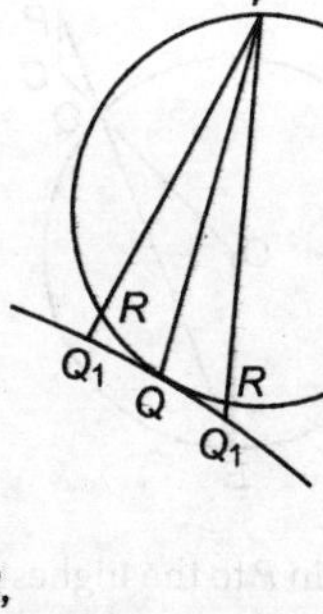

Then, since PQ_1 is > PR,
the time down PQ_1 is > time down PR.
But time down PR = time down PQ (Art. 49),
so that the time down PQ_1 is > time down PQ,
and Q_1 is any point on the given curve.

Hence the time down PQ is less than that down any other straight line from P to the given curve.

Similarly it may be shown that, if we want the chord of quickest descent from a given curve to a given point P, we must describe a circle having the given point P as its lowest point to touch the curve in Q; then QP is the required straight line.

Ex. 1. *To find the straight line of quickest descent from a given point P to a given straight line which is in the same vertical plane as P.*

Let BC be the given straight line. Then we have to describe a circle having its highest point at P to touch the given straight line. Draw PB horizontal to meet BC in B. From BC cut off a portion BQ equal to BP. Then PQ is the required chord; for it is clear that a circle can be drawn to touch BP and BQ at P and Q respectively.

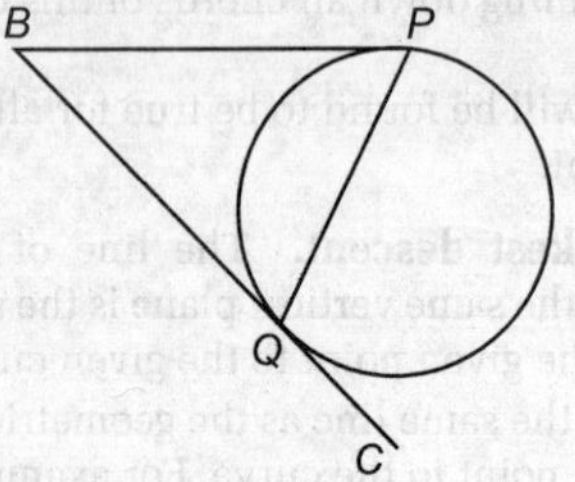

Ex. 2. *To find the line of quickest descent from a given point to a given circle in the same vertical plane.*

Join P to the lowest point B of the given circle to meet the circle again in Q. Then PQ is the required line. For join O, the centre of the circle, to Q and produce to meet the vertical line through P in C.

The $\angle QPC = \angle OBC$, since OB and CP are parallel,

$= \angle OQB = \angle CQP.$

Hence a circle whose centre is C, and radius OP, will have its higher point at P and will touch the given circle at Q.

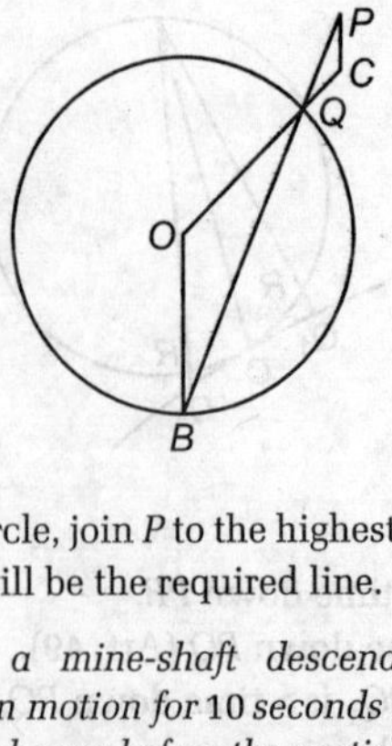

If P be within the given circle, join P to the highest point and produce to meet the circumference in Q; then PQ will be the required line.

52. Ex. 1. *A cage in a mine-shaft descends with* 80 *cm/sec. units of acceleration. After it has been in motion for* 10 *seconds a particle is dropped on it from the top of the shaft. What time elapses before the particle hits the cage?*

Let T be the time that elapses after the second particle starts. The distance it has fallen through is therefore $\frac{1}{2}gT^2$. The cage has been in motion for $(T + 10)$ seconds, and therefore the distance it has fallen through is

$\frac{1}{2} \cdot 80\,(T + 10)^2$ or $40(T + 10)^2$.

Hence we have $40\,(T + 10)^2 = \frac{1}{2}gT^2 = 490T^2$. (assuming $g = 980$ cm/sec^2.)

$$\therefore \qquad T + 10 = 3\frac{1}{2}T.$$

$$\therefore \qquad T = 4 \text{ seconds}.$$

Ex. 2. *A stone is thrown vertically with the velocity which would just carry it to a height of 40 m. Two seconds later another stone is projected vertically from the same place with the same velocity; when and where will they meet?*

Let u be the initial velocity of projection. Since the greatest height is 40 m, we have

$$0 = u^2 - 2g \cdot 40$$

$$\therefore \qquad u = \sqrt{2g \cdot 40} = 28 \text{ m (assuming } g = 9.8 \text{ m/sec}^2.)$$

Let T be the time after the first stone starts before the two stones meet.

Then the distance traversed by the first stone in time T = distance traversed by the second stone in time $(T - 2)$.

$$\therefore \qquad 28T - \frac{1}{2}gT^2 = 28\,(T - 2) - \frac{1}{2}g\,(T - 2)^2$$

$$= 28T - 56 - \frac{1}{2}g(T^2 - 4T + 4)$$

$$\therefore \qquad 56 = \frac{1}{2}g\,(4T - 4) = 4.9\,(4T - 4)$$

$$\therefore \qquad T = 3\frac{6}{7} \text{ seconds}.$$

Also the height at which they meet $= 28T - \frac{1}{2}gT^2$

$$= 108 - 72.9 = 35.1 \text{ m}.$$

The first stone will be coming down and the second stone going upwards.

Examples. VIII.

1. From a balloon, ascending with a velocity of 981 cm per second, a stone is let fall and reaches the ground in 10 seconds; how high was the balloon when the stone was dropped?
2. If a body be let fall from a height of 1962 cm at the same instant that another is sent vertically from the foot of the height with a velocity of 1962 cm per second, what time elapses before they meet?
   If the first body starts 1 sec. later than the other, what time will elapse?
3. A tower is 15696 cm high; one body is dropped from the top of the tower and at the same instant another is projected vertically upwards from the bottom, and

they meet half-way up; find the initial velocity of the projected body and its velocity when it meets the descending body.

4. A body is dropped from the top of a given tower, and at the same instant a body is projected from the foot of the tower, in the same vertical line, with a velocity which would be just sufficient to take it to the same height as the tower; find where they will meet.

5. A particle is dropped from a height h, and after falling $\frac{2}{3}$rds of that distance passes a particle which was projected upwards at the instant when the first was dropped. Find to what height the latter will attain.

6. A body begins to slide down a smooth inclined plane from rest at the top, and at the same instant another body is projected upwards from the foot of the plan with such a velocity that they meet halfway up the plane; find the velocity of projection and determine the velocity of each when they meet.

7. A body is projected upwards with velocity u, and t seconds afterwards another body is similarly projected with the same velocity; find when and where they will meet.

8. A balloon ascends with a uniform acceleration of $122\frac{5}{8}$ cm/sec. units; at the end of half a minute a body is released from it; find the time that elapses before the body reaches the ground.

9. After a ball has been falling under gravity for 5 seconds it passes through a pane of glass and loses half its velocity; if it now reaches the ground in 1 second, find the height of the glass above the ground.

10. The space described by a falling body in the last second of its motion is to that described in the last second but one as 3 : 2; find the height from which the body was dropped, and the velocity with which it strikes the ground.

11. A plane is of length 8829 cm and of height 1962 cm; show how to divide it into three parts so that a particle at the top of the plane may describe the portions in equal times, and find these times.

12. Show that the time that a particle takes to slide down a chord of a vertical circle, starting from one end of horizontal diameter, varies as the square root of the tangent of the inclination of the chord to the vertical.

13. A number of smooth rods meet in a point A and rings placed on them slide down the rods, starting simultaneously from A. Show that after a time t the rings are all on a sphere of radius $\frac{gt^2}{4}$.

14. A number of bodies slide from rest down smooth inclined planes which all commence at the same point and terminate on the same horizontal plane; show that the velocities acquired are the same.

15. Two heavy bodies descend the height and length respectively of a smooth inclined plane; show that the times vary as the spaces described and that the velocities acquired are equal.

16. A heavy particle slides down a smooth inclined plane of given height; show that the time of descent varies as the secant of the inclination of the plane to the vertical.

17. A body slides down smooth chords of a vertical circle ending in its lowest point; show that the velocity on reaching the lowest point varies as the length of the chord.

18. If two circles touch each other at their highest or lowest points, and a straight line be drawn through the point to meet both circles, show that the time of sliding from rest down the portion of this line intercepted between the two circles is constant.

19. A plane, of height h and inclination α to the horizon, has a smooth groove cut in it inclined at an angle β to the line of greatest slope; find the time that a particle would take to describe the groove starting from rest at the top.

20. If a length s be divided into n equal parts at the end of each of which the acceleration of a moving points is increased by $\frac{f}{n}$, find the velocity of particle after describing the distance s if it started from rest with acceleration f.

21. A particle starts from rest with acceleration f; at the end of time t it becomes $2f$; it becomes $3f$ at end of time $2t$, and so on. Find the velocity at the end of time nt, and show that the distance described is

$$\frac{n(n+1)(2n+1)}{12} f \cdot t^2.$$

22. A body starts from rest and moves with uniform acceleration; show that the distance described in the $(n^2 + n + 1)$th second is equal to the distance described in the first n seconds together with the distance described in the first $(n + 1)$ seconds.

23. If a particle occupies n seconds less and acquires a velocity of m feet per second more at one place that at another in falling through the same distance, show that $\frac{m}{n}$ equals the geometrical mean between the numerical values of gravity at the two places.

24. A train goes from rest at one station to rest at another, 1584 metres off, being uniformly accelerated for the first $\frac{2}{3}$ *rds* of the journey and uniformly retarded for the remainder, and takes 3 minutes to describe the whole distance. Find the acceleration, the retardation, and the maximum velocity.

25. An engine-driver suddenly puts on his brake and shuts off steam when he is running at full speed; in the first second afterwards the train travels 2610 cm and in the next 2550 cm. Find the original speed of the train, the time that elapses before it comes to rest, and the distance it will travel in this interval, assuming the brake to cause a constant retardation. Find also the time the train will take, if it be 86 metres 40 cm long, to pass a spectator standing at a point 435 metres 60 cm ahead of the train at the instant when the brake was applied.

26. A railway-train goes from one station to another moving during the first part of the journey with uniform acceleration f; when steam is shut off and the brakes are applied, it moves with uniform retardation f'. If a be the distance between the stations, show that the time the train takes is

$$\sqrt{2a\frac{f+f'}{ff'}}.$$

27. During the first quarter of the journey from a station A to a station B the velocity of a train is uniformly accelerated, and during the last quarter it is uniformly retarded, and the middle half of the journey is performed at a uniform speed. Show that the average speed of the train is $\frac{2}{3}$rds of the full speed.

28. A lift ascending from a pit 600 metres deep rises during the first part of its ascent with uniform acceleration. On nearing the top the upward force is cut off, and the impetus of the lift is just sufficient to carry it to the top. If the whole process occupies 30 sec., find the acceleration during the first part of the ascent, and the maximum velocity attained.

29. A train starts from rest and reaches its greatest speed of 80 km per hour in 5 minutes. This speed is maintained till it is 800 metres from the next stopping place. Find the values of the acceleration and retardation in metre-second units, and the whole time taken for the journey if it be 160 km. Draw also the velocity-time curve for the whole journey.

4

The Laws of Motion

53. In the present chapter we propose to consider the production of motion, and it will be necessary to commence with a few elementary definitions.

Matter is "that which can be perceived by the senses" or "that which can be acted upon by, or can exert, force".

No definition can however be given that would convey an idea of what matter is to anyone who did not already possess that idea. It, like time and space, is a primary conception.

A **particle** is a portion of matter which is infinitely small in all its dimensions, or, at any rate, so small that for the purpose of our investigations the distances between the different portions of it may be neglected. Sometimes bodies of a finite size can be treated as particles, as in the case of a cricket ball thrown into the air, or of a stone falling to the ground. Again in considering the motion of the Earth round the Sun, the Earth itself may be treated as a particle.

A **Body** is a portion of matter which is bounded by surfaces, and which is limited in every direction, so that it consists of a very large number of material particles.

The **Mass** of a body is the quantity of matter in the body.

Force is that which changes, or tends to change, the state of rest or uniform motion of a body.

These definitions may appear to the student to be vague, but we may illustrate their meaning somewhat as follows.

If we have a small portion of any substance, say iron, resting on a smooth table, we may be a push be able to move it fairly easily; if we take a larger quantity of the same iron, the same effort on our part will be able to move it less easily. Again, if we take two portions of platinum and wood of exactly the same size and shape, the effect produced on these two substances by equal efforts on our part will be quite different. Once more, if we have a croquet-ball and a cannon-ball, both of the same size, lying at rest on the ground, and we kick each of them with the same force, the effect on the first is greater than that on the second. So also we can distinguish between a cask full of water, and an empty one of the same size, by watching the effect of equal kicks applied to them.

Thus common experience shows us that the same effort applied to different bodies, under seemingly the same conditions, does not always produce the same result. This is because the *masses* of the bodies are different.

54. If to the same mass we apply two forces in succession, and they generate the same velocity in the same time, the forces are said to be equal.

If the same force be applied to two different masses, and if it produces in them the same velocity in the same time, the masses are said to be equal.

The student will notice that we here assume that it is possible to create forces of equal intensity on different occasions, e.g., we assume that the force necessary to keep a spiral spring stretched through the same distance is the same when other conditions are unaltered.

Hence, by applying the same force in succession, we can obtain a number of masses each equal to a standard unit of mass. The foregoing would be a theoretical method of defining equal masses, applicable under all conditions. In practice, we shall find that equal masses have equal weights, so that the process of weighing is the simplest practical method of comparing masses.

55. The British unit of mass is called the Imperial Pound, and consists of a lump of platinum deposited at Westminster, of which there are in addition several accurate copies kept in other places of safety.

The French, or scientific, unit of mass is called a gramme, and is the one-thousandth part of certain quantity of platinum kept in Paris. The gramme was meant to be defined as the mass of a cubic centimetre of pure water at a temperature of 4°C.

It is a much smaller unit than a Pound.

One Gramme = about 15.432 grains.

One Pound = about 453.6 grammes.

The system of units in which a centimetre, gramme and second, are respectively the units of length, mass, and time, is generally called the C.G.S. system of units.

56. Density. The density of a uniform body is the mass of a unit volume of the body; so that; if m be the mass of volume V of a body whose density is ρ, then

$$m = V\rho.$$

57. The **Weight** of a body is the force with which the earth attracts the body.

It can be shown that every particle of matter in nature attracts every other particle with a force, which varies directly as the product of the masses of the quantities, and inversely as the square of the distance between them; hence it can be deduced that a sphere attracts a particle on, or outside, its surface with a force which varies inversely as the square of the distance of the particle from the centre of the sphere. The earth is not accurately a sphere, and therefore points on its surface are not equidistant from the centre; hence the attraction of the earth for a given mass is not quite the same at all points of its surface, and therefore the weight of a given mass is slightly different at different points of the earth.

58. The **Momentum** of a body is proportional to the product of the mass and the velocity of the body.

If we take as the unit of momentum the momentum of a unit mass moving with unit velocity, then the momentum of a body is mv, where m is the mass and v the velocity of the body. The direction of the momentum is the same as that of the velocity.

Thus the momentum of a body of 100 grammes moving with velocity 275 cm per sec. is 27500 centimetre-gramme-second units of momentum.

59. We can now enunciate what are commonly called Newton's Laws of Motion. "The first two were discovered by Galileo (about the year 1590) and the third in some of its many forms was known to Hooke, Huyghens, Wallis, Wren and others before the publication of the *Principia*." They were put into formal shape by Newton in his *Principia* published in the year 1686.

They are :

Law I. *Every body continues in its state of rest, or of uniform motion in a straight line, except in so far as it be compelled by external impressed force to change that state.*

Law II. *The rate of change of momentum is proportional to the impressed force, and takes place in the direction of the straight line in which the force acts.*

Law III. *To every action there is an equal and opposite reaction.*

No strictly formal proof, experimental or otherwise, can be given of these three laws. On them however is based the whole system of Dynamics, and on Dynamics the whole theory of Astronomy. Now the results obtained, and the predictions made, from the theory of Astronomy agree so well with the actual observed facts of Astronomy that it is inconceivable that the original laws on which the subject is based should be erroneous. For example, the Nautical Almanac is published four years beforehand; the motions of the Moon and the Planets are therein predicted, and the time and place of Eclipses of the Sun and Moon foretold; and the predictions in it are always correct. Hence the real reason for our belief in the truth of the above three laws of motion is that the conclusions drawn from them agree with our experience.

60. Law I. We never see this law actually exemplified on the Earth because it is practically impossible ever to get rid of all forces during the motion of the body. It may be seen approximately in operation in the case of a piece of dry, hard ice projected along the surface of dry, well swept ice. The only forces acting on the fragment of ice, in the direction of its motion, are the friction between the two portions of ice and the resistance of the air. The smoother the surface of the ice the further the small portion will go, and the less the resistance of the air the further it will go. The above law asserts that **if** the ice were perfectly smooth and **if** there were no resistance of the air and no other forces acting on the body, then it would go on for ever in a straight line with uniform velocity.

The law states a principle sometimes called the **Principle of Inertia,** viz.—that a body has no *innate* tendency to change its state of rest or of uniform motion in a straight line. A lump of iron resting on the ground does not move by itself, nor unless it is acted upon by a force external to itself.

If a portion of metal attached to a piece of string be swung round on a smooth horizontal table, then, if the string breaks, the metal, having no longer any force acting on it, proceeds to move in a straight line, viz. the tangent to the circle at the point at which its circular motion ceased.

If a man steps out of a rapidly moving train he is generally thrown to the ground; his feet on touching the ground are brought to rest; but, as no force acts on the upper part of his body, it continues its motion as before, and the man falls to the ground.

If a man be riding on a horse which is galloping at a fairly rapid pace and the horse suddenly stops, the rider is in danger of being thrown over the horse's head.

If a man be seated upon the back seat of a dog-cart, and the latter suddenly starts, the man is very likely to be left behind.

61. (a) Law II. From this law we derive our method of measuring force.

Let m be the mass of a body, and f the acceleration produced in it by the action of a force whose measure is P.

Then, by the second law of motion,

$P \propto$ rate of change of momentum,

$\propto$ rate of change of mv,

$\propto m \times$ rate of change of v (if m is unaltered),

$\propto m \cdot f$.

$\therefore\ P = \lambda \cdot mf$, where λ is some constant.

Now let the unit of force be so chosen that it may produce in unit mass the unit of acceleration.

Hence, when $m = 1$ and $f = 1$, we have $P = 1$,

and therefore $\lambda = 1$.

The unit of force being thus chosen, we have

$$P = m \cdot f.$$

Therefore, when proper units are chosen, the measure of the force is *equal* to the measure of the rate of change of the momentum.

61. (b) The above result can also be deduced by use of calculus as follows :

$$\text{Force} \propto \text{rate of change of momentum.}$$

$$\propto \frac{d}{dt}(mv)$$

$$\propto m\frac{dv}{dt} \text{ (if } m \text{ is unaltered)}$$

$$\propto m \cdot f.$$

$\therefore\ P = \lambda \cdot mf$, where λ is some constant.

Then proceeding as in Art. 61(a), we get $\lambda = 1$.

62. (a) From the preceding Article it follows that the magnitude of the unit of force used in Dynamics depends on the units of mass, and acceleration, that we use. The unit of acceleration, again, depends, by Arts. 9 and 29, on the units of length and time. Hence the unit of force depends on our units of mass, length and time. When these latter units are given the unit of force is a determinate quantity.

When a pound, a foot, and a second are respectively the units of mass, length, and time, the corresponding unit of force is called a **Poundal.**

Hence the equation P = mf is a true relation, m being the number of pounds in the body, P the number of poundals in the force acting on it, and f the acceleration, in ft/sec^2, produced in the mass m by the action of the force P on it.

This relation is sometimes expressed in the form

$$\text{Acceleration} = \frac{\text{Moving Force}}{\text{Mass moved}}.$$

(b) In the M.K.S. system of units, mass is in kilogrammes, acceleration in m/sec^2 and force in newtons.

63. When a gramme, a centimetre, and a second are respectively the units of mass, length, and time, the corresponding unit of force is called a **Dyne.** [This name is derived from the Greek word *δvvαμis*, pronounced Dunamis, which means Force.]

Hence when the equation $P = mf$ is used in this system the force must be expressed in dynes, the mass in grammes, and the acceleration in cm/sec^2.

64. Connection between the unit of force and the weight of the unit of mass. As explained in Art. 42, we know that, when a body drops freely *in vacuo* it moves with an acceleration which we denote by "g"; also the force which causes this acceleration is that which we call its weight.

Now the unit of force acting on the unit of mass produces in it the unit of acceleration.

Therefore g units of force acting on the unit of mass produced in it g units of acceleration (by the second law).

But the weight of the unit of mass is that which produces in it g units of acceleration.

Hence the weight of the unit of mass = g units of force.

N.B. A mass of 1 gramme is said to have a weight of 1 gramme force (1 *gf*).

65. *Foot-Pound-Second System of units.* In this system g is equal to 32.2 approximately.

Therefore the weight of one pound is equal to g units of force, i.e., to g poundals, where $g = 32.2$ approximately.

Hence a poundal is approximately equal to $\frac{1}{32.2}$ times the weight of a pound, i.e., to the weight of about half an ounce.

Since, g has different values at different points of the earth's surface, and since a poundal is a force which is the same everywhere, it follows that **the weight of a pound gramme or kilogramme is not constant, but has different values at different points of the earth.**

66. *Centimetre-Gramme-Second System of units.* In this system g is equal to 981 approximately.

Therefore the weight of one gramme is equal to g units of force, i.e., to g dynes, where

$$g = 981 \text{ approximately.}$$

Hence a dyne is equal to the weight of about $\frac{1}{981}$ of a gramme.

The dyne is a much smaller unit than a poundal. The approximate relation between them may be easily found as follows :

$$\frac{\text{One Poundal}}{\text{One Dyne}} = \frac{\frac{1}{32.2}\text{ wt. of a pound}}{\frac{1}{981}\text{ wt. of a gramme}}$$

$$= \frac{981}{32.2} \times \frac{\text{one pound}}{\text{one gramme}} = \frac{981}{32.2} \times 453.6 \text{ (by Art. 55).}$$

Hence One Poundal = about 13800 dynes.
N.B. 1 gf = g dynes;
1 kgf (kilogram force) = g newtons symbol for 'newton' is N.

Examples. IX.

1. *A mass of 20 gm is acted on by a constant force which in 5 seconds produces a velocity of 15 cm per second. Find the force, if the mass was initially at rest.*
From the equation $v = u + ft$, we have $f = \frac{15}{5} = 3.$
Also, if P be the force expressed in dynes, we have
$$P = 20 \times 3 = 60 \text{ dynes.}$$
Hence, P is equal to the weight of about $\frac{60}{981}$, i.e., $\frac{20}{327}$ gm or P is $= \frac{20}{327}\, g \cdot f.$

2. *A mass of 10 gm is placed on a smooth horizontal plane, and is acted on by a force equal to the weight of 3 gm; find the distance described by it in 10 seconds.*
Here moving force = weight of 3 gm = $3g$ dynes;
and mass moved = 10 gm.
Hence, if cm/sec. units are used, the acceleration $= \frac{3g}{10}$,
So that the distance required $= \frac{1}{2} \cdot \frac{3g}{10} \cdot 10^2 = 14715$ cm.

3. *Find the magnitude of the force which, acting on a kilogramme for 5 seconds, produces in it a velocity of one metre per second.*
Here the velocity acquired = 100 cm per sec.
Hence the acceleration = 20 C.G.S. units.
Hence the force = 1000 × 20 dynes = weight of about $\frac{1000 \times 20}{981}$ or

4. Find the acceleration produced when
(1) A force of 2000 dynes acts on a mass of 4 kg.
(2) A force equal to the weight of 2 kg acts on a mass of 4 kg.
(3) A force of 50 gf acts on a mass of 10 kg.

5. Find the force expressed (1) in dynes, (2) in terms of the weight of a gramme, that will produce in a mass of 9 kg an acceleration of 300 cm/second units.

6. Find the force which, acting horizontally for 5 seconds on a mass of 3924 gm placed on a smooth table, will generate in it a velocity of 15 metres per second.

7. Find the magnitude of the force which, acting on a mass of 18 kg for 10 seconds, will generate in it a velocity of 5 km per hour.

8. A force, equal to the weight of 2 kg, acts on a mass of 40 kg for half a minute; find the velocity acquired, and the space moved through, in this time.

9. A body, acted upon by a uniform force, in ten seconds describes a distance of 7 metres; compare the force with the weight of the body, and find the velocity acquired.

10. In what time will a force, which is equal to the weight of 3 kg, move a mass of 9 kg, through 2616 cm along a smooth horizontal plane, and what will be the velocity acquired by the mass?

11. A body, of mass 200 metric tonnes, is acted on by a force equal to 2×10^9 dynes; how long will it take to acquire a velocity of 47 km 520 metres per hour?

12. In what time will a force, equal to the weight of 10 kg, acting on a mass of 1 metric tonne moves it through 1962 cm?

13. A mass of 100 kg is placed on a smooth horizontal plane, and a uniform force acting on it parallel to the table for 5 seconds causes it to describe 1500 cm in that time; show that the force is equal to about 12×10^6 dynes weight.

14. A heavy truck, of mass 20 metric tonnes, is standing at rest on a smooth line of rails. A horse now pulls at it steadily in the direction of the line of rails with a force equal to the weight of 60 kg. How far will it move in 1 minute?

15. A force equal to the weight of 10 grammes acts on a mass of 27 grammes for 1 second; find the velocity of the mass and the distance it has travelled over. At the end of the first second the force ceases to act; how far will the body travel in the next minute?

16. A force equal to the weight of a kilogramme acts on a body continuously for 10 seconds, and causes it to describe 10 metres in that time; find the mass of the body.

17. A horizontal force equal to the weight of 5 kg acts on a mass along a smooth horizontal plane; after moving through a space of 750 cm the mass has acquired a velocity of 300 cm per second; find its magnitude.

18. A body is placed on a smooth table and a force equal to the weight of 2.7 kg acts continuously on it; at the end of 3 seconds the body is moving at the rate of 14.6 metres per second; find its mass.

19. A body, of mass 1.36 kg, is falling under gravity at the rate of 30.5 metres per second. What is the uniform force that will stop it (1) in 2 seconds, (2) in 0.61 metre?

20. Of two forces, one acts on a mass of 4 kg and in one-eleventh of a second produces in it a velocity of 1.5 m per second, and the other acting on a mass of 600 kg in 1 minute produces in it a velocity of $28\frac{4}{5}$ kms per hour; compare the two forces.

21. A mass of 5 kg falls 300 cm from rest, and is then brought to rest by penetrating 30 cm into some sand; find the average thrust of the sand on it.

22. A cannon-ball of mass 1000 grmames is discharged with a velocity of 45000 centimetres per second from a cannon the length of whose barrel is 200 centimetres; show that the mean force exerted on the ball during the explosion is 5.0625×10^9 dynes.

23. It was found that when 30.5 cm was cut off from the muzzle of a gun firing a projectile of 45.4 kg, the velocity of the projectile was altered from 454 to 405 metres per second. Show that the force exerted on the projectile by the powder-gas at the muzzle, when expanded in the bore, was about 315 tonnes weight.

24. A bullet moving at the rate of 6000 cm per second is fired into a trunk of wood into which it penetrates 22.5 cm; if a bullet moving with the same velocity were fired into a similar piece of wood 12.5 cm thick, with what velocity would it emerge, supposing the resistance to be uniform?

25. A motor car travelling at the rate of 40 kilometres per hour is stopped by its brakes in 4 seconds; show that it will go about 22 metres from the point at which the brakes are first applied, and that the force exerted by them is about 283 times the weight of the car, and would hold the car at rest on an inclined of about 1 in $3\frac{1}{2}$.

67. A poundal and a dyne are called **Absolute Units** because their values are not dependent on the value of g, which varies at different places on the earth's surface. The *weight* of a pound and of a gramme, that is the pound-force and gramme-force, do depend on this value. Hence they are called **Gravitation Units.**

68. *The weight of a body is proportional to its mass and is independent of the kind of matter of which it is composed.* The following is an experimental fact: If we have an air-tight receiver, and if we allow to drop at the same instant, from the same height, portions of matter of any kind whatever, such as a piece of metal, a feather, a piece of paper, etc., all these substances will be found to have always fallen through the same distance, and to hit the base of the receiver at the same time, whatever be the substances, or the height from which they are allowed to fall. Since these bodies always fall through the same height in the same time, therefore their velocities [rates of change of space] and their accelerations [rates of change of velocity] must be always the same.

The student can approximately perform the above experiment without creating a vacuum. Take a penny and a light substance, say a small piece of paper; place the paper on the penny, held horizontally, and allow both to drop. They will be found to keep together in their fall, although, if they be dropped separately, the penny will reach the ground much quicker than the paper. The penny clears the air out of the way of the paper and so the same result is produced as would be the case if there were no air.

Let W_1 and W_2 dynes be the weights of any two of these bodies, m_1 and m_2 their masses. Then since their accelerations are the same and equal to g, we have

$$W_1 = m_1 g,$$

and

$$W_2 = m_2 g;$$

$$\therefore \quad W_1 : W_2 :: m_1 : m_2.$$

or the weight of a body is proportional to its mass.

Hence bodies whose weights are equal have equal masses; so also the ratio of the masses of two bodies is known when the ratio of their weights is known.

The equation $W = mg$ is a numerical one, and means that the number of units of force in the weight of a body is equal to the product of the number of units of mass in the mass of the body, and the number of units of acceleration produced in the body by its weight.

From the result of Art. 61, combined with this article, we have $\frac{P}{W} = \frac{f}{g}$, i.e., the ratio of any force to the weight of a body is the same as the acceleration produced by the force acting on the body to the acceleration produced by gravity.

This form of the relation between P and f is preferred by some.

69. *Distinction between mass and weight.* The student must carefully notice the difference between the mass and the weight of a body. He has probably been so accustomed to estimate the masses of bodies by means of their weights that he has not clearly distinguished between the two. If it were possible to have a cannon-ball at the centre of the earth it would have no weight there; for the attraction of the earth on a particle at its centre is zero. If, however, it were in motion, the same force would be required to stop it as would be necessary under similar conditions at the surface of the earth. Hence we see that it might be possible for a body to have no weight; its mass however remains unaltered.

The confusion is probably to a great extent caused by the fact that the word "gramme" is used in two senses which are scientifically different; it is used to denote both what we more properly call "the mass of one gramme" and "the weight of one gramme". It cannot be too strongly impressed on the student that, strictly speaking, a gramme is a mass and a mass only; when we wish to speak of the force with which the earth attracts this mass we ought to speak of the "gramme-force" (gf). This latter phrase is often shortened into "a pound", but care must be taken to see in which sense this word is used.

It may also be noted here that the expression "a ball of lead weighing 20 g" is, strictly speaking, an abbreviation for "a ball of lead whose weight is equal to the weight of 20 g". The mass of the lead is 20g; its weight of 20 g dynes.

70. *Weighing by Scales and a Spring Balance.* We have pointed out (Art. 42) that the acceleration due to gravity, i.e., the value of g, varies slightly as we proceed from point to point of the earth's surface. When we weigh out a substance (say tea) by means of a pair of scales, we adjust the tea until the weight of the tea is the same as the weight of sundry pieces of metal whose masses are known, and then, by Art. 68, we know that the mass of the tea is the same as the mass of the metal. Hence a pair of scales really measures masses and not weights, and so the apparent weight of the tea is the same everywhere.

When we use a spring balance, we compare the *weight* of the tea with the *force* necessary to keep the spring stretched through a certain distance. If then we move our tea and spring balance to another place, say from London to Paris, the weight of the tea will be different, whilst the force necessary to keep the spring stretched through the same distance as before will be the same. Hence the weight of the tea will pull the spring through a distance different from the former distance, and hence its apparent weight as shown by the instrument will be different.

If we have two places, A and B, at the first of which the numerical value of g is greater than at the second, then a given mass of tea will [as tested by the spring balance] appear to weigh more at A than it does at B.

Ex. 1. At the equator the value of g is 9.78 and in London the value is 9.81; a merchant buys tea at the equator, at a shilling per kg, and sells in London; at what price per kg (apparent) must he sell so that he may neither gain nor lose, if he uses the same spring balance for both transactions?

A quantity of tea which weighs 1 kg at the equator will appear to weight $\frac{9.81}{9.78}$ kg in London. Hence he should sell $\frac{9.81}{9.78}$ kg for one shilling, or at the rate of $\frac{981}{978}$ shillings per kg.

Ex. 2. At a place A, $g = 9.82$, and at a place B, $g = 9.78$. A merchant buys goods at Ꞩ10 per quintal at A and sells at B, using the same spring balance. If he is to gain 20 per cent., show that his selling price must be nearly Ꞩ12.05 per quintal.

71. Physical Independence of Forces. The latter part of the Second Law states that the change of motion produced by a force is in the direction in which the force acts.

Suppose we have a particle in motion in the direction AB and a force acting on it in the direction AC; then the law states that the velocity in the direction AB is unchanged, and that the only change of velocity is in the direction AC; so that to find the real velocity of the particle at the end of a unit of time, we must compound its velocity in the direction AB with the velocity generated in that unit of time by the force in the direction AC. The same reasoning would hold if we had a second force acting on the particle in some other direction, and so for any system of forces. Hence if a set of forces act on a particle at rest, or in motion, their combined effect is found by considering the effect of each force on the particle *just as if the other forces did not exist, and as if the particle were at rest,* and then compounding these effects. This principle is often referred to as that of the *Physical Independence of Forces.*

As an illustration of this principle consider the motion of a ball allowed to fall from the hand of a passenger in a train which is travelling rapidly. It will be found to hit the floor of the carriage at exactly the same spot as it would have done if the carriage had been at rest. This shows that the ball must have continued to move forward with the same velocity that the train had, or, in other words, the weight of the body only altered the motion in the vertical direction, and had no influence on the horizontal velocity of the particle.

Again, if any two small bodies be placed on the edge of a table, and be hit so that they leave the table at the same moment, but with velocities differing as much as possible, then whatever be their masses of their initial velocities, they will be heard to hit the floor at the same instant. It hence follows that the vertical accelerations and velocities produced in the bodies are independent of their masses and also of their initial velocities.

So also, a circus rider, who wishes to jump through a hoop, springs in a vertical direction from the horse's back; his horizontal velocity is the same as that of the horse and remains unaltered; he therefore alights on the horse's back at the spot from which he started.

72. Parallelogram of Forces. We have shown in Art. 30 that if a particle of mass m has accelerations f_1 and f_2 represented in magnitude and direction by lines AB and AC, then its resultant acceleration f_3 is represented in magnitude and direction by AD, the diagonal of the parallelogram of which AB and AC are adjacent sides.

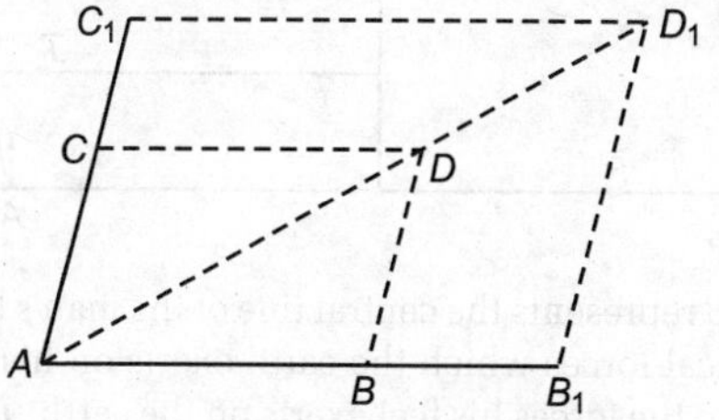

Since the particle has an acceleration f_1 in the direction AB there must be a force P_1 $(= mf_1)$ in that direction, and similarly a force P_2 $(= mf_2)$ in the direction AC. Let AB_1 and AC_1 represent these forces in magnitude and direction. Complete the parallelogram $AB_1D_1C_1$. Then since the forces in the directions AB_1 and AC_1 are proportional to the accelerations in these directions,

$$\therefore \quad AB_1 : AB :: B_1D_1 : BD.$$

Hence, by simple geometry, we have A, D and D_1 in a straight line, and

$$\therefore \quad AD_1 : AD :: AB_1 : AB.$$

It follows that AD_1 represents the force which produces the acceleration represented by AD, and hence is the force which is equivalent to the forces represented by AB_1 and AC_1.

Hence we infer the truth of the Parallelogram of Forces which may be enunciated as follows :

If a particle be acted on by two forces represented in magnitude and direction by the two sides of a parallelogram drawn from a point, they are equivalent to a force represented in magnitude and direction by the diagonal of the parallelogram passing through the point.

Cor. If in Arts. 13-19 which are founded on the Parallelogram of Velocities we substitute the word "force" for "velocity", they will still be true.

73. Law III. *To every action there is an equal and opposite reaction.*

Every exertion of force consists of a mutual action between two bodies. This mutual action is called the stress between the two bodies, so that the Action and Reaction of Newton together form the Stress.

Illustrations. 1. If a book rests on a table, the book presses the table with a force equal and opposite to that which the table exerts on the book.

2. If a man raises a weight by means of a string tied to it, the string exerts on the man's hand exactly the same force that it exerts on the weight, but in the opposite direction.

3. The attraction of the earth on a body is its weight, and the body attracts the earth with a force equal and opposite to its own weight.

4. When a man drags a heavy body along the ground by means of a rope, the rope drags the man back with a force equal to that with which it drags the body forward. [The weight of the rope is neglected.]

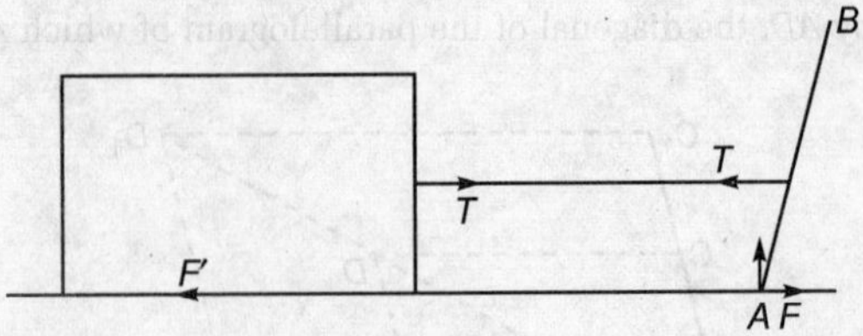

[In the figure AB represents the central line of the man's body. F and R are the horizontal and vertical forces which the earth exerts on his feet, and which are equal and opposite to the forces his feet exerts on the earth. T is the tension of the rope which acts in opposite directions at its ends. F is the horizontal force between the earth and the body.

The man moves because $F > T$.

The body moves because $T > F'$.

Thus at the *commencement* of the motion we have $F > T > F'$.

When the man and body are moving uniformly these three forces are equal.]

5. In the case of a stretched piece of indiarubber, with the ends held in a man's hands, the indiarubber pulls one hand with a force equal and opposite to that with which it pulls the other hand.

The compressed buffers between two railway carriages push one carriage with a force exactly equal and opposite to that with which they push the other carriage.

5

The Laws of Motion (Continued) Applications to Simple Problems

74. Motion of two particles connected by a string.

Two particles, of masses m_1 and m_2, are connected by a light inextensible string which passes over a small smooth fixed pulley. If m_1 be > m_2, find the resulting motion of the system, and the tension of the string.

Let the tension of the string be T dynes; the pulley being smooth, this will be the same throughout the string.

Since the string is inextensible, the velocity of m_2 upwards must, throughout the motion, be the same as that of m_1 downwards.

Hence their accelerations [rates of change of velocity] must be the same in magnitude. Let the magnitude of the common acceleration be f.

Now the force on m_1 downwards in $m_1g - T$ dynes.

Hence $$m_1g - T = m_1f \quad ...(1).$$

So the force on m_2 upwards is $T - m_2g$ dynes;

$\therefore$ $$T - m_2g = m_2f \quad ...(2).$$

Adding (1) and (2), we have $f = \dfrac{m_1 - m_2}{m_1 + m_2} g$, which is the common acceleration.

Also, from (2),

$$T = m_2(f + g) = \frac{2m_1m_2}{m_1 + m_2} g \text{ dynes} \quad ...(3).$$

Since the acceleration is known and constant, the equations of Art. 32 give the space moved through and the velocity acquired in any given time.

Experiment. By using the foregoing result the value of g may be roughly obtained if allowance be made for the friction etc., of the pulley.

Fix a light pulley at a convenient height from the ground, so that the distance through which the masses move may be measured. Round the pulley put a light string having at its ends two equal masses [weights of the shape P, in Art. 82, are convenient]. By trial find the mass R which, when placed on the right-hand P, will make it very slowly and uniformly descend to the ground. This mass R is in general small, and we shall neglect it.

Now place on the same P an additional mass Q so that it descends to the ground with an acceleration f which is given by the previous formula. For $m_1 = P + Q$ and $m_2 = P$.

$$\therefore \qquad f = \frac{m_1 - m_2}{m_1 + m_2} g = \frac{Q}{2P + Q} g.$$

Measure the distance h through which the weight falls, and the time that it takes; then

$$h = \frac{1}{2} ft^2 = \frac{1}{2} \frac{Q}{2P + Q} gt^3.$$

Here everything is known except g which can thus be found.

In an actual experiment the pulley used was a light aluminium one.

The original masses P at the ends of the string were each 265 grammes.

A small mass of the shape Q [Art. 82] equal to 4 grammes when placed on one of the weights P was found to just make it very slowly descend to the ground, so that this weight just overcomes the frictional resistance.

An extra mass of 9 grammes was put on, and the combined weight was then found to descend a distance of 2.4 m to the floor in 5.5 seconds. [This time can be found to a considerable degree of accuracy by a stop-watch or by placing an ordinary watch beating four times per second to the ear; the mean of several determinations should be taken.]

Neglecting the 4 grammes put on in order to overcome the friction we have $m_1 = 265$ and $m^2 = 265 + 9$.

$$\therefore \qquad f = \frac{9}{539} g,$$

and hence
$$240 = \frac{1}{2} \frac{9g}{539} (5.5)^2,$$

$$\therefore \qquad g = \frac{240 \times 92 \times 539 \times 4}{9 \times 121} = \text{about } 951 \text{ cm/sec}^2.$$

This is as accurate a result as we can expect to obtain from this experiment.

That the tension of the string is as found may be **experimentally** verified as follows:

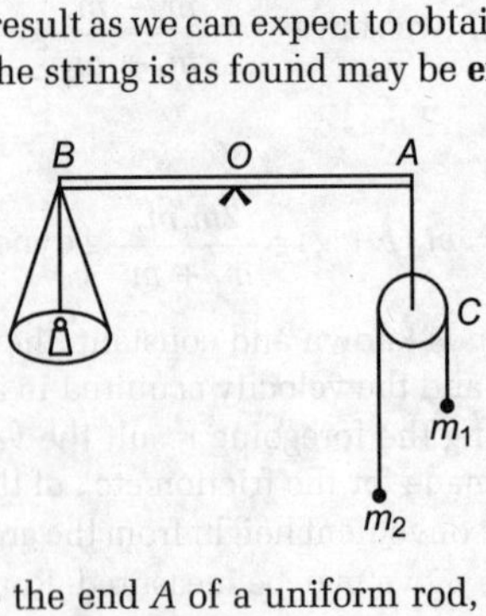

Attach the pulley to the end A of a uniform rod, which can turn about its centre. Then if during the motion the pulley C be at rest, the tension of the string AC must, by result (3),

$$= 2T + \text{wt. of pulley } C = \frac{4m_1 m_2}{m_1 + m_2} g + \text{wt. of pulley},$$

and hence to keep the beam horizontal weights must be put into the scale-pan at B which will just balance this tension.

As a numerical illustration take $m_1 = 70$ and $m_2 = 30$ grammes; let the mass of the pulley C be 40 grammes and that of the scale-pan B be 10 grammes.

During the motion,

$$2T = \frac{4 \cdot 70 \cdot 30}{70 + 30} g = 84 \text{ grammes weight or } gf;$$

therefore total weight to be placed in the scale-pan

= wt. of pulley C + 84 grammes − 10 grammes = 114 grammes.

Put 114 grammes into the scale-pan B; and hold the pulley C, so that it cannot rotate, in such a position that BOA is horizointal; now let motion ensue; the beam will be found to remain horizontal so long as the motion continues; this shows that the tension of the string AC really was 124 grammes as the theory gives.

If the string be slipped off the rim of the pulley, so that no motion can ensue, then, in order to balance m_1 and m_2, the weights that must be put into the scale-pan

= wts. of C, m_1, and m_2 − wt. of the scale-pan

= 40 + 70 + 30 − 10 = 130 grammes.

Hence when there is motion we see, from experiment, that the tension of the string is less than when the pulley is not free to move.

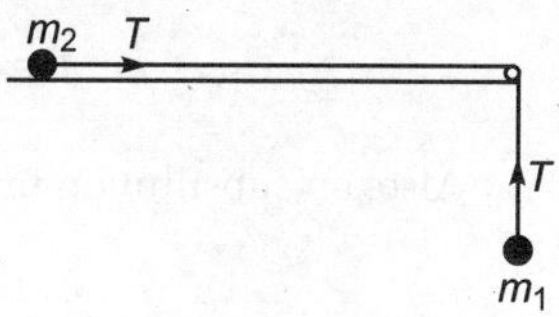

75. *Two particles, of masses m_1 and m_2, are connected by a light inextensible string; m_2 is placed on a smooth horizontal table and the string passes over a light smooth pulley at the edge of the table, m_1 hanging freely; find the resulting motion.*

Let the tension of the string be T dynes.

The velocity and acceleration of m_2 along the table must be equal to the velocity and acceleration of m_1 in a vertical direction.

Let f be the common acceleration of the masses.

The force on m_1 downward is $m_1 g - T$;

$$\therefore \qquad m_1 g - T = m_1 f \qquad \text{...(1).}$$

The only horizontal force acting on m_2 is the tension T; [for the weight of m_2 is balanced by the reaction of the table].

$$\therefore \qquad T = m_2 f \qquad \text{...(2).}$$

Adding (1) and (2), we have

$$m_1 g = (m_1 + m_2) f.$$

$$\therefore \qquad f = \frac{m_1}{m_1 + m_2} g,$$

giving the required acceleration.

Hence, from (2), $T = \dfrac{m_1 m_2}{m_1 + m_2} g$ dynes = weight of a body whose mass is $\dfrac{m_1 m_2}{m_1 - m_2}$.

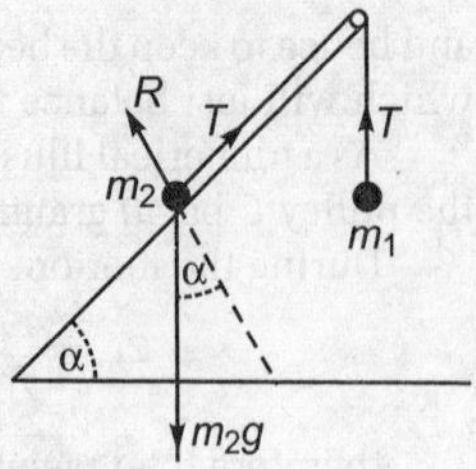

76. *Two masses, m_1 and m_2, are connected by a string; m_2 is placed on a smooth plane inclined at an angle α to the horizon and the string, after passing over a small smooth pulley at the top of the plane, supports m_1, which hangs vertically; if m_1 descends, find the resulting motion.*

Let the tension of the string be T dynes. The velocity and acceleration of m_2 up the plane are clearly equal to the velocity and acceleration of m_1 vertically.

Let f be this common acceleration. For the motion of m_1, we have

$$m_1 g - T = m_1 f \qquad ...(1).$$

The weight of m_2 is $m_2 g$ vertically downwards.

The resolved part of $m_2 g$ perpendicular to the inclined plane is balanced by the reaction R of the plane, since m_2 has no acceleration perpendicular to the plane.

The resolved part of the weight down the inclined plane is $m_2 g \sin\alpha$, and hence the total force up the plane is

$$T - m_2 g \sin\alpha.$$

Hence $$T - m_2 g \sin\alpha = m_2 f \qquad ...(2).$$

Adding (1) and (2), we easily have

$$f = \frac{m_1 - m_2 \sin\alpha}{m_1 + m_2} g.$$

Also, on substitution in (1)

$$T = m_1(g - f) = m_1 g \left[1 - \frac{m_1 - m_2 \sin\alpha}{m_1 + m_2}\right]$$

$$= \frac{m_1 m_2 (1 + \sin\alpha)}{m_1 + m_2} g,$$

giving the tension of the string.

Examples. X.

1. A mass of 9 kg, descending vertically, drags up a mass of 6 kg by means of a string passing over a smooth pulley; find the acceleration of the system and the tension of the string.
2. Two particles, of masses 7 and 9 kg, are connected by a light string passing over a smooth pulley. Find (1) their common acceleration, (2) the tension of the string, (3) the velocity at the end of 5 seconds and (4) the distance described in 5 seconds.
3. Two particles of masses 11 and 13 kg, are connected by a light string over a smooth pulley. Find (1) the velocity at the end of 4 seconds, and (2) the space described in 4 seconds. If at the end of 4 seconds the string be cut, find the distance described by each particle in the next 6 seconds.

4. Masses of 450 and 550 grammes are connected by a thread passing over a light pulley; how far do they go in the first 3 seconds of the motion, and what is the tension of the string?
5. Two masses of 5 and 7 kg are fastened to the ends of a cord passing over a frictionless pulley supported by a hook. When they are free to move, show that the pull on the hook is equal to $11\frac{9}{3}$ kg weight.
6. Two equal masses, of 3 kg each, are connected by a light string hanging over a smooth peg; if a third mass of 3 kg be laid on one of them, by how much is the pressure on the peg increased?
7. Two masses, each equal to *P*, are connected by a light string passing over a smooth pulley, and a third mass *P* is laid on one of them; find by how much the pressure on the peg is increased.
8. Two masses, each equal to *m*, are connected by a string passing over a smooth pulley; what mass must be taken from one and added to the other, so that the system may describe 61 metres in 5 seconds?
9. A mass of 3 kg, descending vertically, draws up a mass of 2 kg by means of light string passing over a pulley; at the end of 5 seconds the string breaks; find how much higher the 2 kg mass will go.
10. A body, of mass $4\frac{1}{2}$ kg, is placed on a smooth table at a distance of $245\frac{1}{2}$ cm from its edge, and is connected, by a string passing over the edge, with a body of mass $\frac{1}{2}$ kg; find

    (1) the common acceleration,

    (2) the time that elapses before the body reaches the edge of the table,

    and (3) its velocity on leaving the table.
11. A mass of 350 grammes is placed on a smooth table at a distance of 245.25 cm from its edge and connected by a light string passing over the edge with a mass of 50 grammes hanging freely; what time will elapse before the first mass will leave the table?
12. A particle, of mass 5 kg, is placed on a smooth plane inclined at 30° to the horizon, and connected by a string passing over the top of the plane with a particle of mass 3 kg, which hangs vertically; find (1) the common acceleration, (2) the tension of the string, (3) the velocity at end of 3 seconds, (4) the space described in 3 seconds.
13. A particle, of mass 2 kg, is placed at the bottom of a plane, inclined at 45° to the horizon and of length 210 cm, and is connected with a mass of 1.5 kg by a string passing over the top of the plane; find the common acceleration of the masses, and the time that elapses before the first arrives at the top of the plane.
14. A body, of mass 6 kg, is placed on an inclined plane, whose height is half its length, and connected by a light string passing over a pulley at the top of the plane with a mass of 4 kg which hangs fréely; find the distance described by the masses in 5 seconds.
15. A mass of 6 grammes slides down a smooth inclined plane, whose height is half its length, and draws another mass from rest over a distance of 1 m in 5 seconds along a horizontal table which is level with the top of the plane over which the string passes; find the mass on the table.

16. A mass of 250 gm is attached by a string passing over a smooth pulley to a larger mass; find the magnitude of the latter so that, if after the motion has continued 3 seconds the string be cut, the former will ascend $54\frac{1}{2}$ cm before descending.

17. Two scale-pans, of mass 1.5 kg each, are connected by a string passing over a smooth pulley; show how to divide a mass of 16.62 kg between the two scale-pans so that the heavier may descend a distance of 16 m in the first 5 seconds.

18. Two strings pass over a smooth pulley on one side they are attached to masses of 3 and 4 kg respectively, and on the other to one of 5 kg; find the tensions of the strings and the acceleration of the system.

19. A string hung over a pulley has at one end a weight of 10 kg and at the other end weights of 8 kg and 4 kg respectively; after being in motion for 5 seconds the 4 kg weight is taken off; find how much further the weights go before they first come to rest.

20. Two unequal masses are connected by a string passing over a small smooth pulley; during the ensuing motion show that the thrust of the axis of the pulley upon its supports is always less than the sum of the weights of the masses.

21. A string passing across a smooth table at right angles to two opposite edges has attached to it at the ends two masses P and Q which hang vertically. Prove that, if a mass M be attached to the portion of the string which is on the table, the acceleration of the system when left to itself will be

$$\frac{P-Q}{P+Q+M}\,g.$$

77. Motion on a rough plane. *A particle slides down a rough plane inclined to the horizon at an angle α; if μ be the coefficient of friction, determine the motion.*

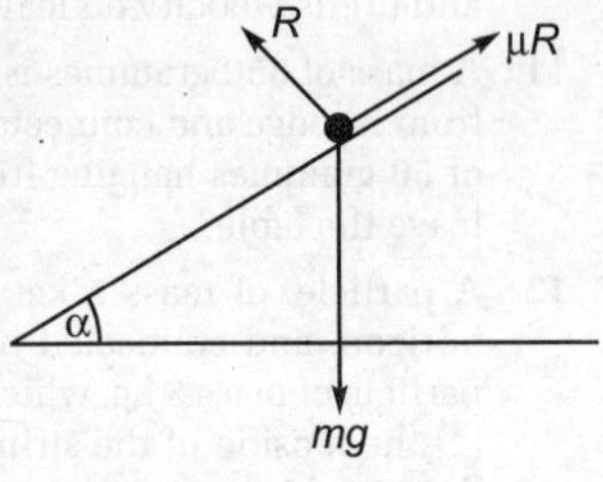

Let m be the mass of the particle, so that its weight is mg dynes; let R be the normal reaction of the plane, and μR the friction.

The total force perpendicular to the plane is $(R - mg\cos\alpha)$ dynes.

The total force down the plane is $(mg\sin\alpha - \mu R)$ dynes.

Now perpendicular to the plane there cannot be any motion, and hence there is no change of motion.

Hence the acceleration, and therefore the total force, in that direction is zero.

$$\therefore \qquad R - mg\cos\alpha = 0 \qquad \text{...(1).}$$

Also the acceleration down the plane

$$= \frac{\text{moving force}}{\text{mass moved}} = \frac{mg\sin\alpha - \mu R}{m} = g(\sin\alpha - \mu\cos\alpha), \text{ by (1).}$$

Hence the velocity of the particle after it has moved from rest over a length l of the plane is, by Art. 32, equal to $\sqrt{2gl(\sin\alpha - \mu\cos\alpha)}$.

Similarly, if the particle were projected up the plane, we have to change the sign of μ, and its acceleration in a direction opposite to that of its motion is

$$g\,(\sin \alpha + \mu \cos \alpha).$$

78. *Two equally rough inclined planes, of equal height, whose inclinations to the horizon are α_1, and α_2, are placed back to back; two masses, m_1 and m_2, are placed on their inclined faces and are connected by a light inextensible string passing over a smooth pulley at the common vertex of the two planes; if m_1 descend, find the resulting motion.*

Let T be the tension of the string, R_1 and R_2 the reactions of the planes, and μ the coefficient of friction.

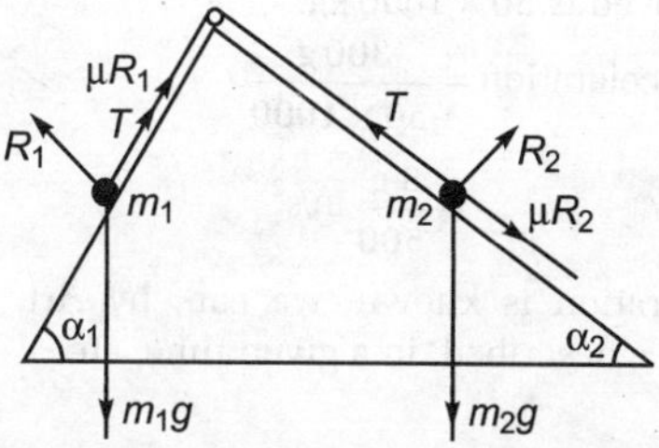

Since m_1 moves *down*, the friction on it acts *up* the plane.
Since m_2 moves *up*, the friction on it acts *down* the plane.
Hence the total force on m_1 down the plane

$$= m_1 g \sin \alpha_1 - T - \mu R_1$$
$$= m_1 g\,(\sin \alpha_1 - \mu \cos \alpha_1) - T.$$

Hence, if f be the common acceleration of the two particles, we have

$$m_1 g\,(\sin \alpha_1 - \mu \cos \alpha_1) - T = m_1 f \qquad \text{...(1).}$$

Similarly, the total force on m_2 up the plane

$$= T - \mu R_2 - m_2 g \sin \alpha_2$$
$$= T - m_2 g\,[\sin \alpha_2 + \mu \cos \alpha_2].$$

Hence

$$T - m_2 g\,(\sin \alpha_2 + \mu \cos \alpha_2)\, m_2 f \qquad \text{...(2).}$$

Adding (1) and (2), we have

$$f\,(m_1 + m_2) = g\begin{bmatrix} m_1(\sin \alpha_1 - \mu \cos \alpha_1) \\ -m_2(\sin \alpha_2 + \mu \cos \alpha_2) \end{bmatrix}$$

giving the required acceleration.

79. *A train, of mass* 50 *metric tons, is ascending an incline of* 1 *in* 100; *the engine exerts a constant tractive force equal to the weight of* 1 *metric ton, and the resistance due to friction, etc. may be taken at* 4 *kg weight per metric ton; find the acceleration with which the train ascends the incline.*

The train is retarded by the resolved part of its weight down the incline, and by the resistance of friction.

The latter is equal to 4×50 or 200 kgf.

The incline is at an angle α to the horizon, where $\sin\alpha = \frac{1}{100}$.

The resolved part of the weight down the incline therefore

$$= W \sin\alpha = 50 \times 1000 \times \frac{1}{100} \text{ kgf}$$

$$= 500 \text{ kgf}$$

Hence the total force to retard the train = 700 kgf

But the engine pulls with a force equal to 1000 kgf.

Therefore the total force to increase the speed equals (1000 – 700) or 300 kgf, i.e., 300 g newtons.

Also the mass moved is 50 × 1000 kg.

Hence the acceleration $= \frac{300\,g}{50 \times 1000}$

$$= \frac{3\,g}{500} \text{ m/s}^2$$

Since the acceleration is known, we can, by Art. 32, find the velocity acquired, and the space described, in a given time, etc.

Examples. XI.

1. A mass of 5 kg on a rough horizontal table is connected by a string with a mass of 8 kg which hangs over the edge of the table; if the coefficient of friction be $\frac{1}{2}$, find the resultant acceleration.
   Find also the coefficient of friction if the acceleration be half that of a freely falling body.
2. A mass Q on a horizontal table, whose coefficient of friction is $\sqrt{3}$, is connected by a string with a mass $3Q$ which hangs over the edge of the table; four seconds after the commencement of the motion the string breaks; find the velocity at this instant.
   Find also the distance of the new position of equilibrium of Q from its initial position.
3. A mass of 200 grammes is moved along a rough horizontal table by means of a string which is attached to a mass of 40 grammes hanging over the edge of the table; if the masses take twice the time to acquire the same velocity from rest that they do when the table is smooth, find the coefficient of friction.
4. A body, of mass 10 kg is placed on a rough plane, whose coefficient of friction is $\frac{1}{\sqrt{3}}$ and whose inclination to the horizon is 30°; if the length of the plane be $122\frac{5}{8}$ cm and the body be acted on by a force, parallel to the plane, equal to 15 kg weight, find the time that elapses before it reaches the top of the plane and its velocity there.
5. If in the previous question the body be connected with a mass of 15 kg, hanging freely, by means of a string passing over the top of the plane, find the time and velocity.

6. A rough plane is 3000 cm long and is inclined to the horizon at an angle $\sin^{-1}\frac{3}{5}$, the coefficient of friction being $\frac{1}{2}$, and a body slides down it from rest at the highest point; find its velocity on reaching the bottom.
If the body were projected up the plane from the bottom so as just to reach the top, find its initial velocity.

7. A particle slides down a rough inclined plane, whose inclination to the horizon is $\frac{\pi}{4}$ and whose coefficient of friction is $\frac{3}{4}$; show that the time of descending any space is twice what it would be if the plane were perfectly smooth.

8. Two rough planes, inclined at 30° and 60° to the horizon and of the same height, are placed back to back; masses of 5 and 10 kg are placed on the faces and connected by a string passing over the top of the planes; if the coefficient of friction be $\frac{1}{\sqrt{3}}$, find the resulting acceleration.

9. If in the previous question the masses be interchanged, what is the resulting acceleration?

10. A train is moving on horizontal rails at the rate of 21 km 650 m per second; if the steam by suddenly turned off, find how far it will go before stopping, the resistance being 4 kg per metric tonne.

11. If a train of 203 metric tonnes, moving at the rate of 48 km per hour, can be stopped in 54 metres, compare the frictional resistances with the weight of a tonne.

12. A train is running on horizontal rails at the rate of 60 kms per hour, the resistance due to friction etc.,being 5 kgf per metric ton; if the steam be shut off, find (1) the time that elapses before the train comes to rest, (2) the distance described in this time.

13. In the previous question if the train be ascending an incline of 1 in 112, find the corresponding time and distance.

14. A train of mass 203 metric tonnes is running at the rate of 64 km per hour down an incline of 1 in 120; find the resistance necessary to stop it in 800 metres.

15. A train runs from rest for 2 kms down a plane whose descent is 1 m vertically for each 100 m of its length; if the resistances be equal to 4 kg per metric ton, how far will the train be carried along the horizontal level at the foot of the incline?

16. A train of mass 142 metric tonnes, travelling at the rate of 24 km per hour, comes to the top of an incline of 1 in 128, the length of the incline being 800 metres, and steam is then shut off; taking the resistance due to friction, etc. as 4.46 kg wt. per metric tonne, find the distance it describes on a horizontal line at the foot of the incline before coming to rest.

17. In the preceding question, if on arriving at the foot of the incline a brake-van, of weight 10.16 metric tonnes, have all its wheels prevented from revolving, find the distance described, assuming the coefficient of friction between the wheels and the line to be 0.5.

18. An engine, of mass 30.2 metric tonnes, pulls after it a train, of mass 132 metric tonnes; supposing the friction to be $\frac{1}{50}$th of the weight of the whole train,

calculate the force exerted by the engine if at the end of the first mile from the start the speed be raised to 72.5 km per hour.
What incline would be just sufficient to prevent the engine from moving the train?
Also down what incline would the train run with constant velocity, neither steam nor brakes being on?

80. *A body, of mass m gm, is placed on a horizontal plane which is in motion with a vertical upward acceleration f; find the reaction between the body and the plane.*

Let R be the reaction between the body and the plane.

Since the acceleration is vertically upwards, the total force acting on the body must be vertically upwards.

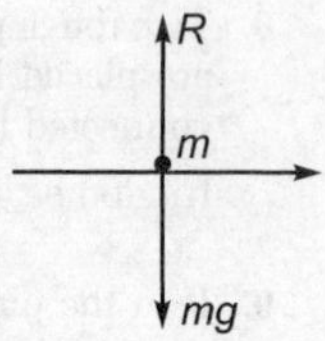

The only force, besides R, acting on the body is its weight mg acting vertically downwards.

Hence the total force is $R - mg$ vertically upwards, and this produces an acceleration; f; hence

$$R - mg = mf, \text{giving } R.$$

In a similar manner it may be shown that, if the body be moving with a downward acceleration f, the reaction R_1 is given by

$$mg - R_1 = mf.$$

We note that the reaction is greater or less than the weight of the body, according as the acceleration of the body is upwards or downwards.

Ex. 1. *The body is of mass 10 kg and is moving with (1) an upward acceleration of 327 cm/sec. units, (2) a downward acceleration of the same magnitude; find the reactions.*

In the first case we have

$$R - 10^4\ g = 10^4 \cdot 327$$

$$\therefore \quad R = 10^4\ (981 + 327)\,\text{dynes} = \text{wt. of } 13333\frac{1}{3}\,\text{gm.}$$

In the second case we have

$$10^4\ g - R_1 = 10^4 \cdot 327.$$

$$\therefore \quad R_1 = 10^4\ (g - 327)\text{dynes} = \text{wt. of } 6666\frac{2}{3}\,\text{gm.}$$

Ex. 2. *Two scale-pans, each of mass M, are connected by a light string passing over a small pulley, and in them are placed masses M_1 and M_2; show that the reactions of the pans during the motion are*

$$\frac{2M_1(M + M_2)}{M_1 + M_2 + 2M} \cdot g \ \text{ and } \ \frac{2M_2(M + M_1)}{M_1 + M_2 + 2M} \cdot g$$

respectively.

Let f be the common acceleration of the system, and suppose $M_1 > M_2$.

Then, as in Art. 74, we have

$$f = \frac{M_1 - M_2}{2M + M_1 + M_2}\, g.$$

Let P be the reaction between M_1 and the scale-pan on which it rests; then the force on the mass M_1, *considered as a separate body*, is $M_1 g - P$. Also its acceleration is f.

Hence $$M_1 g - P = M_1 f,$$

$$\therefore \quad P = M_1(g - f),$$

$$= \frac{2M_1(M + M_2)}{2M + M_1 + M_2} g.$$

81. 7.5 *cm of rainfall in a certain district in* 12 *hours. Assuming that the drops fall freely from a height of a* 400 m. *Find the pressure on the ground per square km of the district due to the rain during the storm, the mass of a cm*^{3} *of water being* 1 *gramme.*

The amount of rain that falls on a square cm during the storm is 7.5 cm^3, and its mass is 7.5 g.

Hence the mass that falls per second.

$$= \frac{7.5}{12 \times 60 \times 60} = \frac{1}{12 \times 8 \times 60} \text{g / cm}^3$$

The velocity of each raindrop on touching the ground is

$\sqrt{2 \times g \times 400}$, or $28\sqrt{10}$ m/sec, assuming

$g = 9.80 \text{m/sec}^2$.

Therefore the momentum that it destroyed per second is

$$28\sqrt{10} \times 10 \text{ cm/sec}^2 \times \frac{1}{12 \times 8 \times 60} \text{g/cm}^2$$

$$= \frac{35\sqrt{10}}{72} \text{ units of momentum per cm}^2.$$

But the number of units of momentum destroyed per second is equal to the number of poundals in the acting force (Art. 61).

Hence the pressure on the ground per cm^2.

$$= \frac{35\sqrt{10}}{72} \text{dynes} = \frac{35\sqrt{10}}{72 \times 981} \text{gf}$$

Hence the pressure per square km.

$$= \text{weight of } \frac{35\sqrt{10} \times 1000^2 \times 100^2}{72 \times 981 \times 1000^2} \text{ metric tons}$$

$$= \text{weight of 15.7 metric tons approximately.}$$

In general, if a jet of water hit a wall, the pressure on the wall per square cm is mv^2 dynes, where v is the velocity in cm per second and m is the mass of a cubic cm of water in g. For a mass mv hits the square cm in each second, and the velocity of each particle of the water is v, so that the total momentum destroyed per second $= mv \times v = mv^2$.

82. Atwood's Machine. This machine is used to verify the laws of motion and to obtain a rough value for g. In its simplest form it consists of a vertical pillar AB firmly clamped to the ground, and carrying as its top a light pulley which will move very freely. This pillar is graduated and carries two platforms, D and F, and

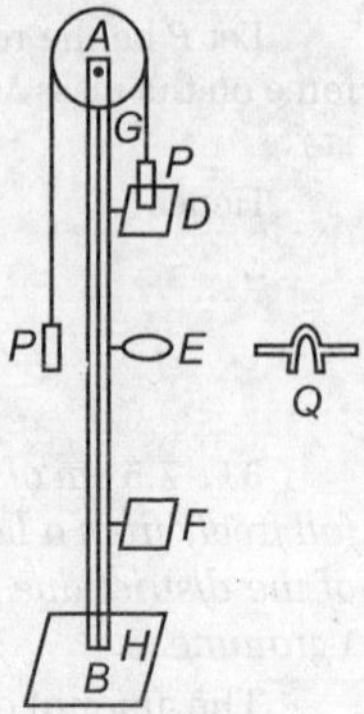

a ring E, all of which can be affixed by screws at any height desired. The platform D can also be instantaneously dropped. Over the pulley passes a fine cord supporting at its ends two long thin equal weights, one of which, P, can freely pass through the ring E. Another small weight Q, called a rider, is provided, which can be laid upon the weight P, but which cannot pass through the ring E.

The weight Q is laid upon P and the platform D is dropped and motion ensues; the weight Q is left behind as the weight P passes through the ring; the weight P then traverses the distance EF with constant velocity, and the time T which it takes to describe this distance is carefully measured.

By Art. 74 the acceleration of the system as the weight falls from D to E is

$$\frac{(Q+P)-P}{(Q+P)+P}g, \quad \text{i.e.,} \quad \frac{Q}{Q+2P}g.$$

Denote this by f, and let $DE = h$.

Then the velocity v on arriving at E is given by

$$v^2 = 2fh.$$

After passing E, the distance EF is described with constant velocity v.

Hence, if $EF = h_1$, we have

$$T = \frac{h_1}{v} = \frac{h_1}{\sqrt{2fh}}.$$

$$\therefore \quad h_1^2 = \frac{2Q}{Q+2P}ghT^2.$$

Since all the quantities involved can be measured, this relation gives us the value of g.

By giving different values to P, Q, h and h_1, we can in this manner verify all the fundamental laws of motion.

In practice, the value of g cannot by this method be found to any great degree of accuracy, and the interest of Atwood's Machine is chiefly of an antiquarian character; the chief causes of discrepancy are the mass of the pulley, which cannot be neglected, the friction of the pivot on which the wheel turns, and the resistance of the air. It is also difficult to accurately measure the times involved in the experiment.

It will be noted that the object of both Galileo's Inclined Plane [Art. 41] and of Atwood's Machine is to lessen the effect of gravity so as to make its results measurable, or, as it has been well expressed, to 'dilute' gravity.

The friction of the pivot may be minimised if its ends do not rest on fixed supports, but on the circumferences of four light wheels, called friction wheels, two on each side, which turn very freely.

There are other pieces of apparatus for securing the accuracy of the experiment as far as possible, e.g., for instantaneously withdrawing the platform D at the required moment.

83. *By using Atwood's machine to show that the acceleration of a given mass is proportional to the force acting on it.*

We shall *assume* that the statement is true and see whether the results we deduce therefrom are verified by experiment.

To explain the method of procedure we shall take a numerical example.

Let P be $49\frac{1}{2}$ g and Q 1 g so that the mass moved is 100 g and the moving force is the weight of 1 g.

The acceleration of the system therefore $= \frac{1}{100} g$ (Art. 74).

Let the distance DE be 40 cm so that the velocity when Q is taken off $= \sqrt{2 \cdot \frac{g}{100} \cdot 40} = 28$ cm per sec., if, for simplicity, we take g equal to 980.

Let the platform F be carefully placed at such a point that the mass will move from E to F in some definite time, say 2 sec.

Then $EF = 28 \times 2 = 56$ cm.

Now alter the conditions. Make P equal to 48 and Q equal to 4 g. The mass moved is still 100 g and the moving force is now the weight of 4 g.

The acceleration is now $\frac{4g}{100}$, and the velocity at E

$$= \sqrt{2 \cdot \frac{4g}{100} \cdot 40} = 56 \text{ cm per second}$$

In 2 seconds the mass would now describe 112 cm, so that, if our hypothesis be correct, the platform F must be twice as far from E as before. *This is found on trial to be correct.*

Similarly if we make $P = 45\frac{1}{2}$ g and $Q = 9$ g, so that the mass moved is still 100 g, the theory would give us that EF should be 168 cm, and this would be found to be correct.

The experiment should now be tried over again *ab initio* and P and Q be given different values from the above; alterations should then be made in their different values so that $2P + Q$ is constant.

By the same method to show that the force varies as the mass when the acceleration is constant.

As before let $P = 49\frac{1}{2}$ g and $Q = 1$ g so that, as in the last experiment, we have $EF = 56$ cm.

Secondly, let $P = 99$ g and $Q = 2$ g, so that the moving force is doubled and the mass moved is doubled. Hence, if our enunciation be correct, the acceleration should be the same, since

$$\frac{\text{second moving force}}{\text{second mass moved}} = \frac{\text{first moving force}}{\text{first mass moved}}.$$

The distance EF moved through in 2 seconds should therefore be the same as before, and this, on trial, *is found to be the case.*

Similarly if we make $P = 148\frac{1}{2}$ g and $Q = 3$ g the same reuslt would be found to follow.

In actual practice some extra weight R must be put on in order to overcome the friction at the pulley, etc. This should be determined before Q is put on; it will be that weight which will just make the P on which it is placed move very slowly and uniformly down to the ground. This weight R must be kept on when Q is added, and must not be counted as part of Q in the above work.

Examples. XII.

1. If I jump off a table with a 10 kg weight in my hand, what is the thrust of the weight on my hand?
2. A mass of 10 kg rests on a horizontal plane which is made to ascend (1) with a constant velocity of 30 cm per second, (2) with a constant acceleration of 30 cm per second; find in each case the reaction of the plane.
3. A man, whose mass is 50 kg, stands on a lift which moves with a uniform acceleration of 327 cm/sec. units; find the reaction of the floor when the lift is (1) ascending, (2) descending.
4. A bucket containing 56 kg of a coal is drawn up the shaft of a coal-pit, and the reaction between the coal and the bottom of the bucket is equal to the weight of 63 kg. Find the acceleration of the bucket.
5. A balloon ascends with a uniformly accelerated velocity, so that a mass of 56 kg produces on the floor of the balloon the same thrust which 58 kg would produce on the earth's surface; find the height which the balloon will have attained in one minute from the time of starting.
6. Two scale-pans, each of mass 30 grammes, are suspended by a weightless string passing over a smooth pulley; a mass of 300 grammes is placed in the one, and 240 grammes in the other. Find the tension of the string and the reactions of the scale-pans.
7. A string, passing over a smooth pulley, supports two scale-pans at its ends, the mass of each scale-pan being 30 g. If masses of 60 and 120 g respectively be placed in the scale-pans, find the acceleration of the system, the tension of the string and the reactions between the masses and the scale-pans.
8. On a certain day 2 cm of rain fell in 3 hours; assuming that the drops are indefinitely small and that the terminal velocity was 300 cm per second, find the impulsive pressure in metric tons per square km consequent on their being reduced to rest, assuming that the mass of a cubic cm of water is 1 g and that the rain was uniform and continuous.
9. Find the pressure in kilogramme wt. per hectare due to the impact of a fall of rain of 7.62 cm in 24 hours, supposing the rain to have a velocity due to falling freely through 122 metres.
10. A jet of water is projected against a wall so that 1200 litres strike the wall per second with a horizontal velocity of 24.5 m per second. Assuming that 1 litre weighs 1 kg and $g = 9.8\ \text{m/sec}^2$, find the reaction of the wall in kgf.

11. The two masses in an Atwood's Machine are each 240 grammes, and an additional mass of 10 grammes being placed on one of them it is observed to descend through 10 metres in 10 seconds; hence show that $g = 980$.

12. Explain how to use Atwood's Machine to show that a body acted on by a constant force moves with constant acceleration.

13. Sixteen balls of equal mass are strung like beads on a string; some are placed on a smooth inclined plane of inclination $\sin^{-1}\frac{1}{3}$, and the rest hang over the top of the plane; how have the balls been arranged if the acceleration at first be $\frac{g}{2}$?

14. Two bodies, of masses P and Q, are connected by a stretched string; P hangs vertically and Q is placed on a smooth plane inclined at 30° to the horizon, the string passing over the top of the plane; if P descend from rest through a given distance in 4 times the time in which it would fall freely from rest through the same distance, find the ratio of P to Q.

15. P hangs vertically and is 9 kg; Q is a mass of 6 kg on a smooth plane whose inclination to the horizon is 30°; show that P will drag Q up the whole length of the plane in half the time that Q hanging vertically would take to draw P up the plane.

16. If the height of an inclined plane be 4 metres and the base $\frac{16}{3}$ metres, find how far a particle will move on a horizontal plane after sliding from rest down the length of the inclined plane, supposing it to pass from one plane to the other without loss of velocity, and that the coefficient of friction for each plane is $\frac{1}{8}$.

17. Show that a train going at the rate of 48 km per hour will be brought to rest in about 77 metres by continuous brakes, if they press on the wheels with a force equal to three-quarters of the weight of the train, the coefficient of friction being 0.16.

18. A train of mass 51 metric tonnes is moving on a level at the rate of 48 km per hour when the steam is shut off, and the brake being applied to the brake-van the train is stopped in 400 metres. Find the mass of the brake-van taking the coefficient of friction between the wheels and rails to be one-sixth, and supposing the unlocked wheels to roll without sliding.

19. A mass m is drawn up a smooth inclined plane, of height h and length l, by means of a string passing over the vertex of the plane, from the other end of which hangs a mass m'. Show that, in order that m may just reach the top of the plane, m' must be detached after m has moved through a distance

$$\frac{m+m'}{m'}\,\frac{hl}{h+l}.$$

20. Two masses are connected by a string passing over a small pulley; show that, if the sum of the masses be constant, the tension of the string is greater, the less the acceleration.

21. A mass m_1 hanging at the end of a string, draws a mass m_2 along the surface of a smooth table; if the mass on the table be doubled the tension of the string is increased by one-half; find the ratio of m_1 to m_2.

22. Two bodies, of masses 9 and 16 kg respectively, are placed on a smooth horizontal table at a distance of 10 m; if they were now to attract each other with a constant force equal to 1 kgf at all distances, find after what time they would meet.

23. In the case of a single movable pulley the free end of the string passes round a fixed pulley and supports a weight P greater than $\frac{1}{2}W$, where W is the weight suspended from the movable pulley. Find the tension of the string during the ensuing motion, the three parts into which it is divided by the pulleys being parallel.

24. A mass m will just supports a mass M in a system of two pulleys in which each string is attached to M, the strings being parallel. A mass m is now attached to M; find the subsequent motion, neglecting the weights of the pulleys.

25. A system of three movable pulleys, in which all the strings are vertical and attached to the beam, is employed to raise a body, of mass 112 kg, by means of one of mass 15 kg attached to a string passing over a smooth fixed pulley. Show that the body will rise with acceleration $\frac{g}{134}$, the masses of the pulleys being neglected.

26. A string, with masses m and m' at its ends, passes over three fixed and under two movable pulleys, each of mass M, hanging down between the fixed pulleys, the parts of the string between the pulleys being vertical. Find the condition that the movable pulleys should neither rise nor fall, and in this case determine the acceleration of m and m'.

27. A rope hangs down over a smooth pulley, and a man of 12 stone lets himself down the portion of rope on one side of the pulley with unit acceleration. Find with what uniform acceleration a man of $11\frac{1}{2}$ stone must pull himself up by the other portion of the rope so that the rope may remain at rest.

28. A man, of mass 60 kg, and a sack of mass 50 kg, are suspended over a smooth pulley by a rope of negligible weight. If the man pulls himself up the rope so as to diminish what would be his acceleration by one-half, find the upward acceleration of the sack in this case, and show that the acceleration upwards of the man relative to the rope is $\frac{g}{10}$.

29. A train, whose mass is 114 metric tonnes, is travelling at the uniform rate of 40 km per hour on a level track, and the resistance due to air friction, etc. is 7.15 kg per tonne. Part of the train, of mass 12.2 metric tonnes, becomes detached. Assuming that the force exerted by the engine is the same throughout, find how much the train will have gained on the detached part after 50 seconds and the velocity of the train when the detached part comes to rest.

30. Two particles, of masses m and $2m$, lie together on a smooth horizontal table. A string which joins them hangs over the edge and supports a pulley carrying a mass $3m$; prove that the acceleration of the latter mass is $\frac{9g}{17}$.

31. *A smooth wedge of mass M, is placed on a horizontal plane, and a particle, of mass m, slides down its slant face, which is inclined at an angle α to the horizon prove that the acceleration of the wedge is*

$$\frac{mg \sin \alpha \cos \alpha}{M + m \sin^2 \alpha}.$$

[Let f_1 be the acceleration of the particle in a direction perpendicular to, and towards, the slant face; f_2 the horizontal acceleration of the wedge; and R the normal reaction between the particle and the slant face; so that R acts in one direction on the particle and in the opposite direction on the wedge. Then

$$mf_1 = mg \cos \alpha - R \qquad \text{...(1)},$$

and

$$Mf_2 = R \sin \alpha \qquad \text{...(2)}.$$

Also, since the particle remains in contact with the slant face, the acceleration f_1 must be the same as the acceleration of the wedge resolved in a direction perpendicular to the slant face.

$$\therefore \qquad f_1 = f_2 \sin \alpha \qquad \text{...(3)}.$$

Solving (1), (2), and (3), we have f_2.]

6

Impulse, Work, and Energy

84. Impulse. Def. *The impulse of a force in a given time is equal to the product of the force (if constant, and the mean value of the force if variable) and the time during which it acts.*

The impulse of a force P acting for a time t is therefore $P \cdot t$.

The impulse of a force is also equal to the momentum generated by the force in the given time. For suppose a particle, of mass m, moving initially with velocity u is acted on by a constant force P for time t. If f be the resulting acceleration, we have $P = mf$.

But, if v be the velocity of the particle at the end of time t, we have

$$v = u + ft.$$

Hence the impulse $= Pt = mft = mv - mu$

= the momentum generated in the given time.

The same result is also true if the force be variable.

Hence it follows that the second law of motion might have been enunciated in the following form :

The change of momentum of a particle in a given time is equal to the impulse of the force which produces it and is in the same direction.

85. Impulsive Forces. Suppose we have a force P acting for a time τ on a body whose mass is m, and let the velocities of the mass at the beginning and end of this time be u and v. Then by the last article

$$P\tau = m(v - u).$$

Let now the force become bigger and bigger, and the time τ smaller and smaller. Then ultimately P will be almost infinitely big and τ almost infinitely small, and yet their product *may* be finite. For example P may be equal to 10^7 dynes, τ equal to $\frac{1}{10^7}$ seconds, and m equal to one gramme, in which case the change of velocity produced is the unit of velocity.

To find the whole effect of a finite force acting for a finite time we have to find two things : (1) the change in the velocity of the particle produced by the force during the time it acts, and (2) the change in the position of the particle during this time. Now in the case of an infinitely large force acting for an infinitely short time, the body moves only a very short distance whilst the force is acting, so that this change of position of the particle may be neglected. Hence the total effect of such a force is known when we know the change of momentum which it produces.

Such a force is called an impulsive force. Hence

Def. *An impulse force is a very great force acting for a very short time, so that the change in the position of the particle during the time the force acts on it may be neglected. Its whole effect is measured by its impulse, or the change of momentum produced.*

In actual practice we never have any experience of an infinitely great force acting for a infinitely short time. Approximate examples are, however, the blow of hammer, and the collision of two billiards balls.

The above will be true even if the force be not uniform. In the ordinary case of the collision of two billiard balls the force generally varies very considerably.

Ex. 1. A body, whose mass is 4.5 kg, is acted on by a force which changes its velocity from 36 km per hour to 54 km per hour. Find the impulse of the force.

Ans. 225×10^4 C.G.S. units of impulse.

Ex. 2. A mass of 2 kg at rest is struck and starts off with a velocity of 10 metres per second; assuming the time during which the blow lasts to be one-hundredth of a second, find the average value of the force acting on the mass.

Ans. 2×10^2 dynes.

Ex. 3. A glass marble, whose mass is $\frac{1}{10}$ kg, falls from a height of 2.5 m, and rebounds to a height of 1.6 m; find the impulse, and the average force between the marble and the floor if the time during which they are in contact be one-tenth of a second.

Ans. 1.26 M.K.S. units of impulse; 13.58 N (newtons).

86. Impact of two bodies. When two masses A and B impinge, then, by the third law of motion, the action of A on B is, at each instant during which they are in contact, equal and opposite to that of B on A.

Hence the impulse of the action of A on B is equal and opposite to the impulse of the action of B on A.

It follows that the change in the momentum of B is equal and opposite to the change in the momentum of A, and therefore the sum of these changes, measured in the same direction, is zero.

Hence, the sum of the momenta of the two masses, measured in the same direction, is unaltered by their impact.

Ex. 1. *A body, of mass* 3 gm, *moving with velocity* 13 cm *per second overtakes a body, of mass* 2 gm, *moving with velocity* 3 cm *per second in the same straight line, and they coalesce and form one body; find the velocity of this single body.*

Let V be the required velocity. Then, since the sum of the moments of the two bodies is unaltered by the impact, we have

$$(3 + 2)V = 3 \times 13 + 2 \times 3 = 45 \text{ units of momentum,}$$

$$\therefore \quad V = 9 \text{ cm per sec.}$$

Ex. 2. *If in the last example the second body be moving in the direction opposite to that of the first, find the resulting velocity.*

In this case the momentum of the first body is represented by 3×13 and that of the second by -2×3. Hence, if V_1 be the required velocity, we have

$$(3 + 2)\,V_1 = 3 \times 13 - 2 \times 3 = 33 \text{ units of momentum,}$$

$$\therefore \quad V_1 = \frac{33}{5} = 6\frac{3}{5} \text{ cm per sec.}$$

87. Motion of a shot and gun. When a gun is fired, the powder is almost instantaneously converted into a gas at a very high pressure, which by its expansion forces the shot out. The action of the gas is similar to that of a compressed spring trying to recover its natural position. The force exerted on the shot forwards is, at any instant before the shot leaves the gun, equal and opposite to that exerted on the gun backwards, and therefore the impulse of this force on the shot is equal and opposite to the impulse of the force on the gun. Hence the momentum generated in the shot is equal and opposite to that generated in the gun, if the latter be free to move.

Ex. *A shot, whose mass is 200 kg, is projected from a gun of mass* 50 *metric tons with a velocity of* 270 *m per second; find the resulting velocity of the gun.*

Since the momentum of the gun is equal and opposite to that of the shot, we have, if v be the velocity communicated to the gun,

$$50 \times 1000v = 200 \times 270$$

$$\therefore \quad v = 1.08 \text{ m per sec.}$$

Examples. XIII.

1. A body, of mass 7 kg, moving with a velocity of 10 metres per second, overtakes a body, of mass 20 kg, moving with a velocity of 2 metres per second in the same direction as the first; if after the impact they move forward with a common velocity, find its magnitude.
2. A body, of mass 8 kg, moving with a velocity of 6 metres per second overtakes a body, of mass 24 kg, moving with a velocity of 2 metres per second in the same direction as the first; if after the impact they coalesce into one body, show that the velocity of the compound body is 3 metres per second.
   If they were moving in opposite directions, show that after impact the compound body is at rest.
3. A body, of mass 10 kg, moving with velocity 4 metres per second meets a body, of mass 12 kg, moving in the opposite direction with a velocity of 7 metres per second; if they coalesce into one body, show that it will have a velocity of 2 metres per second in the direction in which the larger body was originally moving.
4. A shot, of mass 20 gm, is projected with a velocity of 30000 cm per second from a gun of mass 5 kg; find the velocity with which the later begins to recoil.
5. A shot of 400 kg is projected from a 40-metric tonne gun with a velocity of 600 metres per second; find the velocity with which the gun would commence to recoil, if free to move in the line of projection.
6. A shot, of mass 350 kg is fired with a velocity of 490 m per second from a gun of mass 35 metric tons; if the recoil be resisted by a constant force equal to the weight of 16 metric tons, through how many metre will the gun recoil?
7. A shot, whose mass is 400 kg is discharged from an 80 metric tons gun with a velocity of 490 m per second; find the constant force which acting on the gun would stop it after a recoil of 1.6 m.

8. A gun, of mass 1 metric tonne, fires a shot of mass 12.7 kg and recoils up a smooth inclined plane, rising to a height of 1.53 metres; find the initial velocity of the projectile.

88. Work. We have pointed out in Statics, Chapter XI, that a force is said to do work when it moves its point of application in the direction of the force. The work is measured by the product of the force and the distance through which the point of application is moved in the direction of the force. The unit of work used by engineers is a Foot-Pound, which is the work done in raising the weight of one pound through one foot.

The British absolute unit of work is the work done by a poundal is moving its point of application through one foot.

This unit of work is called a **Foot-Poundal.**

With this unit of work the work done by a force of P poundals in moving its point of application through s feet is $P \cdot s$ foot-poundals.

Since the weight of a pound is equal to g-poundals, it follows that a Foot-Pound is equal to g Foot-Poundals.

The C.G.S. unit of work is that done by a dyne in moving its point of application through a centimetre, and is called an **Erg.**

$$\frac{\text{A Foot - Poundal}}{\text{An Erg}} = \frac{\text{Poundal} \times \text{Foot}}{\text{Dyne} \times \text{Centimetre}} = 13800 \times \frac{12}{0.3937} \text{ nearly}$$

[Arts. 66 and 3]

$$= 421390 \text{ approx.}$$

When an agent is performing 1 Joule, i.e., 10^7 Ergs. per second it is said to be working with a power of 1 Watt. One Horse-Power is equivalent to about 746 watts.

89. Ex. 1 *What is the H.P. of an engine which can just keep a train, of mass* 150 *metric tons, moving at a uniform rate of* 72 *km per hour, the resistances to the motion due to friction, the resistance of the air, etc. being taken at* 5 *kg weight per metric ton?*

The force to stop the train is equal to the weight of 150 × 5, i.e., 750 kgf.

Now 72 km per hour is equal to 20 m per second.

Hence a force, equal to 750 kgf, has its point of application moved through 20 m in a second, and hence the work done is 750 × 20 metre-kgf per second.

$\therefore$ The work done per sec. = 750 × 20 × 9.85 /sec.

$$\therefore \quad \text{Number of watts} = 750 \times 20 \times 9.8$$

$$\therefore \quad \text{H.P.} = \frac{750 \times 20 \times 9.8}{746} = 197.0.$$

Ex. 2. *Find the least H.P. of an engine which is able in* 4 *minutes to generate in a train, of mass* 100 *tons, a velocity of* 30 *miles per hour on a level line, the resistances due to friction, etc. being equal to 8 lb. weight per ton, and the puli of the engine being assumed constant.*

Since in 240 seconds a velocity of 44 feet per second is generated the acceleration of the train must be $\frac{14}{240}$ of $\frac{11}{60}$ foot-second units.

Let the force exerted by the engine be P poundals.

The resistance due to friction is equal to 800 pounds weight; hence the total force on the train is $P - 800g$ poundals.

Hence $$P - 800g = 100 \times 2240 \times \frac{11}{60}.$$

$$\therefore \; P = 800\left(g + \frac{154}{3}\right) \text{poundals} = 800\left(1 + \frac{154}{3 \times 32}\right) \text{lb. weight}$$

$$= 800 \times \frac{125}{48} \text{lb. weight.}$$

When the train is moving at the rate of 30 miles per hour, the work done per second must be $800 \times \frac{125}{48} \times 44$ foot-lb.

Hence, if x be the H.P. of the engine, we have

$$x \times 550 = 800 \times \frac{125}{48} \times 44.$$

$$\therefore \qquad x = 166\frac{2}{3}.$$

Ex. 3. *A train, of mass* 100 *metric tons is ascending uniformly an incline of* 1 *in* 250, *and the resistance due to friction, etc. is equal to* 8 *kg per metric ton; if the engine be of* 1.176×10^5 *watts and be working at full power, find the rate at which the train is going.*

The resistance due to friction, etc., is equal to the weight of 800 kg, and the resolved part of the weight of the train down the incline is equal to the weight of $\frac{1}{250}$ of 100 metric tons, or to the weight of 400 kg, so that the total force to impede the motion is equal to the weight of 1200 kg.

Let v be the velocity of the train in m per second. Then the work done by the engine is that done in dragging a force equal to the weight of 1200 kg through v m per second, and is equivalent to $1200v$ m kg per second.

But the total work which the engine can do is 1.176×10^5 Joules per sec.

Hence $$1200v \times 9.8 = 1.176 \times 10^5$$

or $$v = 10,$$

and hence the velocity of the train is 36 km/hr.

Ex. 4. *A particle moving in a straight line is acted by a force which works at a constant rate and changes its velocity from u to v in passing over a distance x. Prove that the time taken is*

$$\frac{3}{2} \cdot \frac{(u+v)\,x}{u^2 + uv + v^2}$$

The rate at which the force acting on the particle does work is given by

$$m\frac{dv}{dt} \times v = K \text{ (a constant)} \qquad \text{...(1).}$$

where m denotes the mass of the particle and v the velocity after time t.

Integrating (1) between the limits 0 and t, we get

$$\frac{1}{2} m\,(v^2 - u^2) = Kt \qquad \text{...(2).}$$

Also from (1) we have

$$mv\frac{dv}{dx} = K$$

Integrating between the limits 0 and x, we get

$$\frac{1}{2} m (v^3 - u^3) = Kx \qquad ...(3).$$

Dividing (2) by (3), we get

$$t = \frac{3}{2} \cdot \frac{(u + v)\, x}{u^2 + uv + v^2}.$$

Examples. XIV.

1. A train, of mass 50 metric tons, is kept moving at the uniform rate of 72 kms per hour on the level,the resistance of air, friction, etc., being 20 kg weight per metric ton. Find the power of the engine.
2. What is the power of an engine which keeps a train going at the rate of 60 kms per hour against a resistance equal to 1050 kgf weight?
3. A train, of mass 100 metric tons travels at 60 kms per hour up an incline of 1 in 200. Find the power of the engine that will draw the train, neglecting all resistances except that of gravity.
4. A train, of mass 200 metric tons, including the engine, is drawn up an incline of 3 in 500 at the rate of 36 kms per hour by an engine of 245000 watts P; find the resistance per ton due to friction, etc.
5. Find the H.P. of an engine which can travel at the rate of 36 kms per hour up an incline of 1 in 100, the mass of the engine and load being 10 metric tons, and the resistances due to friction, etc. being 10 kg weight per metric ton.
6. Determine the rate in H.P. at which an engine must be able to work in order to generate a velocity of 30 km per hour on the level in a train of mass 60 metric tons in 3 minutes after starting, the resistances to the motion being taken at 5 kg per metric ton, and the acceleration being supposed to be constant.
7. A weight of 10 metric tons is dragged in half-an-hour through a length of 110 m up a rough plane inclined at an angle of 30° to the horizon; the coefficient of friction being $\frac{1}{\sqrt{3}}$, find the work expanded, and the power of an engine by which it will be done.
8. Find the work done by gravity on a stone having a mass of 1 kg during the tenth second of its fall from test.
9. A steamer, with engines of 25000 H.P., can be just kept going at the rate of 32 km per hour. What is the resistance of the water to its motion?
10. An engine working at a constant rate of H draws a load M against a resistance R. Show that the maximum speed is $\frac{H}{R}$, and that the time taken to attain half this speed is $\frac{MH}{R^2}\left(\log 2 - \frac{1}{2}\right)$.
11. A mass of m kg moves initially with a velocity of u m per second on a straight line. A constant power equal to H watts is applied so as to increase its velocity; show that the time that elapses before the velocity is n times its original value is $\frac{m(n^2 - 1)\, u^2}{H}$.

12. A body of mass M is propelled in a straight line by an engine producing energy at a constant rate P, against a resistance Kv^2, where v is the velocity and K is a constant. Prove that the space s described from rest is given by $\frac{3sK}{M} = -\log\left(1 - \frac{Kv^3}{P}\right)$.

90. Energy. Def. *The Energy of a body is its capacity for doing work and is of two kinds, Kinetic and Potential.*

The **Kinetic Energy** *of a body is the energy which it possesses by virtue of its motion, and is measured by the amount of work that the body can perform against the impressed forces before its velocity is destroyed.*

A falling body, a swinging pendulum, a revolving flywheel, and a cannon-ball in motion all possess kinetic energy.

Consider the case of a particle, of mass m, moving with velocity u, and let us find the work done by it before it comes to rest.

Suppose it brought to rest by a constant force P resisting its motion, which produces in it an acceleration $-f$ given by $P = mf$.

Let x be the space described by the particle before it comes to rest, so that $0 = u^2 + 2(-f)\cdot x$;

$$\therefore \quad fx = \frac{1}{2}u^2.$$

Hence the kinetic energy of the particle

$$= \text{work done by it before it comes to rest}$$

$$= Px = mfx = \frac{1}{2}mu^2.$$

Hence the kinetic energy of a particle is equal to the product of its mass and one-half the square of its velocity.

91. Theorem. *To show that the change of kinetic energy per unit of space is equal to the acting force.*

If a force P, acting on a particle of mass m, changes its velocity from u to v in time t whilst the particle moves through a space s, we have $v^2 - u^2 = 2fs$, where f is the acceleration produced.

$$\therefore \quad \frac{\frac{1}{2}mv^2 - \frac{1}{2}mu^2}{s} = mf = P \qquad \text{...(1).}$$

This equation proves the proposition when the force is constant.

When the force is variable, the same proof will hold if we take t so small that the force P does not sensibly alter during that interval.

Cor. It follows from equation (1) that the change in the kinetic energy of a particle is equal to the work done on it.

On multiplying the first and third relations of Art. 32 by m, we have

$$m(v - u) = mft = Pt,$$

and

$$\frac{1}{2}m(v^2 - u^2) = mfs = Ps.$$

These are often known as the Momentum and Energy Equations respectively. Expressed in words, they state that

Change of Momentum = Force × Time,

and Change of Kinetic Energy = Force × Space.

92. *The* **Potential Energy** *of a body is the work it can do by means of its position in passing from its present configuration to some standard configuration (usually called its zero position).*

A bent spring has potential energy [as in the case of a watch-spring which, by its uncoiling, keeps a watch going], viz., the work it can do in recovering its natural shape.

A body raised to a height above the ground [e.g., a clock-weight, when the clock is wound up, a stone at the edge of a precipice, or water stored up in a reservoir] has potential energy, viz., the work its weight can do as it falls to the earth's surface, which is usually taken as the zero of potential energy. Compressed air has potential energy, viz., the work it can do in expanding to the volume it would occupy in the atmosphere.

93. *A particle of mass m falls from rest at a height h above the ground; to show that the sum of its potential and kinetic energies is constant throughout the motion.*

Let H be the point from which the particle starts, and O the point where it reaches the ground.

Let v be its velocity when it has fallen through a distance HP $(= x)$, so that $v^2 = 2gx$.

Its kinetic energy at $P = \frac{1}{2} mv^2 = mgx.$

Also its potential energy at P

$$= \text{the work its weight can do as it falls from } P \text{ to } O$$

$$= mg \cdot OP = mg(h - x).$$

Hence the sum of its kinetic and potential energies at P

$$= mgh.$$

But its potential energy when at H is mgh, and its kinetic energy there is zero.

Hence the sum of the potential and kinetic energies is the same at P as at H; and, since P is *any* point, it follows that the sum of these two quantities is the same throughout the motion.

As the particle falls to the ground it will be noted that the potential energy which it has when at its highest point (and which was stored up in it as it was lifted into that position) becomes transformed into kinetic energy, and this goes on continually until the particle reaches the ground, when its store of potential energy becomes exhausted.

In the case of pendulum the potential energy which the bob possesses, when instantaneously at rest in its highest position, becomes converted into kinetic energy as the bob swings down to its lowest position, and is reconverted into potential energy as the bob travels to its next position of instantaneous rest at the end of its swing.

94. The example of the previous article is an extremely simple illustration of the principle of the **Conservation of Energy,** which may be stated as follows :

If a body or system of bodies be in motion under a conservative system of forces, the sum of its kinetic and potential energies is constant.

Forces, of the kind which occur in the material universe, are said to be conservative when they depend on the position or configuration **only** *of the system of bodies, and not on the velocity or direction of motion of the bodies.*

Thus from a conservative system are excluded forces of the nature of friction, or forces such as the resistance of the air which varies as some power of the velocity of the body. Friction is excluded because, if the direction of motion of the body be reversed, the direction of the friction is reversed also.

When the forces are conservative, it is found that the amount of work required to bring a system from one configuration to another is always the same, and does not depend on the path pursued by the system during the alteration of its configuration.

Referring to the case of a particle sliding down a rough plane of length l (Art. 77), we see that the kinetic energy of the particle on reaching the ground is

$$\frac{1}{2}m\,[2gl\,(\sin\alpha - \mu\cos\alpha)],\ \text{i.e.,}\ mgl\sin\alpha - mgl\mu\cos\alpha.$$

Also the potential energy there is zero, so that the sum of the kinetic and potential energies at the foot of the plane is

$$mgl\sin\alpha - \mu mgl\cos\alpha.$$

But the potential energy of the particle when at the top of the plane is $mg \cdot l\sin\alpha$, so that the total loss of visible mechanical energy of the particle in sliding from the top to the bottom of the inclined plane is $\mu mgl\cos\alpha$. This energy has been transformed and appears chiefly in the form of heat, partly in the moving body, and partly in the plane; it is ultimately dissipated into the surrounding air.

Other cases of loss of kinetic energy occur in the examples of Art. 86.

In each case the kinetic energy before impact

$$= \frac{1}{2}\cdot 3\times 13^2 + \frac{1}{2}\cdot 2\times 3^2 = \frac{507+18}{2} = 262\frac{1}{2}\text{cm dynes.}$$

In Ex. 1, the kinetic energy after impact

$$= \frac{1}{2}\cdot 5\cdot 9^2 = \frac{405}{2} = 202\frac{1}{2}\text{cm dynes.}$$

In Ex. 2, the kinetic energy after impact

$$= \frac{1}{2}\cdot 5\times\left(\frac{33}{5}\right)^2 = \frac{1089}{10} = 108.9\text{cm dyne.}$$

Hence in the two cases 60 and 153.6 cm dynes of kinetic energy respectively are lost.

95. Ex. 1. *A bullet, of mass 4 oz., is fired into a target with a velocity of 1200 feet per second. The mass of the target is 20 lb. and it is free to move; find the loss of kinetic energy in foot-pounds.*

Let V be the resulting common velocity of the shot and target. Since no momentum is lost (Art. 36) we have

$$\left(20 + \frac{4}{16}\right)V = \frac{4}{16}\times 1200.$$

$$\therefore \qquad V = \frac{400}{27}.$$

The original kinetic energy $= \frac{1}{2} \cdot \frac{4}{16} \cdot 1200^2 = 180000$ foot-poundals.

The final kinetic energy $= \frac{1}{2}\left(20 + \frac{4}{16}\right) V^2$

$= \frac{20000}{9}$ foot-poundals.

The energy lost $= 180000 - \frac{20000}{9} = \frac{1600000}{9}$ foot-poundals

$= \frac{50000}{9}$ ft/lb.

It will be noted that, in this case, although no momentum is lost by the impact, yet $\frac{80}{81}$ths of the energy is transformed.

It will be found that, in all cases of impact, kinetic energy is lost or rather transformed.

Ex. 2. *Compare the kinetic energies of the shot and gun in the example of Art. 87.*

The kinetic energy of the shot $= \frac{1}{2} \cdot 400 \times (900)^2$ foot-poundals

$= \frac{200 \times 900^2}{32}$ ft/lb. $= \frac{200 \times 900^2}{32 \times 2240}$ ft/tons

$= 2260$ft/tons nearly.

The kinetic energy of the gun

$= \frac{1}{2} \cdot 50 \times 2240 \times \left(\frac{45}{14}\right)^2$ ft/poundals

$= \frac{25}{32} \times \left(\frac{45}{14}\right)^2$ ft/tons $= 8.07$ft/tons nearly.

The kinetic energy of the shot is thus 280 times that of the gun, although their momenta are equal.

It is to this great superiority in kinetic energy of the shot that its destructive power is due.

96. When we take into account the energy which has been transformed into heat, sound, light and other forms which modern Physics recognizes as forms of energy, we find that there is no real loss of energy in an isolated system which is left to itself. This doctrine of the indestructibility of energy is the central Principle of Modern Science. It may be expressed thus;

Energy cannot be created nor can it be destroyed, but it may be transformed into any of the forms which it can take.

As a numerical illustration, it may be stated that 778 foot-pounds of work is equivalent to the heat necessary to raise the temperature of 1 lb. of water by 1° Fahrenheit, i.e., 778 foot-pounds is the **mechanical equivalent of heat.** In the metric system, 4.2 J = 1 calorie (approx.).

Examples. XV.

1. A body, of mass 5 kg, is thrown up vertically with a velocity of 981 cm per second; what is its kinetic energy (1) at the moment of propulsion, (2) after half a second, (3) after one second?
2. Find the kinetic energy measured in foot-pounds of a cannon-ball of mass 25 pounds discharged with a velocity of 200 feet per second.
3. Find the kinetic energy in ergs of a cannon-ball of 10000 grammes discharged with a velocity of 5000 centimetres per second.
4. A cannon-ball, of mass 5000 grammes, is discharged with a velocity of 500 metres per second. Find its kinetic energy in ergs, and, if the cannot be free to move, and have a mass of 100 kilogrammes, find the energy of the recoil.
5. A bullet, of mass 56.7 grammes, is fired into a target with a velocity of 390 metres per second. The mass of the target is 4.53 kg and it is free to move; find the loss of kinetic energy by the impact in foot-pounds.
6. Compare (1) the momenta, and (2) the kinetic energies of a bullet of mass 113.4 grammes and moving with a velocity of 366 metres per second, and a cannon-ball of mass 6.8 kg moving with a velocity of 12.2 metres per second. Find the uniform forces that would bring each to rest in one second and the distance through which each would move.

97. As a further illustration of the use of the Principles of Momentum and Energy, consider the following examples.

Ex. 1. *A hammer, of mass M gm, falls from a height of h cm upon the top of a pile, of mass m gm, and drives it into the ground a distance a cm, find the resistance of the ground, it being assumed to be constant and the pile being supposed inelastic.*

Find also the time during which the pile is in motion, and the kinetic energy lost at the impact.

Let u be the velocity of the hammer on hitting the pile, so that

$$u^2 = 2gh \qquad ...(1).$$

Let v be the velocity of the hammer and pile immediately after the impact. Then the principle of Conservation of Momentum gives

$$(M + m)\, v = Mu \qquad ...(2).$$

If P be the resistance of the ground in dynes, the force to resist the driving of the pile into the ground $= P - (M + m)\, g$.

The Principle of the Conservation of Energy gives

$$\frac{1}{2}(M + m)\, v^2 = [P - (M + m)\, g] \cdot a.$$

$$\therefore \qquad P = (M + m)\, g + (M + m)\frac{v^2}{2a}$$

$$= (M + m)\, g + \frac{M^2}{M + m}\frac{u^2}{2a}, \text{ by (2)},$$

$$= (M + m)\, g + \frac{M^2}{M + m}\, g\, \frac{h}{a}.$$

A weight of slightly more than $\frac{M^2}{M+m} \cdot \frac{h}{a}$ gm placed on the pile would thus slowly overcome the resistance and just drive the pile down.

The principle of Momentum gives the time t during which the pile is in motion. For

$$[P - (M+m)g] \times t = \text{change in the momentum}$$
$$= (M+m)v = Mu,$$

So that
$$t \times \frac{M^2}{M+m}\frac{u^2}{2a} = Mu,$$

and
$$\therefore \quad t = \frac{M+m}{M} \cdot \frac{2a}{u} = \frac{M+m}{M} a \sqrt{\frac{2}{gh}}.$$

The kinetic energy lost at the impact

$$= \frac{1}{2}Mu^2 - \frac{1}{2}(M+m)v^2$$

$$= \frac{1}{2}Mu^2 - \frac{1}{2}\frac{M^2}{M+m}u^2$$

$$= \frac{1}{2}\frac{Mm}{M+m}u^2$$

$$= \frac{m}{M+m} \times \text{energy of the hammer on striking the pile.}$$

The greater that M is compared with m, i.e., the greater is the mass of the hammer compared with that of the pile, the less is the fraction of the energy which is destroyed.

Ex. 2. Motion of a bicycle. *A cyclist, whose weight added to that of his machine is* 100 *kg, is riding on a level road at the rate of* 10 *km an hour; his bicycle is geared up to* 140 *and the length of the cranks is* 14 *cm; if the resistance to his motion be* 3 *kgf find the downward thrust he must exert on his pedals and the rate at which he works compared with a Horse-Power.*

By saying that a bicycle is 'geared up' to 140 cm, we mean that for every revolution of the rider's feet his bicycle advances through a distance equal to the circumference of a wheel of diameter 140 cm, i.e., he advances $\pi \cdot 140$ cm.

Let P be the downward thrust, supposed constant, in kgf.

Then in one complete revolution the work done

$$= 2 \times P \times g \times \frac{14 \times 2}{100} \text{ J}$$

The work done against the resistance to the machine in this time

$$= \frac{\pi \cdot 140}{100} 3\,g \text{ joules}$$

Assuming that no work is lost on account of friction, in other words that the bicycle is a theoretically perfect one, we have by equating these works,

$$2 \times P \times g \times \frac{28}{100} = \pi \times \frac{140}{100} \times 3g,$$

i.e.,
$$P = \frac{15}{2}\pi = 23.6 \text{ kgf nearly.}$$

The work done by the man per hour $= 3g \times 10 \times 1000$ J

$$\therefore \quad \text{work done per second} = \frac{3 \times 9.8 \times 10000}{3600} \text{ W}$$

$$\therefore \quad \text{rate of working} = \frac{3 \times 9.8 \times 10000}{3600 \times 746} = 0.11 \text{ H.P.}$$

If the cyclist were ascending an incline of 1 *in* 50 *at the same rate, find the downward thrust.*

For each complete revolution of the pedals he goes forward $\pi \cdot 140$ cm, i.e., $\frac{\pi \times 140}{100}$ m, and therefore lifts himself and the machine through a vertical distance of $\frac{1}{50} \times \pi \cdot \frac{140}{100}$ m, and in so doing must perform an extra $\frac{100}{50} g \times \pi \times \frac{140}{100}$ J of work. In this case we then have

$$= 2 \times Pg \times \frac{28}{100}$$

$$= \pi \times \frac{140}{100} \times 3g + \frac{200}{50} g \times \pi \times \frac{140}{100}$$

$$\therefore \quad P = 3\frac{5\pi}{2} = 55 \text{ kgf.}$$

Examples. XVI.

1. A shot of mass m is fired from a gun of mass M with velocity u relative to the gun; show that the actual velocities of the shot and gun are $\frac{Mu}{M+m}$ and $\frac{mu}{M+m}$ respectively, and that their kinetic energies are inversely proportional to their masses.
2. A gun is mounted to a gun-carriage movable on a smooth horizontal plane, and the gun is elevated at an angle α to the horizon; a shot is fired and leaves the gun in a direction inclined at an angle θ to the horizon; if the mass of the gun and its carriage be n times that of the shot, show that $\tan\theta = \left(1 + \frac{1}{n}\right)\tan\alpha$.
3. A mass of 560 kg, moving with a velocity of 24000 cm per second, strikes a fixed target and is brought to rest in a hundredth part of a second. Find the impulse of the blow on the target, and supposing the resistance to be uniform throughout the time taken to bring the body to rest, find the distance through which it penetrates.
4. A mass of 203 kg falls from a height of 3.048 metres upon an inelastic pile of mass 609 kg; supposing the mean resistance of the ground to penetration by the pile to be 1.524, metric tonne weight, determine the distance through which the pile is driven at each blow, and the time it takes to travel this distance.
   Find also what fraction of the energy is dissipated to each blow.
5. A bullet, of mass 20 grammes, is shot horizontally from a rifle, the barrel of which is one metre long, with a velocity of 200 metres per second into a mass of 50 kilogrammes of wood floating on water. If the bullet buries itself in the wood without making any splinters or causing it to rotate, find the velocity of the wood immediately after it is struck.
   Find also the average force in grammes' weight which is exerted on the bullet by the powder.

6. A hammer, of mass 203 kg, falls through 122 cm and comes to rest after striking a mass of iron, the duration of the blow being $\frac{1}{50}$th of a second; find the force, supposing it to be uniform, which is exerted by the hammer on the iron.
7. Masses m and $2m$ are connected by a string passing over a smooth pulley; at the end of 3 seconds a mass m is picked up by the ascending body; find the resulting motion.
8. Two equal masses, A and B, are connected by an inelastic thread, $245\frac{1}{4}$ cm long, and are laid close together on a smooth horizontal table $408\frac{3}{4}$ cm from its nearest edge; B is also connected by a stretched inelastic thread with an equal mass C hanging over the edge. Find the velocity of the masses when A begins to move and also when B arrives at the edge of the table.
9. Two masses of 2.26 and 3.17 kg respectively are connected by a string passing over a fixed smooth pulley; at the end of 3 seconds the larger mass impinges on a fixed inelastic horizontal plane; show that the system will be instantaneously at rest at the end of $2\frac{1}{4}$ seconds more.
10. A string over a pulley supports a mass of 2.25 kg on one side and of 0.91 and 1.36 kg on the other, the lower mass 0.91 kg being distant 30.48 cm from the other. The 0.91 kg weight is suddenly raised to the same level as the other and kept from falling. Show that the string will become taut in half a second and that the whole system will then move with a uniform velocity of 97.5 cm per sec.
11. Two equal weights, P and Q, connected by a string passing over a smooth pulley, are moving with a common velocity, P descending and Q ascending. If P be suddenly stopped, and instantly let drop again, find the time that elapses before the string is again tight.
12. A mass M after falling freely through a feet begins to raise a mass m greater than itself and connected with it by means of an inextensible string passing over a fixed pulley. Show that m will have returned to its original position at the end of time

$$\frac{2M}{m-M}\sqrt{\frac{2a}{g}}.$$

Find also what fraction of the visible energy of M is destroyed at the instant when m is jerked into motion.
13. A light inelastic string passes over a light frictionless pulley and has masses of $\frac{4}{10}$ kg and $\frac{3}{10}$ kg attached to its ends. On the $\frac{3}{10}$ kg mass a bar of $\frac{1}{5}$ kg is placed which is removed by a fixed ring after it has descended 2.5 m from rest. How much further will the $\frac{3}{10}$ kg mass descended?

    If whenever the $\frac{3}{10}$ kg mass passes up through the ring it carries the bar with it and whenever it passes down through the ring it leaves the bar behind, find the whole time that elapses before the system comes to rest.
14. Two railway carriages are moving side by side with different velocities; what is the ultimate effect of the interchanging of passengers between the carriages?

15. A man of 84 kg ascends a mountain 3500 m high in 7 hours and the difficulties in his way are equivalent to carrying a weight of 21 kg; one of Watt's horses could pull him up the same height without impediments in 56 minutes; show that the horse does as much work as 6 such men in the same time.

16. A blacksmith, wielding a 6.35 kg sledge, strikes an iron bar 25 times per minute, and brings the sledge to rest upon the bar after each blow. If the velocity of the sledge on striking the iron be 9.75 metres per second, compare the rate at which he is working with a metric horse-power.

17. A steam hammer, of mass 20 tons, falls vertically through 5 feet, being pressed downwards by steam pressure equal to the weight of 30 tons; what velocity will it acquire, and how many foot-pounds of work will it do before coming to rest?

18. A train of 150 tons, moving with a velocity of 50 miles per hour, has its steam shut off and the brakes applied, and is stopped in 363 yards. Supposing the resistance to its motion to be uniform find its value, and find also the mechanical work done by it measured in foot-pounds.

19. A train, of mass 203 metric tonnes, is ascending an incline of 1 in 100 at the rate of 48 km per hour, the resistance of the rails being equal to the weight of 3.56 kg per metric tonne. The steam being shut off, and the brakes applied, the train is stopped in 402.5 metres. Find the weight of the brake-van, the coefficient of sliding friction of iron on iron being $\frac{1}{6}$.

20. If a bicyclist always works with $\frac{1}{10}$ H.P. and goes 12 miles per hour on the level, show that the resistance of the road is 3.125 lb. wt.
If the mass of the machine and its rider be 12 stone, show that up an incline of 1 in 50 the speed will be reduced to about 5.8 miles per hour.

21. A man can bicycle at the rate of $16\frac{1}{2}$ miles per hour on a smooth road. He exerts a down pressure, equal to 20 lb. weight, with each foot during the down stroke, and the length of this stroke is 12 inches. If the machine be geared up to 63, find the work he does per minute.

22. A rifle bullet loses $\frac{1}{20}$th of its velocity in passing through a plank; find how many such uniform planks it would pass through before coming to rest, assuming the resistance of the planks to be uniform.

23. A man sculling does E foot-pounds of work, usefully applied, at each stroke. If the total resistance of the water when the boat is moving n miles per hour be R lb. weight, find the number of strokes he must take per minute to maintain this speed.

24. A bicycle is geared up to 70 inches; the rider works at $\frac{1}{10}$ H.P. and makes 60 revolutions per minute with his feet. Neglecting friction, find the resistance to his motion and the downward thrust on his pedals (supposed constant), if the length of the cranks be $6\frac{3}{4}$ inches.

25. The mass of a rider and his bicycle is 180 lb.; the machine is running freely down an incline of 1 in 60 at a uniform rate of 8 miles per hour; show that to go at the same rate up an incline of 1 in 100 he must work at the rate of 0.1024 H.P.

26. A horizontal jet delivers 100 kgs of water per minute with a velocity of 3 m per second against a fixed vertical plate set at right angles to the direction of the jet. What quantity of momentum is destroyed per second and what is the force, in kfg, on the plate?
Find also the rate at which the jet is delivering energy and express it in terms of a kw (kilo-watts).

27. A hammer, of mass 2 kg, is used to drive a nail, of mass 800 g, into a board, and the hammer when it strikes the nail has a velocity of 2.5 m per second. If each blow drives the nail 1.5 cm into the board, find the resistance against which the nail moves, both nail and hammer being treated as inelastic.

Motion of the centre of inertia of a system of particles.

***98. Theorem.** *If the velocities at any instant of any number of masses $m_1, m_2, \ldots$, parallel to any line fixed in space be $u_1, u_2, u_3, \ldots$, then the velocity parallel to that line of the centre of inertia of these masses at that instant is*

$$\frac{m_1u_1 + m_2u_2 + \ldots}{m_1 + m_2 + \ldots}.$$

At the instant under consideration let $x_1, x_2, x_3, \ldots$ be the distances of the given masses measured along this fixed line from a fixed point in it, and let $\bar{x}$ be the distance of their centre of inertia.

Then (Statics, Art. 111), we have

$$\bar{x} = \frac{m_1x_1 + m_2x_2 + \ldots}{m_1 + m_2 + \ldots}.$$

Let $x'_1, x'_2, \ldots$ be the corresponding distances of these masses at the end of a small time t, the $\bar{x}'$ the corresponding distance of their centre of inertia. Then we have

$$x'_1 = x_1 + u_1t,$$
$$x'_2 = x_2 + u_2t,$$
$$x'_3 = x_3 + u_3t,$$
$$\ldots\ldots\ldots$$

Also
$$\bar{x}' = \frac{m_1x'_1 + m_2x'_2 + \ldots}{m_1 + m_2 + \ldots},$$

$\therefore$
$$\bar{x}' - \bar{x} = \frac{m_1(x'_1 - x_1) + m_2(x'_2 - x_2) + \ldots}{m_1 + m_2 + \ldots}$$
$$= \frac{m_1u_1t + m_2u_2t + \ldots}{m_1 + m_2 + \ldots}.$$

But, if $\bar{u}$ be the velocity of the centre of inertia parallel to the fixed line, we have $\bar{x}' = \bar{x} + \bar{u}t$,

$\therefore$
$$\bar{u} = \frac{\bar{x}' - \bar{x}}{t} = \frac{m_1u_1 + m_2u_2 + \ldots}{m_1 + m_2 + \ldots}.$$

Hence the velocity of the centre of inertia of a system of particles in any given direction is equal to the sum of the momenta of the particles in that direction, divided by the sum of the masses of the particles.

Cor. If a system of particles be in motion in a plane, and their velocities and directions of motion are known, we can, by resolving these velocities parallel to two fixed lines and applying the preceding proposition, find the motion of their centre of inertia.

***99. Theorem.** *If the accelerations at any instant of any number of masses $m_1, m_2, \ldots$, parallel to any line fixed in space, be $f_1, f_2, f_3, \ldots$, then the acceleration of the centre of inertia of these masses parallel to this line is*

$$\frac{m_1 f_1 + m_2 f_2 + \ldots}{m_1 + m_2 + \ldots}.$$

The proof of this proposition is similar to that of the last article. We have only to change x_1, u_1, x'_1, u'_1 into u_1, f_1, u'_1, f'_1, and make similar changes for the other particles.

Ex. 1. *Two masses m_1, m_2 are connected by a light string as in Art. 74; find the acceleration of the centre of inertia of the system.*

The acceleration of the mass m_1 is $\frac{m_1 - m_2}{m_1 + m_2} g$ vertically downwards, and that of m_2 is the same in the opposite direction.

Here then $f_1 = -f_2 = \frac{m_1 - m_2}{m_1 + m_2} g$, so that the acceleration of the centre of inertia

$$= \frac{m_1 f_1 + m_2 f_2}{m_1 + m_2} = \left(\frac{m_1 - m_2}{m_1 + m_2}\right)^2 g.$$

Ex. 2. Two bodies, of masses m and $3m$, are connected by a light string passing over a smooth pulley; show that during the ensuing motion the acceleration of their centre of inertia is $\frac{g}{4}$.

Ex. 3. Find the velocity of the centre of inertia of two masses of 6 and 4 kg which move in parallel lines with velocities of 3 and 8 metres respectively, (1) when they move in the same direction, (2) when they move in opposite directions.

Ans. (1) 5 metres per second; (2) $1\frac{2}{5}$ metres per second in the direction in which the second body is moving.

Ex. 4. Two masses, mn and m, start simultaneously from the intersection of two straight lines with velocities v and nv respectively; show that the path of their centre of inertia is a straight line bisecting the angle between the two given straight lines.

Ex. 5. Two masses move at a uniform rate along two straight lines which meet and are inclined at a given angle; show that their centre of inertia describes a straight line with uniform velocity.

7

Projectiles

100. IN the previous chapters we have considered only motion in straight lines. In the present chapter we shall consider the motion of a particle projected into the air with any direction and velocity. We shall suppose the motion to be within such a moderate distance of the earth's surface, that the acceleration due to gravity may be considered to remain sensibly constant. We shall also neglect the resistance of the air, and consider the motion to be in *vacuo;* for, firstly, the law of resistance of the air to the motion of a particle is not accurately known, and, secondly, even if this law were known, the discussion would require a much larger range of knowledge of pure mathematics than the reader of the present book is supposed to possess.

Def. When a particle is projected into the air, the angle that the direction in which it is projected makes with the horizontal plane through the point of projection is called the **angle of projection;** the path which the particle describes is called its **trajectory;** the distance between the point of projection and the point where the path meets any plane drawn through the point of projection is its **range** on the plane; and the time that elapses before it again meets the horizontal plane through the point of projection is called the **time of flight.**

101. If the earth did not attract a particle to itself, the particle would, if projected into the air, describe a straight line; on account of the attraction of the earth, however the particle describes a curved line. This curve will be proved in Art. 113 to be always a parabola.

Let P be the point of projection, u the velocity and α the angle of projection; also let PAP' be the path of the particle, A being the highest point, and P' the point where the path again meets the horizontal plane through P.

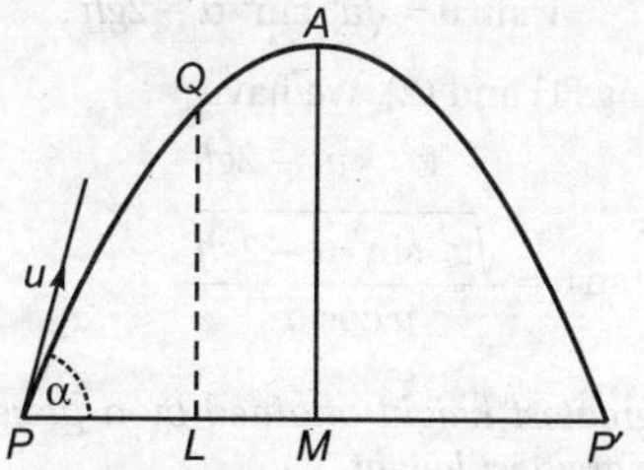

By the principle of the Physical Independence of Forces (Art. 71), the weight of the body only has effect on the motion of the body in the vertical direction; it therefore has no effect on the velocity of the body in the horizontal direction, and this horizontal velocity therefore remains unaltered.

The horizontal and vertical components of the initial velocity of the particle are $u \cos \alpha$ and $u \sin \alpha$ respectively.

The horizontal velocity is, therefore, throughout the motion equal to $u \cos \alpha$.

In the vertical direction the initial velocity is $u \sin \alpha$ and the acceleration is $-g$, [for the acceleration due to gravity is g vertically *downwards*, and we are measuring our positive direction *upwards*]. Hence the vertical motion is the same as that of a particle projected vertically upwards with velocity $u \sin \alpha$, and moving with acceleration $-g$.

The resultant motion of the particle is the same as that of a particle projected with a vertical velocity $u \sin \alpha$ inside a vertical tube of small bore, whilst the tube moves in a horizontal direction with velocity $u \cos \alpha$.

102. *To find the velocity and direction of motion after a given time has elapsed.*

Let v be the velocity, and θ the angle which the direction of motion at the end of time t makes with the horizontal.

Then $\quad v \cos \theta =$ horizontal velocity at end of time t

$= u \cos \alpha$, the constant horizontal velocity.

Also $\quad v \sin \theta =$ the vertical velocity at end of time t

$= u \sin \alpha - gt.$

Hence, by squaring and adding,

$$v^2 = u^2 - 2ugt \sin \alpha + g^2t^2,$$

and, by division, $\tan \theta = \dfrac{u \sin \alpha - gt}{u \cos \alpha}.$

103. *To find the velocity and direction of motion at a given height.*

Let v be the magnitude, and θ the inclination to the horizon, of the velocity of the particle at a given height h. The horizontal and vertical velocities at this point are therefore $v \cos \theta$ and $v \sin \theta$.

Hence

$v \cos \theta = u \cos \alpha$, the constant horizontal velocity ...(1).

Also, by Art. 32,

$$v \sin \theta = \sqrt{u^2 \sin^2 \alpha - 2gh} \qquad ...(2).$$

Squaring and adding (1) and (2), we have

$$v^2 = u^2 - 2gh$$

Also, by division, $\tan \theta = \dfrac{\sqrt{u^2 \sin^2 \alpha - 2gh}}{u \cos \alpha}.$

104. *To find the greatest height attained by a projectile, and the time that elapses before it is at its greatest height.*

Let A (Fig. Art. 101), be the highest point of the path. The projectile must at A be moving horizontally, and hence the vertical velocity at A must be zero.

Hence, by Art. 32,

$$0 = u^2 \sin^2 \alpha - 2g \cdot MA.$$

$$\therefore \qquad MA = \frac{u^2 \sin^2 \alpha}{2g},$$

giving the greatest height attained.

Let T be the time from P to A; then T is the time in which a vertical velocity $u \sin \alpha$ is destroyed by gravity.

Hence, by Art. 32, $0 = u \sin \alpha - gT$.

$$\therefore \qquad T = \frac{u \sin \alpha}{g}.$$

giving the required time.

105. *To find the range on the horizontal plane and the time of flight.*

When the projectile arrives at P' (Fig. Art. 101), the distance it has described in a vertical direction is zero.

Hence, if t be the time of flight, we have by Art. 32 (1)

$$0 = u \sin at - \frac{1}{2} gt^2.$$

$$\therefore \qquad t = \frac{2\, u \sin \alpha}{g} = \text{twice the time to the highest point.}$$

During this time t the horizontal velocity remains constant and equal to $u \cos \alpha$.

$$\therefore \qquad PP' = \text{horizontal distance described in time } t$$

$$= u \cos \alpha \cdot t = \frac{2\, u^2 \sin \alpha \cos \alpha}{g}.$$

Hence the range is equal to twice the product of the initial vertical and horizontal velocities divided by g.

106. *For a* **given** *velocity of projection, u, to find the maximum horizontal range, and the corresponding direction of projection.*

If α be the angle of projection, the horizontal range, by the previous article,

$$= \frac{2u^2 \sin \alpha \cos \alpha}{g} = \frac{u^2 \sin 2\alpha}{g}.$$

Also $\sin 2\alpha$ is greatest when $2\alpha = 90°$, that is, when $\alpha = 45°$.

Hence the range on a horizontal plane is greatest when the initial direction of projection is at an angle of 45° with the horizontal through the point of projection.

The magnitude of this maximum horizontal range is

$$\frac{u^2}{g} \sin 90°, \text{ i.e., } \frac{u^2}{g}.$$

107. *To show that, with a given velocity of projection, there are for a given horizontal range in general two directions of projection, which are equally inclined to the direction of maximum projection.*

By Art. 105, the range, when the angle of projection is α, is $\frac{u^2}{g}\sin 2\alpha$.

Also, when the angle of projection is $\frac{\pi}{2}-\alpha$, the range

$$=\frac{u^2}{g}\sin 2\left(\frac{\pi}{2}-\alpha\right)=\frac{u^2}{g}\sin(\pi-2\alpha)=\frac{u^2}{g}\sin 2\alpha$$

Hence we have the same horizontal range for the angles of projection α and $\frac{\pi}{2}-\alpha$.

These directions are equally inclined to the horzion and the vertical respectively, and are therefore equally inclined to the direction of maximum range, which bisects the angle between the horizontal and the vertical.

106. Ex. 1. *A bullet is projected, with a velocity of* 19620 *cm per second, at an angle of* 30° *with the horizontal; find* (1) *the greatest height attained,* (2) *the range on a horizontal plane and the time of flight, and* (3) *the velocity and direction of motion of the bullet when it is at a height of* 29430 *cm.*

The initial horizontal velocity

$$= 19620\cos 30° = 19620\times\frac{\sqrt{3}}{2} = 9810\sqrt{3}\text{cm per second}$$

The initial vertical velocity = 19620 sin 30° = 9810 cm per second.

(1) If h be the greatest height attained, then h is the distance through which a particle, starting with velocity 9810 cm per second and moving with acceleration $-g$, goes before it comes to rest.

$$\therefore \quad 0 = 9810^2 - 2gh;$$

$$\therefore \quad h = \frac{9810^2}{2\times 981} = 49050\,\text{cm}.$$

(2) If t be the time of flight, the vertical distance described in time t is zero.

$$\therefore \quad 0 = 9810\,t - \frac{1}{2}gt^2;$$

$$\therefore \quad t = \frac{9810\times 2}{g} = 20\,\text{seconds}.$$

The horizontal range = the distance described in 20 seconds by a particle moving with a constant velocity of $9810\sqrt{3}$ cm per sec.

$$= 20\times 9810\sqrt{3} = 196200\sqrt{3}\,\text{cm}.$$

(3) If v be the velocity, and θ the inclination to the horizontal, at a height of 29430 cm, we have

$$v^2\sin^2\theta = 9810^2 - 2g\cdot 29430 = 981^2\times 40,$$

and $$v^2\cos^2\theta = (9810\sqrt{3})^2 = 981^2\times 300.$$

Hence, by addition, we have $v = 981\times\sqrt{340} = 1962\sqrt{85}$ cm per sec.

Also, by division,

$$\tan\theta = \sqrt{\frac{2}{15}}$$

$$\therefore \quad \theta = \tan^{-1}\sqrt{\frac{2}{15}}.$$

Ex. 2. *A cricket ball is thrown with a velocity of* 2943 *cm per second; find the greatest range on the horizontal plane, and the two directions in which the ball may be thrown so as to give a range of* $4414\frac{1}{2}$ *cm.*

If the angle of projection be α, the range, by Art. 105,

$$= \frac{2.2943^2 \cdot \sin\alpha \cos\alpha}{g} = \frac{2942^2 \cdot \sin 2\alpha}{g}.$$

The maximum range is obtained when α = 45°, and therefore

$$\frac{2943^2}{981} = 8829 \text{cm}.$$

When the range of $4414\frac{1}{2}$ cm, the angle α is given by

$$\frac{2943^2}{g} \sin 2\alpha = 4414\frac{1}{2}.$$

$$\therefore \quad \sin 2\alpha = \frac{8829 \times 981}{2 \times 2943^2} = \frac{8829}{6 \times 2943} = \frac{1}{2}.$$

$$\therefore \quad 2\alpha = 30°, \text{or } 150°.$$

$$\therefore \quad \alpha = 15°, \text{ or } 75°.$$

Ex. 3. *A cannon ball is projected horizontally from the top of a tower,* 1962 *cm high, with a velocity of* 2943 *cm per second. Find*

(1) *the time of flight,*

(2) *the distance from the foot of the tower of the point at which it hits the ground, and*

(3) *its velocity when it hits the ground.*

(1) The initial vertical velocity of the ball is zero, and hence *t*, the time of flight, is the time in which a body, falling freely under gravity, would describe 1962 cm.

Hence
$$1962 = \frac{1}{2} \cdot 981^2$$

$$\therefore \quad t^2 = 4$$

$$\therefore \quad t = 2 \text{ seconds}.$$

(2) During this time the horizontal velocity is constant, and therefore the required distance from the foot of the tower

$$= 2943 \times 2 = 5886 \text{cm}.$$

(3) The vertical velocity at the end of 2 seconds = 2 × 981 = 1962 cm per second, and the horizontal velocity is 2943 cm per second;

$$\therefore \text{ The required velocity} = \sqrt{2943^2 + 1962^2} = 981\sqrt{13} \text{ cm per second}$$

Ex. 4. *From the top of a cliff,* 24.5 *m high, a stone is thrown so that it starts with a velocity of* 39.2 *m per second, at an angle of* 30° *with the horizon; find where it hits the ground at the bottom of the cliff.*

The initial vertical velocity is 39.2 sin 30°, or 19.6 m per second, and the initial horizontal velocity is 39.2 cos 30°, or $19.6 \times \sqrt{3}$ m per second.

Let *T* be the time that elapses before the stone hits the ground.

Then *T* is the time in which a stone, projected with vertical velocity 19.6 and moving with acceleration −*g*, describes a distance −24.5 m.

$$\therefore \qquad -24.5 = 19.6\,T - \frac{1}{2} \times 9.8\,T^2$$

Hence $T = 5$ seconds.

During this time the horizontal velocity remains unaltered, and hence the distance of the point, where the stone hits the ground, from the foot of the cliff $= 98\sqrt{3}$ = about 170 m.

Examples. XVII.

1. A particle is projected at an angle α to the horizon with a velocity of u cm per second; find the greatest height attained, the time of flight, and the range on a horizontal plane, when
   (1) $u = 1962, \alpha = 30°$;
   (2) $u = 2452\frac{1}{2}, \alpha = 60°$;
   (3) $u = 2943, \alpha = 75°$;
   (4) $u = 6131\frac{1}{4}, \alpha = \sin^{-1}\frac{3}{5}$.
2. Find the greatest range on a horizontal plane when the velocity of projection is (1) 981, (2) 2943, (3) 4905 cm per second.
3. A shot leaves a gun at the rate of 160 metres per second; calculate the greatest distance to which it could be projected; and the height to which it would rise.
4. If a man can throw a stone 80 metres, how long is it in the air, and to what height does it rise?
5. A body is projected with a velocity of 49 m per sec. in a direction making an angle $\tan^{-1} 3$ with the horizon; show that it rises to a vertical height of $110\frac{1}{4}$ m, that its direction of motion is inclined to the horizon at an angle of 60° when its vertical height above the ground is 73.5 m and that its time of flight is about $9\frac{1}{2}$ sec.
6. A projectile is fired horizontally from a height of 1962 cm from the ground, and reaches the ground at a horizontal distance of 4905 cm. Find its initial velocity.
7. A stone is thrown horizontally, with velocity $\sqrt{2gh}$, from the top of a tower of height h. Find where it will strike the level ground through the foot of the tower. What will be its striking velocity?
8. A stone is dropped from a height of 274.3 cm above the floor of a railway carriage which is travelling at the rate of 48 km per hour. Find the velocity and direction of the particle in space at the instant when it meets the floor of the carriage.
9. A ship is moving with a velocity of $490\frac{1}{2}$ cm per second, and a body is allowed to fall from the top of its mast, which is $4414\frac{1}{2}$ cm high; find the velocity and direction of motion of the body, (1) at the end of two seconds, (2) when it hits the deck.

10. A shot is fired from a gun on the top of a cliff, 17658 cm high, with a velocity of 8829 cm per second, at an elevation of 30°. Find the horizontal distance from the vertical line through the gun of the point where the shot strikes the water.

11. From the top of a vertical tower, whose height is $\frac{13}{2} g$ cm, a particle is projected, the vertical and horizontal components of its initial velocity being $6g$ and $8g$ respectively; find the time of flight, and the distance from the foot of the tower of the point at which it strikes the ground.

12. A gun is aimed so that the shot strikes horizontally the top of the spire of Strasburg Cathedral, which is 141 metres high; show that, if the angle of projection be $\cot^{-1} 5$, then the velocity of projection is nearly 268 metres per second.

13. Find the velocity and direction of projection of a shot which passes in a horizontal direction just over the top of a wall which is 3924 cm off and 1962 cm high.

14. A particle is projected at an angle of elevation $\sin^{-1} \frac{4}{5}$, and its range on the horizontal plane is 3 km; find the velocity of projection, and the velocity at the highest point of its path.

15. Two balls are projected from the same point in directions inclined at 60° and 30° to the horizontal; if they attain the same height, what is the ratio of their velocities of projection?
What is this ratio if they have the same horizontal range?

16. The velocity of a particle when at its greatest height is $\sqrt{\frac{2}{5}}$ of its velocity when at half its greatest height; show that the angle of projection is 60°.

17. Find the angle of projection when the range of a horizontal plane is (1) 4, (2) $4\sqrt{3}$ times the greatest height attained.

18. Find the angle of projection when the range is equal to the distance through which the particle would have to fall in order to acquire a velocity equal to its velocity of projection.

109. Range on an inclined plane. *From a point on a plane, which is inclined at an angle β to the horizon, a particle is projected with a velocity u, at an angle α with the horizontal, in a plane passing through the normal to the inclined plane and the line of greatest slope; to find the range on the inclined plane.*

Let PQ be the range on the inclined plane, PT the direction of projection, and QN the perpendicular on the horizontal plane through P.

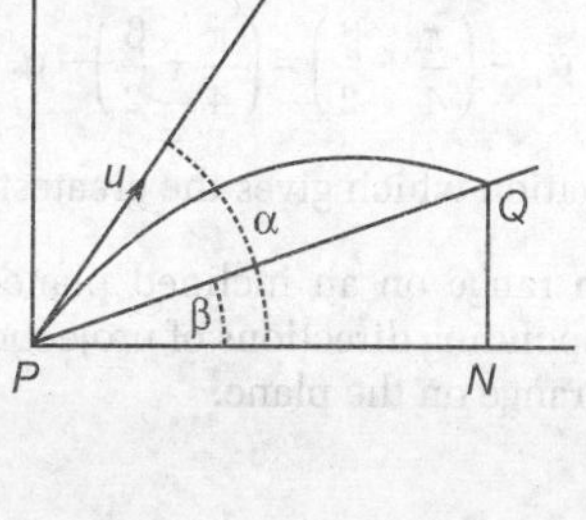

The initial component of the velocity perpendicular to PQ is $u \sin(\alpha - \beta)$, and the acceleration in this direction is $-g \cos \beta$.

Let T be the time which the particle takes to go from P to Q. Then in time T the space described in a direction perpendicular to PQ is zero.

Hence $0 = u \sin(\alpha - \beta).T - \frac{1}{2} g \cos \beta \cdot T^2$, and therefore

$$T = \frac{2u}{g} \frac{\sin(\alpha - \beta)}{\cos \beta}$$

During this time the horizontal velocity $u \cos \alpha$ remains unaltered; hence $PN = u \cos \alpha \cdot T$, so that the range

$$PQ = \frac{PN}{\cos \beta} = \frac{u \cos \alpha}{\cos \beta} \cdot T = \frac{2u^2}{g} \frac{\cos \alpha \sin(\alpha - \beta)}{\cos^2 \beta}.$$

110. Maximum range. *To find the direction of projection which gives the maximum range on the inclined plane, and to show that for any given range there are two directions of projection, which are equally inclined to the direction for maximum range.*

From the preceding article the range

$$= \frac{2u^2}{g} \frac{\cos \alpha \sin(\alpha - \beta)}{\cos^2 \beta} = \frac{u^2}{g \cos^2 \beta} \{\sin(2\alpha - \beta) - \sin \beta\} \quad ...(i).$$

Now u and β are given; hence the range is a maximum when $\sin(2\alpha - \beta)$ is greatest, or when $2\alpha - \beta = \frac{\pi}{2}$.

In this case $\alpha - \beta = \frac{\pi}{2} - \alpha$, i.e., the angles TPQ and LPT are equal.

Hence, *the direction for maximum range bisects the angle between the vertical and the inclined plane.*

Also the maximum range

$$= \frac{u^2}{g \cos^2 \beta}(1 - \sin \beta) = \frac{u^2}{g(1 + \sin \beta)}.$$

Again, the range with an angle of elevation α_1 is, by (i), the same as that with elevation α, if

$$\sin(2\alpha_1 - \beta) = \sin(2\alpha - \beta),$$

i.e., if
$$2\alpha_1 - \beta = \pi - (2\alpha - \beta),$$

i.e., if
$$\alpha_1 = \frac{\pi}{2} + \beta - \alpha,$$

i.e., if
$$\alpha_1 - \left(\frac{\pi}{4} + \frac{\beta}{2}\right) = \left(\frac{\pi}{4} + \frac{\beta}{2}\right) - \alpha.$$

But $\frac{\pi}{4} + \frac{\beta}{2}$ is the elevation which gives the greatest range.

Hence for any **given** range on an inclined plane there are two angles of projection, the two corresponding directions of projection being equally inclined to that for the maximum range on the plane.

111. Ex. 1. *From the foot of an inclined plane, whose rise is 7 in 25, a shot is projected with a velocity of 196 m per second at an angle of 30° with the horizontal, (1) up the plane, (2) down the plane. Find the range in each case.*

Let β be the inclination of the plane, so that

$$\sin\beta = \frac{7}{25} \text{ and } \cos\beta = \frac{24}{25}.$$

(1) By Art. 109, the range in the first case

$$= 2\,\frac{196^2}{9.8}\,\frac{\cos 30^\circ \sin(30^\circ - \beta)}{\cos^2\beta}$$

$$= \frac{196^2}{4.9} \times \frac{\frac{\sqrt{3}}{2}\left(\frac{1}{2}\cdot\frac{24}{25} - \frac{\sqrt{3}}{2}\cdot\frac{7}{25}\right)}{\frac{24^2}{25^2}}$$

$$= 4 \times 196 \times 10 \times \frac{25\sqrt{3}\,(24 - 7\sqrt{3})}{4 \times 576}$$

$$= \frac{1225}{48}(3\sqrt{3} - 7)$$

$$= 195.8 \text{ m approximately.}$$

(2) The initial velocity perpendicular to the inclined plane is $u \sin(30^\circ + \beta)$ and the acceleration is $-g\cos\beta$. Hence the time of flight, T, is $2\,\frac{u}{g}\,\frac{\sin(30^\circ + \beta)}{\cos\beta}$. Hence, as in Art. 109, if R_1 be the range, we have $R_1 \cos\beta = u \cos 30^\circ \cdot T$.

$$\therefore \quad R_1 = 2\,\frac{u^2}{g}\,\frac{\cos 30^\circ \sin(30^\circ + \beta)}{\cos^2\beta}$$

$$= \frac{1225}{48}(8\sqrt{3} + 7), \text{ as in (i),}$$

$$= 511.4 \text{ m}$$

N.B. The range *down* an inclined plane may also be obtained from the formula of Art. 109, by changing β into –β, so that it is

$$\frac{2u^2}{g}\,\frac{\cos\alpha \sin(\alpha + \beta)}{\cos^2\beta}.$$

Ex. 2. *In the previous example, find the greatest range.*

The angle of projection α must

$$= \frac{1}{2}\left(\frac{\pi}{2} + \beta\right) = \frac{\pi}{4} + \frac{\beta}{2}.$$

$$\text{The range now} = \frac{u^2}{g\cos^2\beta}(1 - \sin\beta)$$

$$= \frac{u^2}{g}\,\frac{1}{1 + \sin\beta} = 3920\,\frac{1}{1 + \frac{7}{25}}$$

$$= \frac{3920 \times 25}{32} = 6125 \text{ m.}$$

Similarly the greatest range down the inclined plane would be found to be $3920 \dfrac{1}{1-\dfrac{7}{25}}$, i.e., 5444.4 m

Ex. 3. *A particle is projected at an angle α with the horizontal from the foot of a plane, whose inclination to the horizon is β; show that it will strike the plane at right angles, if* $\cot\beta = 2\tan(\alpha-\beta)$.

Let u be the velocity of projection, so that $u\cos(\alpha-\beta)$ and $u\sin(\alpha-\beta)$ are the initial velocities respectively parallel and perpendicular to the inclined plane.

The acceleration in these two directions are $-g\sin\beta$ and $-g\cos\beta$.

Then, as in Art. 109, the time, T, that elapses before the particle reaches the plane again is $\dfrac{2u\sin(\alpha-\beta)}{g\cos\beta}$.

If the direction of motion at the instant when the particle hits the plane by perpendicular to the plane, then the velocity at that instant parallel to the plane must be zero.

Hence $$u\cos(\alpha-\beta) - g\sin\beta\cdot T = 0.$$

$$\therefore \quad \frac{u\cos(\alpha-\beta)}{g\sin\beta} = T = \frac{2u\sin(\alpha-\beta)}{g\cos\beta}$$

$$\therefore \quad \cos\beta = 2\tan(\alpha-\beta).$$

112. Motion upon an inclined plane. *A particle moves upon a smooth plane which is inclined at an angle β to the horizon, being projected from a point in the plane with velocity in a direction inclined at an angle α to the intersection of the inclined plane with a horizontal plane; find the motion.*

Resolve the acceleration due to gravity into two components; one, $g\sin\beta$, in the direction of the line of greatest slope and the other, $g\cos\beta$, perpendicular to the inclined plane. The latter acceleration is destroyed by the reaction of the plane.

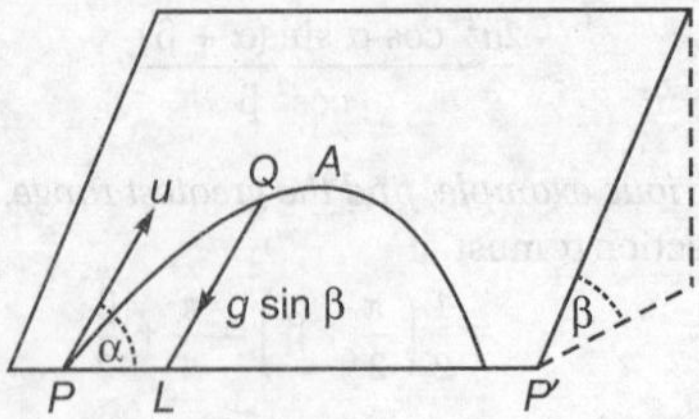

The particle therefore moves upon the inclined plane with an acceleration $g\sin\beta$ parallel to the line of greatest slope.

Hence the investigation of the motion is the same as that in Arts. 101-107, if we substitute "$g\sin\beta$" for "g", and instead of "vertical distances" read "distances measured on the inclined plane parallel to the line of greatest slope."

Examples. XVIII.

1. A plane is inclined at 30° to the horizon; from its foot a particle is projected with a velocity of $18393\frac{3}{4}$ cm per second in a direction inclined at an angle of 60° to the horizon; find the range on the inclined plane and the time of flight.

2. A particle is projected with velocity V, at an angle of 75° to the horizon, from the foot of a plane whose inclination is 30°. Find where it will strike the plane. Find also the maximum range of the particle on the inclined plane.

3. A particle is projected with velocity 1962 cm per second at an angle of 45° with the horizon; find its range on a plane inclined at 30° to the horizontal and its time of flight. Find also its greatest range on the inclined plane with the given initial velocity.

4. A particle is projected with a velocity of 39240 cm per second at an angle of 45° with the hoizontal; find its range on a plane inclined to the horizon at an angle $\sin^{-1}\frac{3}{5}$, when projected (i) up, (ii) down, the plane.

5. The velocity of projection of a rifle ball is 196 m per second. Find its greatest range and the corresponding time of flight on planes inclined to the horizon at angles of

(1) 45°, (2) 60°, (3) $\sin^{-1}\frac{3}{5}$, (4) $\sin^{-1}\frac{5}{13}$.

6. The greatest range of a particle, projected with a certain velocity, on a horizontal plane is 4905 metres; find its greatest range on an inclined plane whose inclination is 45°.

Find also the greatest range when the particle is projected down the inclined plane.

7. The greatest range, with a given velocity of projection, on a horizontal plane is 1000 metres; show that the greatest ranges up and down a plane inclined at 30° to the horizon are respectively $666\frac{2}{3}$ and 2000 metres.

8. From a point on a plane inclined at (1) 30°, (2) 60°, to the horizon a particle is projected at right angles to the plane with a velocity of 25 metres per second; find the range on the plane in the two cases.

***113.** *A particle is projected into the air with a given velocity and direction of projection; to show that its path is a parabola.*

As in Art. 101, let u be the velocity and α the angle of projection, PP' the horizontal range, A the highest point and AM the perpendicular on PP'. Then, by Art. 104,

$$AM = \frac{u^2 \sin^2 \alpha}{2g} \qquad \text{...(1)}.$$

Also $\qquad PM$ = horizontal distance described in time $\frac{u \sin \alpha}{g}$

$$= \frac{u^2 \sin \alpha \cos \alpha}{g} \qquad \text{...(2)}.$$

Let Q be any point on the path, and let QN and QL be the perpendiculars on AM and PP' respectively. Let t be the time from P to Q.

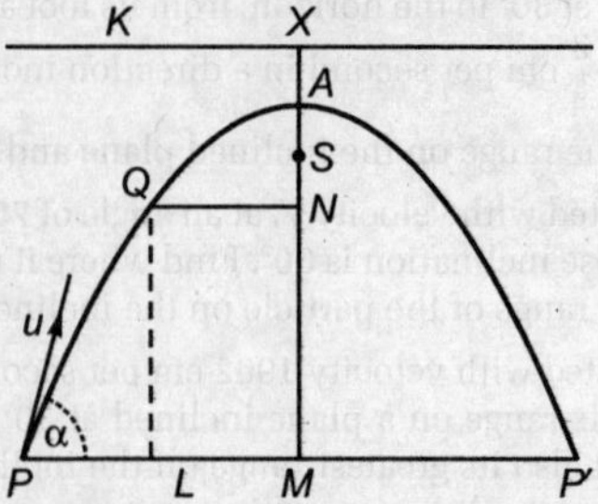

Then QL = vertical distance described in time t

$$= u \sin\alpha \cdot t - \frac{1}{2} g t^2 \quad \text{...(3),}$$

and $\quad PL = u\cos\alpha \cdot t \quad$ ...(4).

Hence from (1) and (3),

$$AN = AM - NM = AM - QL$$

$$= \frac{u^2 \sin^2\alpha}{2g} - \left(u\sin\alpha \cdot t - \frac{1}{2} g t^2\right) = \frac{g}{2}\left(\frac{u \sin\alpha}{g} - t\right)^2.$$

Also, from (2) and (4),

$$QN = PM - PL = \frac{u^2 \sin\alpha\cos\alpha}{g} - u\cos\alpha \cdot t$$

$$= u\cos\alpha \cdot \left(\frac{u\sin\alpha}{g} - t\right)$$

$$\therefore \quad QN^2 = u^2\cos^2\alpha \left(\frac{u\sin\alpha}{g} - t\right)^2 = u^2\cos^2\alpha \cdot \frac{2AN}{g}$$

$$= \frac{2u^2\cos^2\alpha}{g} \cdot AN.$$

Measure AS vertically downwards and equal to $\dfrac{u^2\cos^2\alpha}{2g}$.

$$\therefore \quad QN^2 = 4AS \cdot AN.$$

But this is the fundamental property of the curve known as a parabola.

Hence Q lies on a parabola whose axis is vertical, whose vertex is at A, and whose latus rectum

$$= 4AS = \frac{2u^2\cos^2\alpha}{g}.$$

Cor. I. It will be noted that the latus rectum, and therefore the *size*, of the parabola depends only on the initial horizontal velocity and is independent of the initial vertical velocity.

Cor. II. The height of the focus S above the horizontal line through $P = SM = AM - AS$

$$= \frac{u^2 \sin^2 \alpha}{2g} - \frac{u^2 \cos^2 \alpha}{2g} = -\frac{u^2}{2g} \cos 2\alpha.$$

Hence, if α be less than 45°, this distance is negative and the focus of the path is then situated *below* the horizontal line drawn through the point of projection.

114. *To show that the velocity at any point is equal in magnitude to that which would be acquired by a particle in falling freely through the height from the directrix to the point.*

In the figure of Art. 113, produce MA to X, making AX equal to AS, and draw XK horizontal. Then XK is the directrix.

If v be the velocity at Q, we have, by Art. 102,

$$v^2 = (u \sin \alpha - gt)^2 + (u \cos \alpha)^2$$

$$= u^2 - 2ug \sin \alpha \cdot t + g^2 t^2$$

$$= 2g \left[\frac{u^2}{2g} - \left(u \sin \alpha \cdot t - \frac{1}{2} gt^2 \right) \right].$$

But $\quad MX = MA + AX = \dfrac{u^2 \sin^2 \alpha}{2g} + \dfrac{u^2 \cos^2 \alpha}{2g} = \dfrac{u^2}{2g},$

and $\quad MN = QL = u \sin \alpha \cdot t - \dfrac{1}{2} gt^2.$

$\therefore \quad v^2 = 2g\,[MX - MN] = 2g \cdot NX.$

Hence v is equal to the velocity that would be acquired in falling through the vertical distance from the directrix to the point Q.

115. Experimental Proof *that the path of a projectile is a parabola.*

Let AC be a curved board with a groove in it down which a small ball will run when released. Fix it firmly in front of a vertical blackboard. Mark a point C on the groove, and let the ball always start from the same point C, and after running down the groove to A describe a path freely in the air just in front of the blackboard.

Fix to the board a number of small paper or cardboard hoops, so that the ball just passes through them; the hoops are adjusted by trial. After letting the ball run down the groove two or three times the position of the first hoop is ascertained; and then after similar experiments the positions of the rest on the hoops are found.

The ball must always be started very carefully from the same point C.

Draw a curve, $AP_1P_2P_3$ ... passing through the centres of the hoops. This will be easily done by freehand drawing if a good many hoops are fixed in their proper positions.

Draw vertical lines P_1M_1, P_2M_2, P_3M_3, ... to meet in M_1, M_2, ... the horizontal line through A.

Measure off the distances AM_1, AM_2, ... and P_1M_1, P_2M_2, ...

Then on taking the squares of $AM_1, AM_2, AM_3, \ldots$ and dividing them respectively by $P_1M_1, P_2M_2, \ldots$ we shall find that the results obtained are very approximately the same.

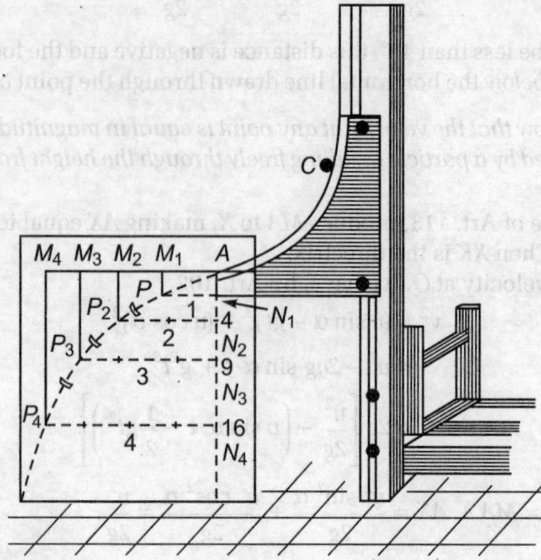

Hence for *any* point P on the curve we find that $\dfrac{AM^2}{PM}$ is the same, i.e., that $\dfrac{PN^2}{AN}$ is the same.

Hence PN^2 varies as AN.

But this is the fundamental property of the parabola.

Hence the curve is a parabola.

If we start the ball from a different point C we shall obtain the same result, but the parabola will vary in shape according to the position of the starting-point C.

By arranging the grooved board so that its direction at A is not horizontal, we can in a similar manner show that the path with any direction and velocity of projection at A is still a parabola.

Examples. XIX.

1. On the moon there seems to be no atmosphere, and gravity there is about one-sixth of that on the earth. What space of country would be commanded by the guns of a lunar fort able to project shot with a velocity 49050 cm per second?
2. A tennis-ball is served from a height of 2.4 m; it just touches the net at a point where it is 1 m high and hits the service-line 6.3 m from the net; the horizontal distance of the server from the foot of the net being 11.7 m, show that the horizontal velocity of the ball is about 51.3 m per second and find the angle of projection.

3. A plane, of length 183 cm, is inclined at an angle of 30° to the horizon, and a particle is projected straight up the plane with a velocity of 4.88 metres per second; find the greatest height attained by the particle after leaving the plane, and the range on a horizontal plane passing through the foot of the inclined plane.
4. If a stone be hurled from a sling which has been swung in a horizontal circle of 70 cm radius, at a height of $122\frac{5}{6}$ cm from the ground, and at the steady rate of 21 revolutions in 2 seconds, find the range on the ground.
5. Two guns are pointed at each other, one upwards at the angle of elevation 30°, and the other downwards at the same angle of depression, the muzzles being 30 m apart. If the charges leave the guns with velocities 330 m and 270 m per second respectively, find when and where they will meet.
6. A projectile, aimed at a mark which is in the horizontal plane through the point of projection, falls a cm short of it when the elevation is α, and goes b cm too far when the elevation is β. Show that, if the velocity of projection be the same in all cases, the proper elevation is
$$\frac{1}{2}\sin^{-1}\frac{a\sin 2\beta + b\sin 2\alpha}{a+b}.$$
7. A hill is inclined at an angle of 30° to the horizon; from a point on the hill one projectile is projected up the hill and another down, both starting with the same velocity; the angle of projection in each case is 45° with the horizon; show that the range of one projectile is nearly $3\frac{3}{4}$ that of the other.
8. A particle is projected from a point on an inclined plane in a direction making an angle of 60° with the horizon; if the range on the plane be equal to the distance through which another particle would fall from rest during the time of flight of the first particle, find the inclination of the plane to the horizon.
9. From a point in a given inclined plane two bodies are projected with the same velocity in the same vertical plane at right angles to one another; show that the difference of their ranges is constant.
10. The angular elevation of an enemy's position on a hill h cm high is β, show that, in order to shell it, the initial velocity of the projectile must not be less than $\sqrt{gh}\,(1 + \operatorname{cosec}\beta)$.
11. Show that the greatest range on an inclined plane passing through the point of projection is equal to the distance through which the particle would fall freely during the corresponding time of flight.
12. A particle, projected with velocity u, strikes at right angles a plane through the point of projection inclined at an angle β to the horizon. Show that the height of the point struck above the horizontal plane through the point of projection is $\frac{2u^2}{g}\frac{\sin^2\beta}{1+3\sin^2\beta}$, that the time of flight is $\frac{2u}{g\sqrt{1+3\sin^2\beta}}$, and that the range on a horizontal plane through the point of projection would be
$$\frac{u^2\sin 2\beta}{g}\cdot\frac{1+\sin^2\beta}{1+3\sin^2\beta}.$$

13. Show that four times the square of the number of seconds in the time of flight in the range on a horizontal plane equals the height in feet of the highest point of the trajectory.

14. If the maximum height of a projectile above a horizontal plane passing through the point of projection be h, and α be the angle of projection, find the interval between the instants at which the height of the projectile is $h \sin^2 \alpha$.

15. Find the direction in which a rifle must be pointed so that the bullet may strike a body let fall from a balloon at the instant of firing; find also the point where the bullet meets the body, supposing the balloon to be 198 m high, the angle of its elevation from the position of the rifleman to be 30°, and the velocity of projection of the bullet to be 396 m per second. [The balloon is at rest.]

16. Two particles are projected simultaneously, one with velocity V up a smooth plane inclined at an angle of 30° to the horizon, and the other with a velocity $\frac{2V}{\sqrt{3}}$ at an elevation of 60°. Show that the particles will be relatively at rest at the end of $\frac{2V}{3g}$ seconds from the instant of projection.

17. The radii of the front and hind wheels of a carriage are a and b, and c is the distance between the axle-trees; a particle of dust driven from the highest point of the hind wheel is observed to alight on the highest point of the front wheel. Show that the velocity of the carriage is

$$\sqrt{\frac{(c+b-a)(c+a-b)}{4(b-a)}g}.$$

18. Find the charge of powder required to send a 30.84 kg shot, with an elevation of 15°, to a range of 2740 metres, given that the velocity communicated to the same shot by a charge of 4.53 kg is 487.5 metres per second, and assuming that the kinetic energy of the shot is proportional to the magnitude of the charge.

19. A body, of mass 1 kg, is projected with a velocity of 6 m per second at an angle of 60° to the horizon; another body, of mass 5 kg, is at the same time projected from the same point with a velocity of 12 m per second at an angle of 30° to the horizon. Find to two places of decimals the height to which their common centre of gravity rises, and the distance of the point at which it meets the horizontal plane through the point of projection.

20. A train is travelling at the rate of 72.4 km per hour, and a passenger throws up a ball vertically with an initial velocity of 366 cm per second; find the latus rectum of the path which it describes. If the ball be projected with the same velocity at 60° to the horizontal (1) in the same direction, (2) in the opposite direction, with the motion of the train, find the latus rectum in each case.

21. In a trajectory find the time that elapses before the particle is at the end of the latus rectum.

22. A particle is projected so as to enter in the direction of its length a small straight tube of small bore fixed at an angle of 45° to the horizon and to pass out at the other end of the tube; show that the latera recta of the paths which the particle describes before entering and leaving the tube differ by $\sqrt{2}$ times the length of the tube.

23. A particle is projected horizontally from the top of a tower, 1962 cm high, and the focus of the parabola which it describes is in the horizontal plane through the foot of the tower; find the velocity of projection.

24. A particle is projected with velocity $2\sqrt{ag}$ so that it just clears two walls, of equal height a, which are at a distance $2a$ from each other. Show that the latus rectum of the path is $2a$, and that the time of passing between the walls is $2\sqrt{\frac{a}{g}}$.

25. Show that the locus of the foci of all trajectories which pass through two given points is a hyperbola.

26. If t be the time in which a projectile reaches a point P of its path, and t' be the time from P till it strikes the horizontal plane through the point of projection, show that the height of P above the plane is $\frac{1}{2}gtt'$.

27. If at any point of a parabolic path the velocity be u and the inclination to the horizon be θ, show that the particle is moving at right angles to its former direction after a time $\frac{u}{g \sin \theta}$.

8

Collision of Elastic Bodies

116. If a man allows a glass ball to drop from his hand upon a marble floor it rebounds to a considerable height, almost as high as his hand; if the same ball be allowed to fall upon a wooden floor, it rebounds through a much smaller distance.

If we allow an ivory billiard ball and a glass ball to drop from the same height, the distances through which they rebound will be different.

If again we drop a leaden ball upon the same floors, the distances through which it rebounds are much smaller than in either of the former cases.

Now the velocities of these bodies are the same on first touching the floor; but since they rebound through different heights, their velocities on leaving the floor must be different.

The property of the bodies which causes these differences in their velocities after leaving the floor is called their **Elasticity.**

In the present chapter we shall consider some simple cases of the impact of elastic bodies. We can only discuss the cases of particles in collision with particles or planes, and of smooth homogeneous spheres in collision with smooth planes or smooth spheres.

117. Def. Two bodies are said to *impinge directly* when the direction of motion of each is along the common normal at the point at which they touch.

They are said to *impinge obliquely* when the direction of motion of either, or both, is not along the common normal at the point of contact.

The direction of this common normal is called the *line of impact.*

In the case of two spheres the common normal is the line joining their centres.

118. Newton's Experimental Law. Newton found, by experiment, that, if two bodies impinge directly, their relative velocity after impact is in a constant ratio to their relative velocity before impact, and is in the opposite direction. [The experiment is described in Art. 151.]

If the bodies impinge obliquely, their relative velocity resolved along their common normal after impact is in a constant ratio to their relative velocity before impact resolved in the same direction, and is of opposite sign.

This constant ratio depends on the substances of which the bodies are made, and is independent of the masses of the bodies. It is generally denoted by e and is called the Modulus or Coefficient of Elasticity, Restitution, or Resilience. Either of the two latter terms is better than the first.

If u and u' be the component velocities of two bodies before impact along their common normal (as in the figure of Art. 122), and v and v' the component velocities of the bodies *in the same direction* after impact, the law states that

$$v - v' = -e(u - u') \qquad \text{...(1).}$$

This experimental law may also be expressed in the form.

Velocity of Separation $= e$ times the Velocity of Approach, these two velocities being measured in the direction of the common normal at the point of impact.

Thus in the case of Art. 122 the left-hand sphere caught up the right-hand sphere and the velocity of approaches was $u - u'$; also after the impact the right-hand sphere must move away from the other, and the velocity of separation is $v' - v$; this second form of enunciation of the law therefore gives

$$v' - v = e(u - u'),$$

which is the same as (1).

The value of e has widely different values for different bodies; for two glass balls e is .94; for two ivory ones it is .81; for two of cork it is .65; for two of cast-iron about .66; whilst for two balls of lead it is about .20, and for two balls, one of lead and the other of iron, the value is .13.

Bodies for which the coefficient of restitution is zero are said to be "inelastic", whilst "perfectly elastic" bodies are those for which the coefficient is unity. Probably there are no bodies in nature coming strictly under either of these headings; approximate examples of the former class are such bodies as putty or dough, whilst probably the nearest approach to the latter class is in the case of glass balls.

More careful experiments have shown that the ratio of the relative velocities before and after impact is not absolutely constant, but that it decreases very slightly for very large velocities of approach of the bodies. In any case, however, the law is only an approximate one, and cannot be taken as rigorously true.

119. *Motion of two smooth bodies perpendicular to the line of impact.*

When two smooth bodies impinge, there is no tangential action between them, so that the stress between them is entirely along their common normal, i.e., the line which is perpendicular to both surfaces at their point of contact. Hence there is no force perpendicular to this common normal, and therefore no change of velocity in that direction.

Hence the component velocity of each body in a direction perpendicular to the common normal is unaltered by the impact.

120. *Motion of two bodies along the line of impact.*

From Art. 86 it follows that, when two bodies impinge, the sum of their momenta along the line of impact is the same after impact as before.

The two principles enunciated in this and the previous articles, together with Newton's experimental law, are sufficient to find the change in the motion of particles and smooth spheres produced by a collision.

We shall now proceed to the discussion of particular cases.

121. Impact on a fixed plane. *A smooth sphere, or particle, whose mass is m and whose coefficient of restitution is e, impinges obliquely on a fixed plane; find the change in its motion.*

Let AB be the fixed plane, C the point at which the sphere impinges, and CN the normal to the plane at C so that CN passes through the centre, O, of the sphere.

Let DO and OE be the direction of motion of the centre of the sphere before and after impact, and let the angles NOD and NOE be α and θ. Let u and v be the velocities of the sphere before and after impact as indicated in the figure.

Since the plane is smooth, there is no force parallel to the plane; hence the velocity of the sphere resolved in a direction parallel to the plane is unaltered.

$$\therefore \quad v \sin\theta = u \sin\alpha \qquad \text{...(1).}$$

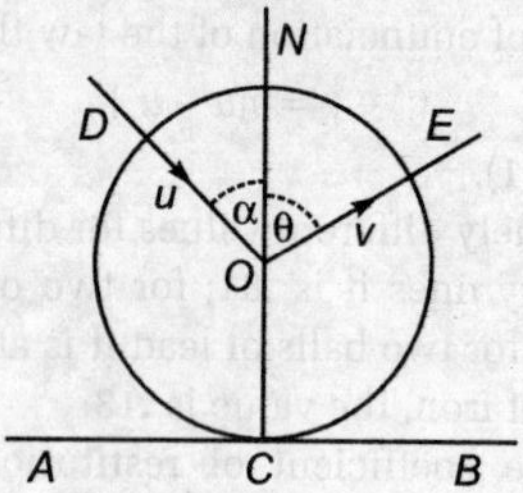

By Newton's experimental law, the normal velocity of separation is e times the normal velocity of approach.

$$\text{Hence} \quad v\cos\theta - 0 = e\,(u\cos\alpha - 0)$$

$$\therefore \quad v\cos\theta = eu\cos\alpha \qquad \text{...(2).}$$

From (1) and (2), by squaring and adding, we have

$$v = u\sqrt{\sin^2\alpha + e^2\cos^2\alpha},$$

and, by division, $\cot\theta = e\cot\alpha$.

These two equations give the velocity and direction of motion after impact.

The impulse of the force of impact on the plane is equal and opposite to the impulse of the force of impact on the sphere, and is therefore measured by the change of the momentum of the sphere perpendicular to the plane.

Hence the impulse of the blow $= mu\cos\alpha + mv\cos\theta$

$$= m(1+e)u\cos\alpha.$$

Cor. 1. If the impact be direct, we have $\alpha = 0$.

$$\therefore \quad \theta = 0, \text{ and } v = eu$$

Hence, *The direction of motion of a sphere, which impinges directly on a smooth plane, is reversed and its velocity reduced in the ratio* $1 : e$.

Cor 2. If the coefficient of restitution be unity, we have $\theta = \alpha$, and $v = u$.

Hence *when the plane is perfectly elastic the angle of reflexion is equal to that of incidence, and the velocity is unaltered in magnitude.*

Cor 3. If the coefficient of restitution be zero, we have

$$\theta = 90°, \text{ and } v = u\sin\alpha.$$

Hence *A sphere after impact with an inelastic plane slides along the plane with its velocity parallel to the plane unaltered.*

Ex. *A ball, moving with a velocity of* 10 *metres per second impinges on a smooth fixed plane at an angle of* 45°; *if the coefficient of restitution be* $\frac{4}{5}$, *find the velocity and direction of motion of the ball after the impact.*

Let its velocity after the impact be v at an angle θ with the fixed plane.

Its component velocities along and perpendicular to the plane, before impact, are each $10 \times \frac{1}{\sqrt{2}}$, i.e., $5\sqrt{2}$. After impact its component velocities in the same two directions are $v \cos\theta$ and $v \sin\theta$.

Hence we have $$v \cos\theta = 5\sqrt{2}$$

$$v \sin\theta = e \cdot 5\sqrt{2} = 4\sqrt{2}$$

Therefore, by squaring and adding,

$$v^2 = 82, \text{ so that } v = \sqrt{82} = 9.06$$

Also, by division, $\tan\theta = \frac{4}{5}$, so that, by the table of natural tangents, $\theta = 38°40'$ nearly. Hence, after the impact, the ball moves with a velocity of 9.06 metres per sec. at an angle of 38°40′ with the plane.

Examples. XX.

1. A glass marble drops from a height of 300 cm upon a horizontal floor; if the coefficient of restitution be .9, find the height to which it rises after the impact.
2. An ivory ball is dropped from a height of 500 cm upon a horizontal slab; if it rebounds to a height of 320 cm, show that the coefficient of restitution between the slab and the ball is .8.
3. A heavy elastic ball drops from the ceiling of a room and after rebounding twice from the floor reaches a height equal to one-half that of the ceiling; show that the coefficient of restitution is $\sqrt{\frac{1}{2}}$.
4. From a point in one wall of a room a ball is projected along the smooth floor to hit the opposite wall and returns to the point from which it started; if the coefficient of restitution be $\frac{1}{2}$, show that the ball takes twice as long in returning as it took in going.
5. From a point in the floor of a room a ball is projected vertically with velocity $981\sqrt{3}$ cm per second; if the height of the room be $490\frac{1}{2}$ cm, and the coefficients of restitution between the ball and the ceiling and the ball and the floor be each $\frac{1}{\sqrt{2}}$, show that the ball, after rebounding from the ceiling and the floor, will again just reach the height of the ceiling.

6. A ball moving with a velocity of 8 metres per sec. impinges at an angle of 80° on a smooth plane, find its velocity and direction of motion after the impact, the coefficient of restitution being $\frac{1}{2}$.

7. A sphere moving with a velocity of 5 metres per sec. hits against a smooth plane, its direction of motion being inclined at an angle $\sin^{-1}\frac{3}{5} = (36°52')$ to the plane; show that after impact its velocity is $2\sqrt{5}$ (= 4.47) metres per sec. at an angle $\tan^{-1}\frac{1}{2}$ (= 26°34′) with the plane, if the coefficient of restitution be $\frac{2}{3}$.

8. A ball falls from a height of 110 mt upon a plane inclined at (1) 30°, (2) 45° and (3) 60°, to the horizon; find the velocity and direction of motion after the impact in the three cases, the coefficient of restitution being $\frac{3}{4}$.

122. Direct impact of two spheres. *A smooth sphere, of mass m, impinges directly with velocity u on another smooth sphere, of mass m′, moving in the same direction with veloity u′. If the coefficient of restitution be e, find their velocities after the impact.*

Let v and v' be the velocities of the two spheres after impact.

The velocity of approach is $u - u'$, and the velocity of separation is $v' - v$, so that by Newton's experimental law we have

$$v' - v = e(u - u') \qquad \text{...(1).}$$

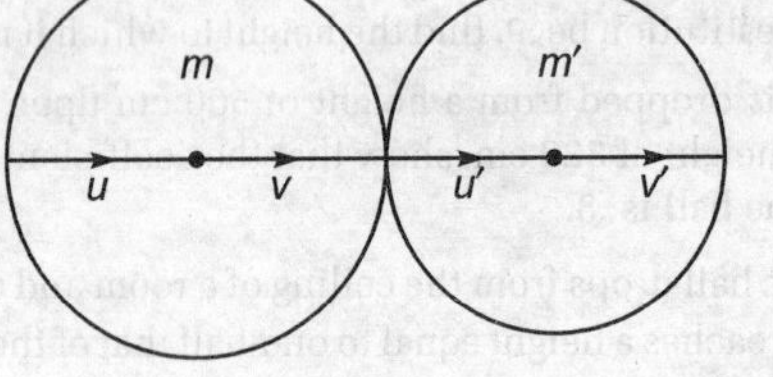

Again, the only force acting on the bodies during the impact is the blow along the line of centres. Hence, by Art. 120, the total momentum in that direction is unaltered.

$$\therefore \qquad mv + m'v' = mu + m'u' \qquad \text{...(2).}$$

Multiplying (1) by m', and subtracting from (2), we have

$$(m + m')v = (m - em')u + m'(1 + e)u'$$

Again multiplying (1) by m, and adding to (2), we have

$$(m + m')v' = m(1 + e)u + (m' - em)u'$$

These two equations give the velocities after impact.

If the second sphere be moving in a direction opposite to that of the first, we must change the sign of u'.

Also the impulse of the blow on the ball m

$$= \text{the change produced in its momentum}$$

$$= m(u - v) = \frac{mm'}{m + m'}(1 + e)(u - u')$$

The impulse of the blow on the other ball is equal and opposite to this.

Cor. If we put $m = m'$ and $e = 1$, we have

$$v = u', \text{ and } v' = u$$

Hence, *If two equal perfectly elastic balls impinge directly they interchange their velocities.*

123. Ex. 1. *A ball of mass 8 kg and moving with velocity 4 metres per second, overtakes a ball, of mass 10 kg moving with velocity 2 metres per second in the same direction; if e be* $\frac{1}{2}$, *find the velocities of the balls after impact.*

Let v and v' be the required velocities.

Since the total momentum is unaltered,

$$\therefore \quad 8v + 10v' = 8 \times 4 + 10 \times 2 = 52$$

By Newton's Law,

$$v' - v = \frac{1}{2}(4 - 2) = 1$$

Hence, by solving, $v = 2\frac{1}{3}$, and $v' = 3\frac{1}{3}$, metres per second.

Ex. 2. *If in the previous question, the second ball be moving in a direction opposite to the first, find the velocities.*

Here the equations are

$$8v + 10v' = 8 \times 4 - 10 \times 2 = 12,$$

and $$v' - v = \frac{1}{2}(4 + 2) = 3,$$

since $v' - v$ is the velocity of separation and $4 + 2$ is the velocity of approach.

Hence, on solving, $v = -1$ and $v' = 2$ metres per second, so that each ball turns back after the impact, since the velocities are reckoned positively in the direction in which the first was going before impact.

124. Oblique impact of two spheres. *A smooth sphere, of mass m, impinges with a velocity u obliquely on a smooth sphere, of mass m′, moving with velocity u′. If the directions of motion before impact make angles α and β respectively with the line joining the centres of the spheres, and if the coefficient of restitution be e, find the velocities and directions of motion after impact.*

Let the velocities of the spheres after impact be v and v' in directions inclined at angle θ and ϕ respectively to the line of centres.

Since the spheres are smooth, there is no force perpendicular to the line joining the centres of the two balls, and therefore the velocities in that direction are unaltered.

Hence $$v \sin \theta = u \sin \alpha \qquad ...(1),$$

and $$v' \sin \phi = u' \sin B \qquad ...(2).$$

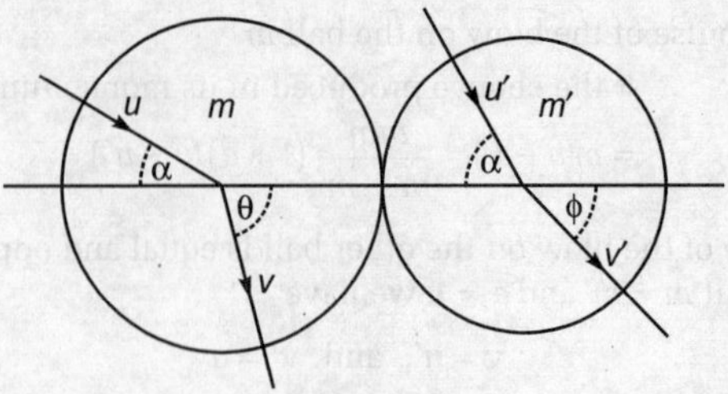

Since $u \cos \alpha - u' \cos \beta$ is the normal velocity of approach, and $v' \cos \phi - v \cos \theta$ is the normal velocity of separation, we have, by Newton's law

$$v' \cos \phi - v \cos \theta = e(u \cos \alpha - u' \cos \beta) \quad ...(3).$$

Again, the only force acting on the spheres during the impact is the blow along the line of centres. Hence (Art. 120) the total momentum in that direction is unaltered.

$$\therefore \quad mv \cos \theta + m'v' \cos \phi = mu \cos \alpha + m'u' \cos \beta \quad ...(4).$$

The equations (1), (2), (3) and (4) determine the unknown quantities v, v', θ and ϕ.

Multiply (3) by m', subtract from (4), and we obtain

$$v \cos \theta = \frac{(m - em')u \cos \alpha + m'(1 + e)u' \cos \beta}{m + m'} \quad ...(5).$$

So multiplying (3) by m, and adding to (4), we get

$$v' \cos \phi = \frac{m(1 + e)u \cos \alpha + (m' - em)u' \cos \beta}{m + m'} \quad ...(6).$$

From (1) and (5) by squaring an adding we obtain v^2, and by division we have $\tan \theta$.

Similary from (2) and (6) we obtain v'^2 and $\tan \phi$.

Hence the motion is completely determined.

The impulse of the blow on the first ball

$$= \text{the change produced in its momentum}$$

$$= m(u \cos \alpha - v \cos \theta)$$

$$= \frac{mm'}{m + m}(1 + e)(u \cos \alpha - u' \cos \beta) \text{ on reduction.}$$

The impulse of the blow on the other ball is equal and opposite to this.

Cor 1. If $u' = 0$, we have from equation (2) $\phi = 0$, and hence the sphere m' moves along the lines of centres. This follows independently, since the only force on m' is along the line of centres.

Cor 2. If $m = m'$, and $e = 1$, we have

$$v \cos \theta = u' \cos \beta, \text{ and } v' \cos \phi = u \cos \alpha$$

Hence, *If two equal perfectly elastic spheres impinge they interchange their velocities in the direction of the line of centres.*

125. Ex. 1. *A ball, of mass* 5 *kg and moving with velocity* 15 *metres per sec., impinges on a ball, of mass* 10 *kg and moving with velocity* 5 *metres per sec.; if their* velocities before impact be parallel and inclined at an angle of 30° to the line joining their centres at the instant of impact, find the resulting motion, the coefficient of restitution being $\frac{1}{2}$.

Let the velocities after impact be v and v' at angles θ and ϕ to the line joining the centres.

Since the velocities perpendicular to the line of centres are unaltered, we have

$$v \sin\theta = 15 \sin 30° = \frac{15}{2} \quad ...(1),$$

and

$$v' \sin\phi = 5 \sin 30° = \frac{5}{2} \quad ...(2).$$

By Newton's Law,

$$v' \cos\phi - v\cos\theta = \frac{1}{2}[15\cos 30° - 5\cos 30°] = 5\frac{\sqrt{3}}{2} \quad ...(3).$$

Since the momentum along the line of impact is unaltered,

$$\therefore \quad 5v\cos\theta + 10v'\cos\phi = 5.15\frac{\sqrt{3}}{2} + 10.5\frac{\sqrt{3}}{2}$$

$$\therefore \quad v\cos\theta + 2v'\cos\phi = 25\frac{\sqrt{3}}{2} \quad ...(4).$$

Solving (3) and (4), we have

$$v\cos\theta = 5\frac{\sqrt{3}}{2} \quad ...(5),$$

and

$$v'\cos\phi = 5\sqrt{3} \quad ...(6).$$

From (1) and (5), we have $v = 5\sqrt{3} = 8.66$ metres per sec. nearly, and $\theta = 60°$.

From (2) and (6), we have $v' = \frac{5}{2}\sqrt{13} = 9$ metres per sec. nearly, and $\tan\phi = \frac{1}{2\sqrt{3}} = \frac{\sqrt{3}}{6}$, so that, by the table of natural tangents, $\phi = 16°6'$.

Ex. 2. *Two smooth balls, one of mass double that of the other, are moving with equal velocities in opposite parallel directions and impinge, their directions of motion at the instant of impact making angles of* 30° *with the line of centres. If the coefficient of restitution be* $\frac{1}{2}$, *find the velocities and directions of motion after the impact.*

Let the masses of the balls be $2m$ and m and let the velocities after impact be v and v' respectively at angles θ and ϕ to the line of centres.

Since the velocities perpendicular to the line of centres are unaltered,

$$\therefore \quad v\sin\theta = u\sin 30° = \frac{u}{2} \quad ...(1),$$

and

$$v'\sin\phi = u\sin 30° = \frac{u}{2} \quad ...(2).$$

The normal velocity of approach is $u\cos 30° + u\cos 30°$, and the normal velocity of separation is $v'\cos\phi - v\cos\theta$, so that by newton's Law, we have

$$v'\cos\phi - v\cos\theta = e\,[u\cos 30° + u\cos 30°] = u\frac{\sqrt{3}}{2} \quad ...(3).$$

Since the momentum resolved parallel to the line of centres remains unaltered,

$\therefore$ $$2mv \cos\theta + mv' \cos\phi = 2mu \cos 30° - mu \cos 30°,$$

$\therefore$ $$2v \cos\theta + v' \cos\phi = u\frac{\sqrt{3}}{2} \quad ...(4),$$

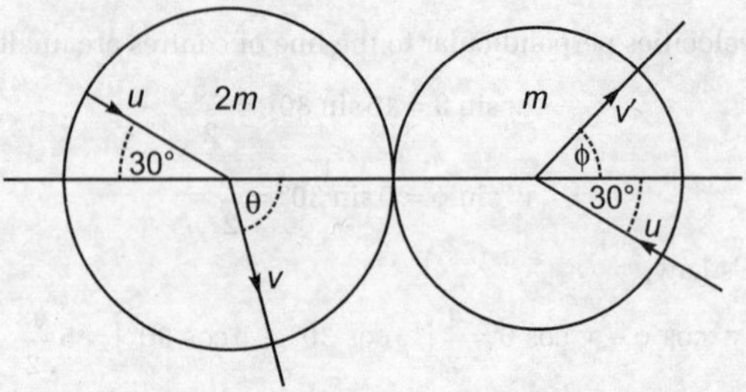

Solving (3) and (4), we have $v \cos\theta = 0$ and $v' \cos\phi = u\frac{\sqrt{3}}{2}$.

From these equations and (1) and (2), we obtain

$$\theta = 90°,\ v = \frac{u}{2};\ \phi = 30°,\ v' = u.$$

Hence after impact the larger ball starts off in a direction perpendicular to the line of centres with half its former velocity, and the smaller ball moves as if it were a perfectly elastic ball impinging on a fixed plane.

Examples. XXI.

1. A sphere, of mass 4 kg and moving with velocity 5 metres per sec., overtakes a sphere of mass 3 kg and moving with velocity 4 metres per sec.; if the impact he direct and the coefficient of restitution be $\frac{1}{2}$, find the velocities of the spheres after impact.
2. A ball, of mass 10 kg and moving with velocity 6 metres per sec., overtakes a sphere of mass 8 kg and moving with velocity 3 metres per sec.; if the impact be direct and the coefficient of restitution be $\frac{3}{4}$, find the velocities of the spheres after impact.
3. A sphere, moving with velocity 12 metres per sec., meets an equal sphere moving in the same line with a velocity of 6 metres per sec. in the opposite direction; if the coefficient of restitution be $\frac{1}{2}$, find their velocities after two impact.
4. If a ball overtakes a ball of twice its own mass moving with one-seventh of its velocity; and if the coefficient of restitution between them be $\frac{3}{4}$, show that the first ball will, after striking and second ball, remain at rest.

5. If the masses of two balls be as 2 : 1, and their respective velocities before impact be as 1 : 2 and in opposite directions, and e be $\frac{5}{6}$, show that each ball will after direct impact move back with $\frac{5}{6}$ths of its original velocity.

6. A sphere impinges directly on an equal sphere at rest; if the coefficient of restitution be e, show that their velocities after the impact are as $1 - e : 1 + e$.

7. A ball, of mass m and moving with velocity u, impinges on a ball, of mass em and moving with velocity eu in the opposite direction; if the impact be direct and e be the coefficient of restitution, show that the velocity of the second ball after impact is the same as that of the first ball before impact.

8. A ball, of mass 2 kg, impinges directly on a ball, of mass 1 kg, which is at rest; find the coefficient of restitution if the velocity with which the larger ball impinges be equal to the velocity of the smaller ball after impact.

9. A ball of mass m impinges directly upon a ball of mass m_1 at rest; the velocity of m after impact is $\frac{3}{5}$ths of its velocity before impact and the coefficient of restitution is $\frac{3}{5}$; compare (i) the masses of the two balls, and (ii) the velocities of m and m_1 after impact.

10. Three spheres, whose masses are 2 kg, 6 kg and 12 kg respectively, and whose velocities are 12, 4 and 2 metres per second respectively, are moving in a straight line in the above order. If the coefficient of restitution be unity, show that the first two spheres will be brought to rest by the collisions which will take place.

11. A ball is let fall from a height of 19.5 metres, and at the same instant an equal ball is projected from the ground with a velocity of 20 metres per second to meet it in direct impact : if the coefficient of restitution be $\frac{1}{2}$, find the times that elapse after the impact before the balls reach the ground.

12. An inelalstic sphere impinges obliquely on a second sphere at rest, whose mass is twice its own, in a direction making an angle of 30° with the line joining the centres of the spheres; show that its direction of motion is turned through an angle of 30°.

13. Two equal balls moving with equal speeds impinge, their directions being inclined at 30° and 60°, to the line joining their centres at the instant of impact; if the coefficient of restitution be unity, show that after impact they are moving in parallel directions inclined at 45° to the line of centres.

14. Two equal balls, moving with equal velocities, impinge; if their directions of motion before impact make angles of 30° and 90° respectively with the line joining the centres at the instant of impact, and if the coefficient of restitution be $\frac{1}{3}$, show that after impact the balls are moving in parallel directions, and that the velocity of one is double that of the other.

15. Two equal perfectly elastic balls impinge; if their directions of motion before impact be at right angles, show that their directions of motion after impact are at right angles also.

16. A sphere, moving with velocity $u\sqrt{3}$, impinges on an equal sphere, moving with velocity u, their directions of motion before impact making angles of 30° and 60° with the line of centres; show that, if the coefficient of restitution be unity, their directions of motion after impact make angles of 60° and 30° respectively with the line of centres.

17. A sphere, of mass $5m$ and moving with velocity $13\,u$, impinges on a sphere, of mass m and moving with velocity $5\,u$, their directions of motion being inclined at angles of $\sin^{-1}\frac{5}{13}$ and $\sin^{-1}\frac{3}{5}$ respectively to the line of centres; if the coefficient of restitution be $\frac{1}{2}$, find their velocities and directions of motion after the impact.

126. Action between two elastic bodies during their collision. When two elastic bodies impinge, the time during which the impact lasts may be divided into two parts, during the first of which the bodies are compressing one another, and during the second of which they are recovering their shape.

That the bodies are compressed may be shown experimentally by dropping a billiard ball upon a floor which has been covered with fine coloured powder. At the spot where the ball hits the floor, the powder will be found to be removed not from a geometric point only, but from a small circle; this shows that at some instant during the compression the part of the ball in contact with the floor was a circle; it follows that the ball was then deformed and afterwards recovered its shape.

It is also found that the small circle is increased in size if the distance through which the ball is dropped be increased, in which case the velocity of the ball on hitting the floor is increased. Hence the greater the velocity at impact, the greater is the temporary deformation of the billiard ball.

The first portion of the impact lasts until the bodies are instantaneously moving with the same velocity; forces then come into play tending to make the bodies recover their shape. The mutual action between the bodies during the first portion of the impact is often called "the force of compression," and that during the second portion "the force of restitution."

We have no means of finding out what is the actual magnitude of the force between two bodies during an impact; we only know that it must vary very considerably, being zero at the commencement of the impact and zero at the end, and that it must be large at some instant during which the impact lasts. But, by Newton's Third Law, the force at *each instant* must be the same in magnitude for each body, but opposite in direction; hence; the impulses of the forces acting on the two bodies must be equal, but in opposite directions.

127. It is easy to show that the ratio of the impulses of the forces of restitution and compression is equal to the quantity e, which we have defined as the coefficient of restitution.

Consider the case of one sphere impinging directly on another, as in Art. 122, and use the same notation.

U be the common velocity of the bodies at the instant when the compression is finished. Then

$m(u - U)$ is the loss of momentum by the first ball,

and $m'(U-u')$ is the gain by second ball.

Hence, if I be the impulse of the force of compression, we have

$$I = m(u-U) = m'(U-u'),$$

$$\therefore \qquad \frac{I}{m} + \frac{I}{m'} = u - U + U - u' = u - u' \qquad ...(1).$$

Again, the loss of momentum by the first ball during the period of restitution is $m(U-v)$, and the gain by the second ball is $m'(v'-U)$.

Hence, if I' be the impulse of the force of restitution,

$$I' = m(U-v) = m'(v'-U),$$

$$\therefore \qquad \frac{I'}{m} + \frac{I'}{m'} = U - v + v' - U = v' - v \qquad ...(2).$$

Hence, from (1) and (2), $\dfrac{I'}{I} = \dfrac{v'-v}{u-u'}$,

i.e., $\dfrac{\text{Impulse of the force of restitution}}{\text{Impulse of the force of compression}}$

$$= \frac{\text{Normal velocity of separation}}{\text{Normal velocity of approach}} = e.$$

$$\therefore \qquad I' = eI.$$

128. Loss of Kinetic Energy by Impact. *Two spheres of given masses moving with given velocities impinge; to show that there is a loss of kinetic energy and to find the amount.*

I. Let the collision be direct and the notation as in Art. 122.

Then we have

$$mv + m'v' = mu + m'u \qquad ...(1),$$

$$v' - v = e(u-u') \qquad ...(2).$$

To the square of (1) add the square of (2) multiplied by mm'; we then have

$$(m^2 + mm')v^2 + (m'^2 + mm')v'^2 = (mu + m'u')^2 + e^2 mm'(u-u')^2,$$

i.e., $(m+m')(mv^2 + m'v'^2)$

$$= (mu + m'u')^2 + mm'(u-u')^2 - (1-e^2)mm'(u-u')^2$$

$$= (m+m')(mu^2 + m'u'^2) - (1-e^2)mm'(u-u')^2.$$

$$\therefore \quad \frac{1}{2}mv^2 + \frac{1}{2}m'v'^2 = \frac{1}{2}mu^2 + \frac{1}{2}m'u'^2 - \frac{1-e^2}{2}\frac{mm'}{m+m'}(u-u')^2.$$

Hence the kinetic energy after impact

$$= \text{kinetic energy before impact} - \frac{1-e^2}{2}\frac{mm'}{m+m'}(u-u')^2:$$

Hence the loss of kinetic energy is

$$\frac{1-e^2}{2}\frac{mm'}{m+m'}(u-u')^2,$$

and this loss does not vanish unless $e = 1$, that is, unless the balls are perfectly elastic.

II. Let the collision be oblique and the notation as in Art. 124.

As in I., we have

$$\frac{1}{2}mv^2\cos^2\theta + \frac{1}{2}m'v'^2\cos^2\phi = \frac{1}{2}mu^2\cos^2\alpha + \frac{1}{2}m'u'^2\cos^2\beta$$

$$-\frac{1-e^2}{2}\frac{mm'}{m+m'}(u\cos\alpha - u'\cos\beta)^2 \qquad ...(3).$$

Also, since $v\sin\theta = u\sin\alpha$, and $v'\sin\phi = u'\sin\beta$, we have

$$\frac{1}{2}mv^2\sin^2\theta + \frac{1}{2}m'v'^2\sin^2\phi = \frac{1}{2}mu^2\sin^2\alpha$$

$$+\frac{1}{2}m'u'^2\sin^2\beta \qquad ...(4).$$

Adding (3) and (4), we have

The kinetic energy after impact = kinetic energy before impact $-\dfrac{1-e^2}{2}\dfrac{mm'}{m+m'}(u\cos\alpha - u'\cos\beta)^2$.

Hence we see that in any impact, unless the coefficient of restitution be unity, some kinetic energy is lost, or, rather, is transformed.

This missing kinetic energy is converted into molecular energy and chiefly reappears in the shape of heat.

Cor. Suppose, as in the case of a nail hit by a hammer, that the object struck was at rest.

In this case $u' = 0$ and $e = 0$. Hence, by the result of I., the energy lost, or transformed,

$$= \frac{1}{2}\frac{mm'(1-e^2)}{m+m'}u^2.$$

$$\therefore \frac{\text{Mechanical energy lost by the blow}}{\text{Mechanical energy before the blow}}$$

$$= \frac{1}{2}\frac{mm'(1-e^2)}{m+m'}u^2 \div \frac{1}{2}mu^3 = \frac{m'}{m+m'}(1-e^2).$$

This latter expression is made smaller if the ratio of m to m' be made bigger, *i.e.*, the bigger the mass of the hammer compared with that of the nail, the smaller is the loss of mechanical energy at the impact.

129. Ex. 1. *A particle falls from a height h upon a fixed horizontal plane; if a be the coefficient of restitution, show that the whole distance described by the particle before it has finished rebounding is* $\dfrac{1+e^2}{1-e^2}h$, *and that the time that elapses is* $\sqrt{\dfrac{2h}{g}}\,\dfrac{1+e}{1-e}$.

Let u be the velocity of the particle when it first hits the plane, so that $u^2 = 2gh$.

By Art. 121, Cor. 1, the particle rebounds with velocity eu.

The velocity when it again hits the plane is eu, and the velocity after the second rebound is e^2u.

Similarly the velocity after the third, fourth ... rebounds is $e^2u, e^4u, \ldots$

The height to which the particle ascends after the first, second, ... rebounds are

$$\frac{e^2u^2}{2g}, \frac{(e^4u)^2}{2g}, \frac{(e^6u)^2}{2g}, \ldots, \text{ i.e., } e^2h, e^4h, e^6h, \ldots$$

Hence the whole space described

$$= h + 2(e^2h + e^4h + e^6h + \ldots \; ad. \, inf.)$$

$$= h + 2h\frac{e^2}{1-e^2},$$

by summing the infinite geometric progression,

$$= h\frac{1+e^2}{1-e^2}.$$

Also the time of falling originally $= \sqrt{\dfrac{2h}{g}}$.

The times of ascending after the impacts are the times in which the velocities $eu, e^2u, e^3u, \ldots$ are destroyed by gravity.

Hence these times are $\dfrac{eu}{g}, \dfrac{e^2u}{g}, \dfrac{e^3u}{g}, \ldots$, i.e., $e\sqrt{\dfrac{2h}{g}}, e^2\sqrt{\dfrac{2h}{g}}, \ldots$

Hence the whole time during which the particle is in motion

$$= \sqrt{\frac{2h}{g}} + 2\cdot\sqrt{\frac{2h}{g}}\,[e + e^2 + e^3 + \ldots \; ad \; inf.]$$

$$= \sqrt{\frac{2h}{g}}\left[1 + 2\frac{e}{1-e}\right] = \sqrt{\frac{2h}{g}}\,\frac{1+e}{1-e}.$$

In theory therefore we have an infinite number of rebounds taking place in a finite time; in practice after a few rebounds the velocity of the ball becomes destroyed.

Since the height to which the particle rebounds after the first impact is e^2h, i.e., e^2 times the height from which it fell,

$$\therefore \qquad e^2 = \frac{\text{height of rebound}}{\text{height of falling}}.$$

Hence the value of e for a given ball and a given floor may be easily found by experiment. For, if the ball be let fall from a given suitable height, it will be easy to find the height of rebound after a few trials, and then we easily have e^2.

Ex. 2. *From a point in a smooth horizontal plane a particle is projected with velocity u at an angle α to the horizon; if the coefficient of restitution between the particle and the plane be e, show that the distance described along the plane before the particle ceases to rebound is* $\dfrac{u^2}{g}\dfrac{\sin 2\alpha}{1-e}$.

The initial vertical velocity is $u \sin \alpha$.

The initial vertical velocities after the first, second, ... rebounds are, as in the last example, $eu \sin \alpha, e^2u \sin \alpha, e^3u \sin \alpha \ldots$

Hence the time between the first and second rebounds is, as in Art. 105, $2\dfrac{eu \sin \alpha}{g}$.

So the times in the other trajectories are $2\dfrac{e^2u\sin\alpha}{g}, 2\dfrac{e^3u\sin\alpha}{g}\ldots$

Hence the total time that elapses before the particle ceases to rebound

$$= \frac{2u\sin\alpha}{g} + \frac{2\,eu\sin\alpha}{g} + \frac{2e^2u\sin\alpha}{g}\ldots ad\ inf.$$

$$= \frac{2u\sin\alpha}{g}[1 + e + e^2 + \ldots] = \frac{2u\sin\alpha}{g}\frac{1}{1-e}.$$

During this time the horizontal velocity, being unaltered by the impacts, is always $u\cos\alpha$.

Hence, the horizontal distance described

$$= \frac{2u\sin\alpha}{g}\frac{1}{1-e} \times u\cos\alpha = \frac{u^2\sin 2\alpha}{g(1-e)}$$

After the particle has ceased to rebound, it moves along the plane with constant velocity $u\cos\alpha$.

Examples. XXII.

1. An elastic particle is projected so that it hits a vertical wall and returns after impact to the point from which it was projected without hitting the ground. If the angle of projection be α, and the direction of the path of the particle when it again reaches the point of projection make an angle β with the horizontal, show that $\tan\alpha = e\tan\beta$, where e is the coefficient of restitution.

2. Show that an elastic sphere let fall from a height of $490\frac{1}{2}$ cm above a fixed horizontal table will come to rest in 8 seconds, after describing $1992\frac{21}{32}$ cm, supposing the coefficient of restitution to be $\frac{7}{9}$.

3. A ball falls from a height of $1471\frac{1}{2}$ cm upon an elastic horizontal plane; if the coefficient of elasticity be $\frac{1}{3}$, find the total space described by the sphere before it finally comes to rest, and the time that elapses.

4. A particle is projected from a point in a horizontal plane with a velocity of 1962 cm per second at an angle of 30° with the horizon; if the coefficient of restitution be $\frac{3}{4}$, find the distance described by it horizontally before it ceases to rebound, and the time that elapses.

5. A ball falls vertically for 2 seconds and hits a plane inclined at 30° to the horizon; if the coefficient of restitution be $\frac{3}{4}$, show that the time that elapses before it again hits the plane in 3 seconds.

6. A perfectly elastic ball is dropped from the top of a tower of height h, and when it has fallen half-way to the ground it strikes a smooth rigid projecting stone inclined at 45° to the horizon; find where it will reach the ground.

7. A ball, at rest on a smooth horizontal plane at the distance of 1 m from a wall, is impinged on directly by another equal ball moving at right angles to the wall with a velocity of 1 m per second. If the coefficients of restitution between the balls, and the balls and wall, be each $\frac{1}{5}$, show that they will impinge a second time at the end of 0.9 second, the radii of the balls being of inconsiderable magnitude.
8. Two equal marbles, A and B, lie in a smooth horizontal circular groove at opposite ends of a diameter; A is projected along the groove and at the end of time t impinges on B; show that a second impact will occur at the end of time $\frac{2t}{e}$.
9. Two marbles, of equal diameter but of masses $10m$ and $11m$, are projected from the same point with velocities, equal in magnitude but opposite in direction, along a circular groove; where will the second impact take place if the coefficient of restitution be $\frac{3}{4}$?
10. A sphere, of mass m, impinges obliquely on a sphere, of mass M, which is at rest. Show that, if $m = eM$, the directions of motion of the spheres after impact are at right angles.
11. A sphere impinges on a sphere of equal mass which is at rest; if the directions of motion after impact be inclined at angles of 30° to the original direction of motion of the impinging sphere, show that the coefficient of restitution is $\frac{1}{3}$.
12. A ball impinges on another equal ball moving with the same speed in a direction perpendicular to its own, the line joining the centres of the balls at the instant of impact being perpendicular to the direction of motion of the second ball : if e be the coefficient of restitution, show that the direction of motion of the second ball is turned through an angle $\tan^{-1}\frac{1+e}{2}$.
13. Two equal smooth elastic spheres, moving in opposite parallel directions with equal speeds, impinge on one another; if the inclination of their directions of motion to the line of centres be $\tan^{-1}\sqrt{e}$, where e is the coefficient of restitution, show that their directions of motion will be turned through a right angle.
14. Two equal balls are in contact on a table; a third equal ball strikes them simultaneously and remains at rest after the impact; show that the coefficient of restitution is $\frac{2}{3}$.
15. The masses of five balls at rest in a straight line form a geometrical progression whose ratio is 2, and their coefficients of restitution are each $\frac{2}{3}$. If the first ball be started towards the second with velocity u, show that the velocity communicated to the fifth is $\left(\frac{5}{9}\right)^4 u$.
16. A ball of given elasticity slides from rest down a smooth inclined plane, of length l, which is inclined at an angle α to the horizon, and impinges on a fixed smooth horiziontal plane at the foot of the former; find its range on the horizontal plane.

17. A heavy elastic ball falls from a height of n m and meets a plane inclined at an angle of 60° to the horizon; find the distance between the first two points at which it strikes the plane.

18. An inelastic ball, of small radius, sliding along a smooth horizontal plane with a velocity of 4.9 m per second, impinges on a smooth horizontal rail at right angles to its direction of motion; if the height of the rail above the plane be one half the radius of the ball, show that latus rectum of the parabola subsequently described is nearly 0.4 m in length.

19. A particle is projected along a smooth horizontal plane from a given point A in it, so that after impinging on an imperfectly elastic vertical plane it may pass through another given point B of the horizontal plane; give a geometrical construction for the direction of projection.

20. A smooth circular table is surrounded by a smooth rim whose interior surface is vertical. Show that a ball, whose coefficient of restitution is e, projected along the table from a point in the rim in a direction making an angle $\tan^{-1}\sqrt{\dfrac{e^3}{1+e+e^2}}$ with the radius through the point, will return to the point of projection after two impacts on the rim. Prove also that when the ball returns to the point of projection its velocity is to its original velocity as $e^{\frac{3}{2}} : 1$.

If the angle that its direction of projection makes with the radius be $\tan^{-1} e^{\frac{3}{2}}$, show that it will return to the point of projection after three rebounds.

21. Two elastic particles are projected simultaneously from a point in a smooth horizontal plane; show that their centre of gravity will describe a number of arcs of the same parabola in different positions.

9

The Hodograph and Normal Accelerations

130. In the following chapter we shall consider the motion of a particle which moves in a curve. It will be convenient, as a preliminary, to explain how the velocity, direction of motion, and acceleration of a particle moving in any manner may be mapped out by means of another curve.

131. Hodograph. Def. *If a particle be moving in any path whatever, and if from any point O, fixed in space, we draw a straight line OQ parallel and proportional to the velocity at any point P of the path, the curve traced out by the end Q of this straight line is called the hodograph of the path of the particle.*

[The word Hodograph is derived from two Greek words δ′δ*os* (pronounced Hodos) meaning "a path", and γρ*α*′ φεω (pronounced Graphein) meaning "to write"]

It is so called because it represents graphically to the eye the velocity and acceleration of the moving point.

132. Theorem. *If the hodograph of the path of a moving point P be drawn, then the velocity of the corresponding point Q in the hodograph represents, in magnitude and direction, the acceleration of the moving point P in its path.*

Let P and P' be two points on the path close to one another; draw OQ and OQ' parallel to the tangents at P and P' and proportional to the velocities there, so that Q and Q' are two points on the hodograph very close to one another.

Whilst the particle has moved from P to P' its velocity has changed from OQ to OQ', and therefore, as in Art. 27, the change of velocity is represented by QQ'.

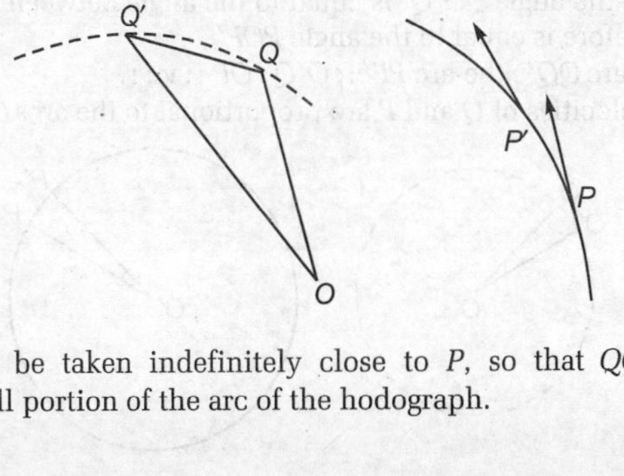

Now let P' be taken indefinitely close to P, so that QQ' becomes an indefinitely small portion of the arc of the hodograph.

If τ be the time of describing the arc PP', then, by Art. 28, the acceleration of

$$P = \frac{\text{change of velocity in time } \tau}{\tau}$$

$$= \frac{QQ'}{\tau} = \text{velocity of } Q \text{ in the hodograph.}$$

Hence the velocity of Q in the hodograph represents, in magnitude and direction, the acceleration of P in the path.

133. Examples. 1. The hodograph of a point describing a circle with uniform speed is another circle which the corresponding point describes with uniform speed. For, in this case, since the magnitude of the velocity of P is constant, the line OQ is constant in length, and therefore Q always lies on a circle whose centre is O. Also, since the point P describes its circle uniformly, the tangent at P turns through equal angles in equal times, and therefore the line OQ turns through equal angles in equal times.

2. The hodograph of a point describing a straight line with constant acceleration is a straight line, which the corresponding point describes with constant velocity. For, in this case, the line OQ is always drawn in a fixed direction and the velocity of Q, being equal in magnitude to the constant acceleration of P, is also constant.

Normal Acceleration.

134. We have learnt from the First Law of Motion that every particle, once in motion and acted on by no forces, continues to move in a straight line with uniform velocity. Hence it will not describe a curved line unless acted upon by some external force. If it describes a curve with uniform speed, there can be no force in the direction of the tangent to its path, or otherwise its speed would be altered, and so the only force acting on it is normal (that is, perpendicular) to its path. If its speed be not constant, there must in addition be a tangential force.

In the following articles we shall investigate the simple case of the normal acceleration of a particle moving in a circle with constant speed.

135. Theorem. *If a particle describes a circle of radius r with uniform speed v, show that its acceleration is* $\frac{v^2}{r}$ *directed toward the centre of the circle.*

Let P and P' be two consecutive positions of the moving particle and Q and Q' the corresponding points on the hodograph. Since the speed of P is constant, the line $O'Q$ is of constant length, and therefore the point Q moves on a circle whose radius is v; also the angle $QO'Q'$ is equal to the angle between the tangents at P and P' and therefore is equal to the angle POP'.

Hence the arc QQ' : the arc $PP' :: O'Q : OP :: v : r$.

Also the velocities of Q and P are proportional to the arcs QQ' and PP'.

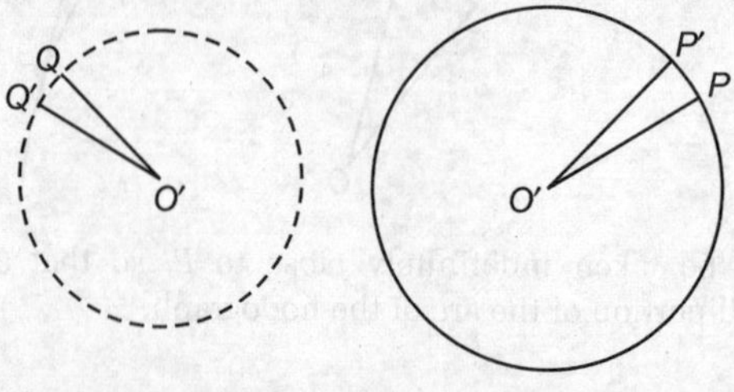

Hence the velocity of Q in the hodograph : $v :: v : r$.

$\therefore$ $$\text{velocity of } Q = \frac{v^2}{r}.$$

But the point Q is moving in a direction perpendicular to $O'Q$ and therefore parallel to PO; also the acceleration of the point P is equal to the velocity of Q (Art. 132).

Hence the acceleration of P is $\frac{v^2}{r}$ in the direction PO.

If the speed v be not constant but variable it can be shown (*Elementary Dynamics*, Art. 157) that the normal acceleration is still $\frac{v^2}{r}$.

Cor. 1. If ω be the angular velocity of the particle about the centre O, we have $v = r\omega$, and the normal acceleration is therefore $\omega^2 r$.

Cor. 2. The force required to produce the normal acceleration is $m\frac{v^2}{r}$, where m is the mass of the particle.

136. Without the use of the hodograph, a proof of the very important theorem of the last article can be given as follows.

Let P' be a point on the circle very close to P. Draw the tangent $P'T$ at P' to meet the tangent, Px, at P in T.

Join P and P' to the centre, O of the circle.

Since, the angles at P and P' are right angles, a circle will go through the points O, P, T and P', and hence $\angle P'Tx$

$$= \text{supplement of } \ P'TP = POP' = \theta.$$

Let v be the speed in the circle, and let τ be the time of describing the arc PP'.

In time τ a velocity parallel to PO has been generated equal to $v \sin\theta$.

Hence the acceleration in the direction $PO = \frac{v\sin\theta}{\tau}$ (when τ, and therefore, θ, is taken very small)

$$= \frac{v\cdot\theta}{\tau} = \frac{v}{\tau}\cdot\frac{\text{arc } PP'}{OP} = \frac{v}{\tau}\cdot\frac{\text{arc } PP'}{\tau}.$$

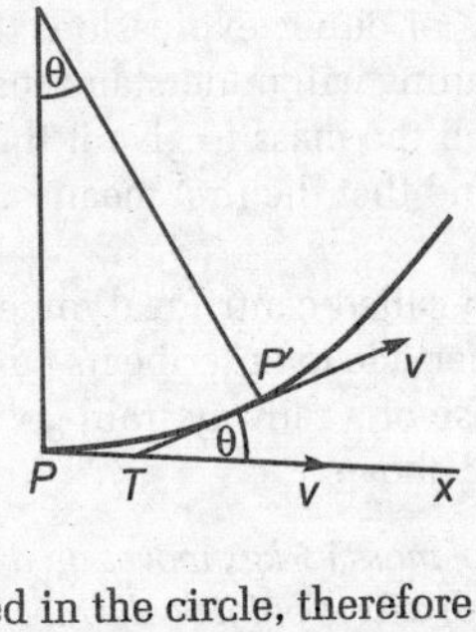

But, since v is the speed in the circle, therefore $\frac{\text{arc } PP'}{\tau} = v$.

Hence the required acceleration $= \dfrac{v^2}{\tau}$.

As in Art. 135, Cor. 1, this acceleration is equal to $\tau\omega^2$, where ω is the angular velocity.

Also the force towards the centre must be $m\dfrac{v^2}{\tau}$.

137. The force spoken of in the preceding articles, which is required to cause the normal acceleration of a body, may be produced in many ways.

For example, the body may be tethered by a string, extensible or inextensible, to a fixed point.

Again, the force may be caused by the pressure of a material curve by means of which the body is constrained to move in a curve; for example, a train may be made to describe the curved portion of a railway line by means of the pressure of the rails on the flanges of its wheels.

The force may also be of the nature of an attraction such as exists between the sun and earth, and which compels the earth to describe a curve about the sun.

138. When a man whirls in a circle a mass tied to one end of a string, the other end of which is in his hand, the tension of the string exerts the necessary force on the body to give it the required normal acceleration. But, by the third law of motion, the string exerts upon the man's hand a force equal and opposite to that which it exerts upon the particle; these two forces form the action and reaction of which Newton speaks. It *appears* to the man that the mass is trying to get away from his hand. For this reason a force, equal and opposite to the force necessary to give the particle its normal acceleration, is often called "its centrifugal force," i.e., centre-avoiding force. This may however be a somewhat misleading term; it seems to imply that the force *belongs* to the mass instead of being an external force acting on the mass. It also appears to imply that the particle wants to get away from the centre of the curve and is prevented from doing so; this is clearly not so; the particle would, if it were not prevented, move along the tangent to the curve, i.e., along the line *Px* of the figure of Art. 136; it has no wish, or tendency, to move in the direction *OP*.

A somewhat less misleading term is "centripetal force", i.e., centre-seeking force.

We shall avoid the use of either expression; the student who meets with them in the course of his reading will understand that the second of them means "the force which must act on the mass to give it the acceleration normal to the curve in which it moves", and that the first means a force equal and opposite to this.

This latter force (the so-called centrifugal force) is the force which acts on the body which causes the particle to describe its curved path, e.g., it is the force acting on the *rails* in the case of a railway train going round a curve, or on the *man's hand* in the case cited above.

139. Ex. 1. *A particle, of mass 1.5 kg., moves on a smooth table with a velocity of 2 m per second, being attached to a fixed point on the table by a string of length 2.5 m; find the tension of the string.*

Here $v = 2$, and $r = 2.5$.

Therefore, by Art. 135, the acceleration toward the fixed point is

$$\frac{v^2}{2.5}, \text{ i.e., } \frac{8}{5}$$

Hence the tension of the string

$$= 1.5 \times \frac{8}{5} = 2.4 \text{ newtons.}$$

Ex. 2. *A particle, of mass m, moves on a horizontal table and is connected by a string, of length l, with a fixed point on the table; if the greatest weight that the string can support be that of a mass of M kg, find the greatest number of revolutions per second that the particle can make without breaking the string.*

Let n be the required number of revolutions, so that the velocity of the mass is $n \cdot 2\pi l$.

Therefore the tension of the string $= m \cdot \dfrac{4\pi^2 n^2 l^2}{l}$ newtons.

Hence $Mg = 4m\pi^2 n^2 l$, so that $n = \dfrac{1}{2\pi}\left(\dfrac{Mg}{ml}\right)^{\frac{1}{2}}$.

If the number of revolutions were greater than this number, the tension of the string would be greater than the string could exert, and it would break.

Examples. XXIII.

1. A string is 90 cm long, and has one end attached to a fixed point on a smooth horizontal table; if a mass of 2943 gm tied at the other end of the string describe uniformly a horizontal circle with speed 180 cm per second, find the tension of the string.
2. A string is 109 cm long can just support a weight of 1600 gm; a mass of 900 gm is tied at its end and revolves uniformly on a horizontal table, the other end of the string being attached to a fixed point on the table; find the greatest number of revolutions per minute that can be made by the string without its breaking.
3. A string, 109 cm long, can just sustain a weight of 10 kg : if the revolving mass be 900 gm, determine the greatest number of complete revolutions that can be made in one minute by the string without its breaking.
4. A string, 0.5 m long, has a mass of one kg attached to one end and the other end is attached to a fixed point; if the mass be whirled round in a horizontal circle, whose centre is the fixed point, and if the resulting tension of the string be equal to the weight of 5 kg, show that the string is making about $94\frac{1}{2}$ revolutions per minute.
5. The tension of a string, one end of which is fixed and to the other end of which is attached a mass which revolves uniformly, is 9 times the weight of the revolving mass; find the velocity of the mass if the length of the string be 109 cm.
6. With what number of turns per minute must a mass of 10 grammes revolve horizontally at the end of a string, half a metre in length, to cause the same tension in the string as would be caused by a mass of one gramme hanging vertically?

7. A locomotive engine, of mass 10.16 metric tonnes, moves on a curve, of radius 182.9 metres, with a velocity of 48.3 km per hour; what force tending toward the centre of the curve must be exerted by the rails so that this may be the case?
8. If, in the previous question, the mass of the engine be 12.2 metric tonnes, its velocity 95.56 km per hour, and the radius of the curve 366 metres, what is the required force?

140. The Conical Pendulum. If a particle be tied by a string to a fixed point *O*, and move so that it describes a circle in a horizontal plane, the string describing a cone whose axis is the vertical line through *O*, then the string and particle together are called a conical pendulum.

When the motion is uniform, the relations between the velocity of the particle and the length and inclination of the string are easily found.

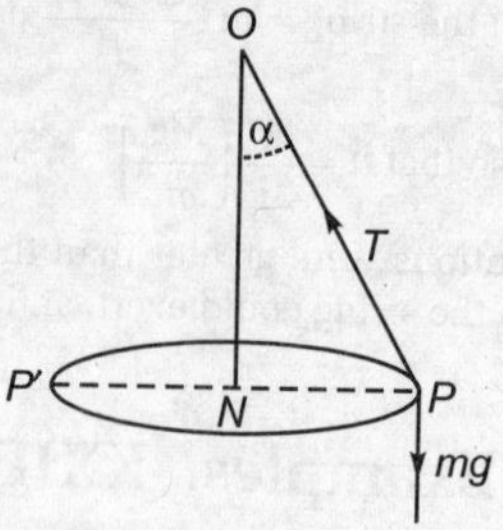

Let *P* be the particle tied by a string *OP*, of length *l*, to a fixed point *O*. Draw *PN* perpendicular to the vertical through *O*. Then *P* describes a horizontal circle with *N* as centre [*dotted in the figure*].

Let *T* be the tension of the string, α is inclination to the vertical, and v the velocity of the particle.

By Art. 135, the acceleration of *P* in the direction *PN* is $\frac{v^2}{PN}$, and hence the force in that direction must be

$$m\frac{v^2}{l\sin\alpha}.$$

Now the only forces acting on the particle are the tension, *T*, of the string and the weight, *mg*, of the particle.

Since, the particle has no acceleration in a vertical direction, the forces acting upon it in that direction must balance, and hence we have

$$T\cos\alpha = mg \qquad \text{...(1)}.$$

Also $T\sin\alpha$ is the only force in the direction *PN*, and hence

$$T\sin\alpha = \frac{mv^2}{l\sin\alpha} \qquad \text{...(2)}.$$

From (1) and (2), we have $\frac{v^2}{l\sin^2\alpha} = \frac{g}{\cos\alpha}$.

If the particle makes n revolutions per second, then

$$v = n \cdot 2\pi PN = 2\pi nl \sin\alpha$$

$$\therefore \quad 4\pi^2 n^2 l = \frac{g}{\cos\alpha}, \text{that is,} \cos\alpha = \frac{g}{4\pi^2 n^2 l} \qquad ...(3).$$

Hence, by (1),

$$T = 4m\pi^2 n^2 l \text{ dynes} \qquad ...(4).$$

Hence the tension of the string : weight of the particle

$$:: 4\pi^2 n^2 l : g.$$

The equations (3) and (4) give α and T.

The time of revolution of the particle

$$= \frac{2\pi l \sin\alpha}{v} = 2\pi\sqrt{\frac{l\cos\alpha}{g}} = 2\pi\sqrt{\frac{ON}{g}},$$

and therefore varies as the square root of the depth of the particle below the fixed point.

141. Governors of steam engines. It is generally desirable that engines of the stationary kind should run at a constant speed. Their speed is therefore usually controlled by a Governor; this generally consists of two heavy revolving balls which are attached at the ends of light rods, the other ends of which are connected with a vertical shaft driven by the engine.

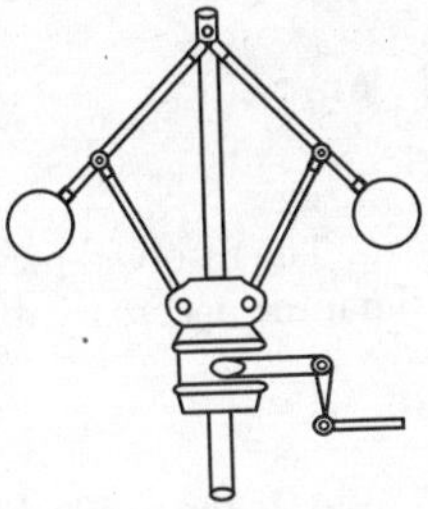

A simple form, known as Watt's Governor, is shown in the figure. When the shaft runs too fast the balls rise and lift the mechanism at c; by means of levers attached to it the valve regulating the supply of steam is partially closed and the speed is lessened; so when the shaft runs too slowly the balls fall and the supply of steam is increased. The governor thus automatically regulates the supply of steam, so that the engine runs at approximately a constant speed.

From the last result of Art. 140 it follows that, for a governor of a steam engine rotating 60 times per minute, the height is about 25 cm : for one making 100 revolutions per minute the height is 0.12 cm : this latter height is too small for practical purposes except for extremely small engines.

In order that governors may run at a high speed they are therefore usually loaded by means of a spring or weight so adjusted as to keep c lower than it would be in an unloaded governor.

142. Motion of bicycle rider on a circular path. When a man is riding a bicycle on a curved path he always inclines his body inwards towards the centre of his path. By this means the reaction of the ground becomes inclined to the vertical. The vertical component of this reaction balances his weight, and the horizontal component tends towards the centre of the path described by the centre of inertia of the man and his machine, and supplies the necessary normal acceleration.

143. Motion of a railway carriage on a curved portion of the railway line. When the rails are level, the force to give the carriage the necessary acceleration toward the centre of curvature of its path is given by the action of the rails on the flanges of the wheels with which the rails are in contact. In order, however, to avoid the large amount of friction that would be brought into play, and the consequent wearing away of the rails, the outer rail is generally raised so that the floor of the train is not horizontal. The necessary inclination of the floor, in order that there may be no action on the flanges, may be easily found as follows.

Let v be the velocity of the train, and r the radius of the circle described by its centre of inertia G.

Let the figure represent a section of the carriage in the vertical plane through the line joining its centre of inertia to the centre, O, of the circle which it is describing, and let the section meet the rails in the points A and B.

[*The wheels are omitted for the continuous of the figure.*]

Let R and S be the reactions of the rails perpendicular to the floor AB, and let θ be the inclination of the floor to the horizon.

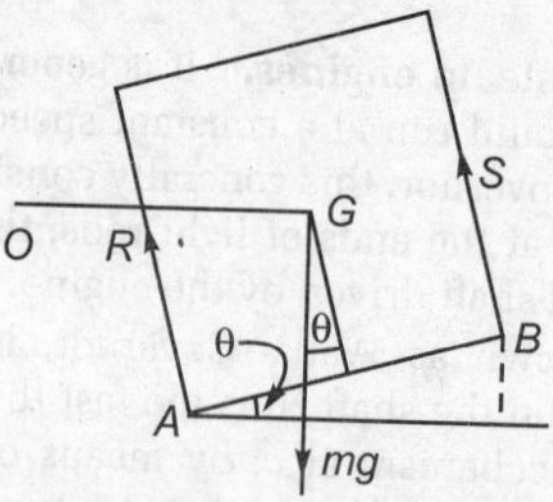

The resolved part, $(R + S)\sin\theta$, of the reactions in the direction GO supplies the force necessary to cause the acceleration towards the centre of the curve.

$$\therefore \qquad (R+S)\sin\theta = m\frac{v^2}{r} \qquad \text{...(1).}$$

Also the vertical components of the reactions balance the weight

$$\therefore \qquad (R+S)\cos\theta = mg \qquad \text{...(2).}$$

From (1) and (2).

$$\tan\theta = \frac{v^2}{rg} \qquad \text{...(3),}$$

giving the inclination of the floor.

If the width AB be given, we can now easily determine the height of the outer rail above the inner; for it is equal to $AB \sin\theta$.

It will be noted that the height through which the outer rail must be raised in order that there may be no horizontal thrust on the flanges depends on the velocity of the train. In practice the height is adjusted so that there is no thrust for trains moving with moderate velocities. For trains moving with higher velocities, the horizontal thrust of the rails on the flanges supplies the additional force required.

This thrust may be found as follows. Assuming that the height of the outer rail has been so adjusted that there is no side thrust for trains travelling with velocity v, let X be the side thrust, reckoned from B towards A, when the velocity of the train is V. Then instead of equations (1) and (2) we have, (if the above figure be used with the addition of a force X along BA),

$$(R+S)\sin\theta + X\cos\theta = m\frac{V^2}{r} \qquad \ldots(4),$$

and

$$(R+S)\cos\theta - X\sin\theta = mg \qquad \ldots(5).$$

Hence we have

$$X = m\frac{V^2}{r}\cos\theta - mg\sin\theta$$

$$= m\cos\theta\left[\frac{V^2}{r} - g\tan\theta\right]$$

$$= m\cos\theta\left[\frac{V^2 - v^2}{r}\right], \text{ by equation (3).}$$

If V exceed v, X is positive, and the side thrust is caused by the outer rail at B. If V be less than v, X is negative and therefore acts from A to B, so that the side thrust is in this case caused by the inner rail at A.

144. Rotating sphere. *A smooth hollow sphere is rotating with uniform angular velocity ω about a vertical diameter; to show that a heavy particle placed inside, and rotating with it, will only remain resting against the side of the sphere at one particular level, and that, if the angular velocity fall short of a certain limit, the particle will only rest at the lowest point of the sphere.*

Let AB be the axis of rotation of the sphere, A being the highest point, and let O be the centre; let P be the position of the particle when in relative equilibrium and PN the perpendicular on AB.

Now P describes a circle about N as centre with angular velocity ω, and therefore the force towards N must be $m\omega^2 . PN$, or $m\omega^2 a\sin\theta$, where a is the radius of the sphere and θ the angle POB.

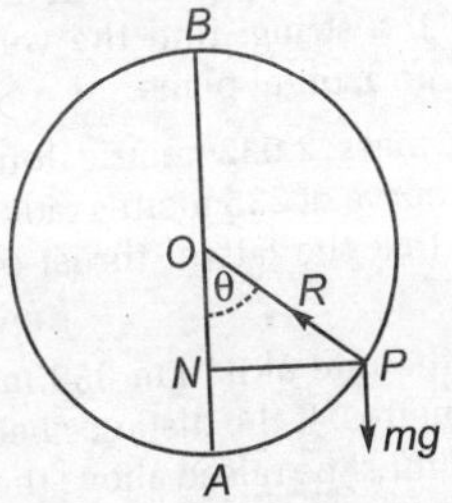

The horizontal component of the normal reaction, R, at P supplies this horizontal force, and the vertical component balances the weight of the particle.

Hence

$$R\sin\theta = m\omega^2 a\sin\theta \qquad \ldots(1),$$

and

$$R\cos\theta = mg \qquad \ldots(2).$$

From equation (1) we have, either $\sin\theta = 0$, or $R = m\omega^2 a$.

Substituting for R in (2), we have

$$\cos\theta = \frac{g}{\omega^2 a} \qquad ...(3).$$

Hence the particle is either at the lowest point, where $\sin\theta = 0$, or at a point determined by equation (3).

The value of θ given by (3) is impossible unless $g < \omega^2 a$, i.e., unless the angular velocity ω is greater than $\left(\frac{g}{a}\right)^{\frac{1}{2}}$. If the angular velocity be less than this quantity, the only position of relative rest of the particle is at the lowest point of the sphere.

Examples. XXIV.

1. A mass of 2 kg is tied at the end of a string of length 109 cm, and revolves as a conical pendulum, the string being always inclined to the vertical at an angle of 60°; find the tension of the string and the velocity of the particle.
2. Show that the inclination to the vertical of the string of a conical pendulum, when the string is 20 inches long and the pendulum revolves 200 times per minute, is
$$\cos^{-1}\frac{9}{20\pi^2}, \text{ i.e., about } 87°24'.$$
3. A string, of length 1.2 m, and having one end attached to a fixed point and the other to a mass of 20 kg, revolves, as a conical pendulum, 30 times per minute; show that the tension of the string is 24π newtons, and that its inclination to the vertical is $\cos^{-1}\left(\frac{49}{6\pi^2}\right)$, i.e., about 34°11′.
4. A heavy particle which is suspended from a fixed point by a string, 0.30 m long, is raised until the string, which is kept tight, makes an angle of 60° with the vertical, and is then projected horizontally in the direction perpendicular to the vertical plane through the string; find the velocity of projection so that the particle may move in a horizontal plane.
5. A railway carriage, of mass 2.032 metric tonnes, is moving at the rate of 96.56 km per hour on a curve of 235 metres radius; if the outer rail be not raised above the inner, show that the lateral thrust of the outer rail is equal to the weight of about 640 kg.
6. A train is travelling at the rate of 63 km 360 metres per hour on a curve, the radius of which is 396 metres. If the distance between the rails be 150 cm, find how much the outer rail must be raised above the inner, so that there may be no lateral thrust on the rails.
7. A train is travelling at the rate of 47 km 520 metres per hour on a curve the radius of which is 360 metres. If the distance between the rails be 150 cm, find how much the outer rails must be raised above the inner so that there may be no lateral thrust on the rails.
8. A railway carriage moves on a circular curve; find to what height the outer rail must be raised above the inner so that there may be no lateral thrust on the rails

if the radius of the curve be 396 metres, the breadth between the rails 150 cm, and the carriage has a velocity of 71 km 280 metres per hour.

9. A mass is hung from the roof of a railway carriage by means of a string, 2 m long; show that, when the train is moving on a curve of radius 100 m at the rate of 48 km per hour, the mass will move from the vertical through a distance of 35.7 cm.

10. A bowl, 76.2 mm deep, is made from a spherical surface whose radius is 152.4 mm and rotates about its vertical axis. Find the greatest number of revolutions which it can make in a minute, if a particle can rest on its surface without being thrown out.

11. If 2θ be the vertical angle of a smooth hollow cone, whose axis is vertical and vertex downwards, show that the distance from its axis of a body, moving in a circle on its surface and making n revolutions per second, is

$$\frac{g \cot \theta}{4\pi^2 n^2}.$$

12. The sails of a windmill are about 9 metres long, and revolve 10 times per minute; show that a man clinging to the outer end of one of these sails would, at the highest point of his path, experience no reaction from the sail, and therefore could for a moment leave go without falling.

13. A heavy particle is connected by an inextensible string, 91.4 cm, to a fixed point, and describes a circle in a vertical plane passing through the fixed point, making 600 revolutions per minute; neglecting the small variations in the speed of the particle, find the ratios of the tensions of the string in its two vertical positions and in its horizontal position.

14. Two particles, of the same mass, are fastened respectively to the middle point and one extremity of a weightless string, and are laid upon a smooth table, the other end of the string being fastened to a point in the table.

If the string be pulled tight, and the particles be so projected that they always remain in a straight line, show that the tensions in the two portions of the string are as 3 : 2.

15. A train, moving in a straight line with velocity v, comes to a curve of radius r; show that the mean slope of the surface of the water in a fixed tumbler carried by the train, or the mean deflection of a plummet attached by a short cord, will be

$$\tan^{-1} \frac{v^2}{gr}.$$

16. A particle, of mass m, is fastened by a string, of length l, to a point at a distance b above a smooth table; if the particle be made to revolve on the table n times per second, find the reaction of the table. What is the greatest value of n, so that the particle may remain in contact with the table?

17. A wet open umbrella is held with its handle upright and made to rotate about it at the rate of 14 revolutions in 33 seconds. If the rim of the umbrella be a circle of one m in diameter, and its height above the ground be 1.225 m, show that the drops shaken off from the rim meet the ground in a circle of $1\frac{2}{3}$ m in diameter. If the mass of a drop be 0.3 g, show that the force necessary to keep it attached to the umbrella is about 313 dynes and is inclined at an angle about $\tan^{-1} 0.363$ to the vertical.

18. A particle, of mass m, on a smooth table is fastened to one end of a fine string which passes through a small hole in the table and supports at its other end a particle of mass $2m$, the particle m being held at a distance c from the hole. Find the velocity with which m must be projected, so that it may describe a circle of radius c.

19. Two masses, m and m', are placed on a smooth table and connected by a light string passing through a small ring fixed to the table. If they be projected with velocities v and v' respectively at right angles to the portions of the string, which is initially tight, find the ratio in which the string must be divided at the ring, so that both particles may describe circles about the ring as centre.

20. Two masses, m and m', are connected by a string, of length l, which passes through a small ring; find how many revolutions per second the smaller mass, m', must make, as a conical pendulum, in order that the greater mass may hang at rest at a distance a from the ring.

21. A string, passing through a small hole in a smooth horizontal table, has a small sphere, of mass m, attached to each end of it; the upper sphere revolves in a circle on the table when suddenly it strikes an obstacle and loses half its velocity; find what diminution must be made in the mass of the lower sphere, so that the upper one may continue rotating in a circle.

22. A string PAQ passes through a hole A in a smooth table, the portion AP lying on the table, and AQ being at an angle of 45° to the vertical, and below the table, so that P and Q are in the same vertical line. If masses be attached at P and Q and, the strings being stretched, be each projected horizontally, find the ratio of the masses, so that the plane PAQ may always be vertical and the angle PAQ always 45°. If the string be 1.225 m in length, find the time of revolution.

23. A body, of mass m, moves on a horizontal table being attached to a fixed point on the table by an extensible string whose modulus of elasticity is λ; given the original length a of the string, find the velocity of the particle when it is describing a circle of radius r.

24. A particle is attached to a point A by an elastic string, whose modulus of elasticity is twice the weight of the particle and whose natural length is l, and whirled so that the string describes the surface of a cone whose axis is the vertical line through A. If the distance below A of the circular path during steady motion be l, show that the velocity of the particle must be $\sqrt{3}\,gl$.

25. In Ex. 8 find the lateral thrust when the velocity is (1) 47 km 520 metres, (2) 95 km 40 metres per hour, the mass of the carriage being 10 metric tonnes. In each case state which rail causes the thrust.

10

Motion on a Smooth Curve Under the Action of Gravity

145. THE general case of the motion of a particle, constrained to move on a given curve under any given forces, is beyond the scope of the present book; so also is the motion of a particle constrained to move under gravity on a given curve.

There is one proposition, however, relating to the motion of a particle under gravity which we can prove in an elementary manner, and which is very useful for determining many of the circumstances of the motion.

146. Theorem. *If a particle slides down an arc of any smooth curve in a vertical plane, and if u be its initial velocity and v its velocity after sliding through a vertical distance h, show that* $v^2 = u^2 + 2gh$.

Let A be the point of the curve from which the particle starts, and B the point whose distance from A, measured vertically, is h. Draw AM and BN horizontal to meet any vertical line in M and N.

Let P and Q be two points on the curve, very close to one another, and draw PR and QS perpendicular to MN. Then PQ is very approximately a small portion of a straight line. Draw QV vertical to meet PR in V.

The acceleration at P along PQ is $g \cos VQP$ and hence, if v_P and v_Q be the velocities at P and Q, we have

$$v_Q^2 = v_P^2 + 2g \cos VQP \cdot PQ = v_P^2 + 2g \cdot VQ$$

$$\therefore \qquad v_Q^2 - v_P^2 = 2g \cdot VQ,$$

i.e., the change in the square of the velocity is due to the vertical height between P and Q. Since this is true for every element of arc, is true for the whole arc AB.

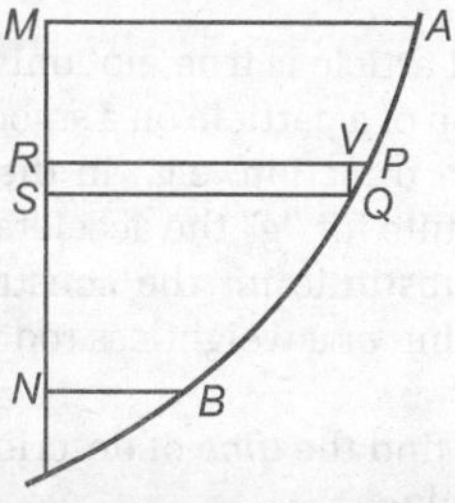

Hence the change in the square of the velocity in passing from A to B is that due to the vertical height h, so that $v^2 = u^2 + 2gh$.

The theorem in the preceding article may be deduced directly from the Principle of the Conservation of Energy.

For, since the curve is smooth, the reaction of the arc is always perpendicular to the direction of motion of the particle. Hence, by *Statics,* Art. 196, no work is done on the body by the pressure of the curve. The only force that does work is the weight of the particle.

Hence, since the change of energy is equal to the work done, we have

$$\frac{1}{2}mv^2 - \frac{1}{2}mu^2 = \text{work done by the weight} = mgh.$$

$$\therefore \qquad v^2 = u^2 + 2gh.$$

147. If, instead of sliding *down* the smooth curve, the particle be started along it with velocity u, so that it moves *upwards,* the velocity v when its vertical distance from the starting point is h is, similarly, given by the equation

$$v^2 = u^2 - 2gh.$$

Hence the velocity of the particle will not vanish until it arrives at a point of the curve whose vertical height above the point of projection is $\frac{u^2}{2g}$.

It will be noticed that the height to which the particle will ascend is independent of the *shape* of the constraining curve, nor need it continually ascend. The particle may first ascend, then descend, then ascend again, and so on; the point at which it comes to rest finally will be at a height $\frac{u^2}{2g}$ above the point at which its velocity is u.

It follows that, if a particle slides from rest upon a smooth arc, it will come to rest when it is at the same vertical height as the starting point. An approximate example is the Switch-back railway in which the car almost rises to the same height as that of the point at which it started. The slight difference beween theory and experiment is caused by the resistance of the air and the friction of the rails which, although small, are not quite negligible.

The heavier the car, the less will be found to be the difference between theory and experiment.

The expression for the velocity when the particle is at a vertical distance h from the starting point is the same, whether the particle be at that instant ascending or descending.

The theorem of the last article is true, not only of motion under gravity, but also in any case of the motion of a particle on a smooth curve under the action of a constant force in a constant direction, e.g., in the case of motion on a smooth inclined plane, if we substitute for "g" the acceleration caused by the forces.

It is also true if we substitute for the constraining curve an inextensible string fastened to a fixed point, or a weightless rod which is always normal to the path of the particle.

We cannot, in general, find the *time* of describing any given arc without the use of the Differential Calculus.

148. Galileo's Experiment. It is not easy to accurately perform experiments on a body sliding down a smooth curve; for it is practically impossible to get a smooth curve. We can however in the analogous case of a particle tied by a string verify experimentally the theorem of Art. 146.

Tie a heavy body, such as a lead sphere, to one end of a light flexible string the other end of which is attached to a fixed point A. Let the body swing about this point as centre in front of a blackboard.

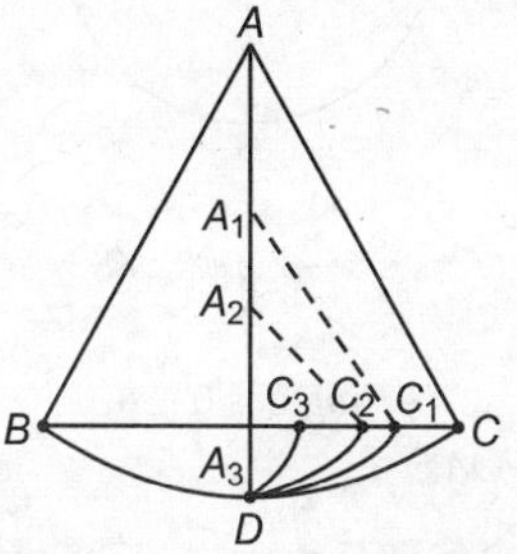

Mark the point B on the blackboard from which the sphere is allowed to start and through it draw a horizontal line BA_3C. If the sphere be now allowed to swing about A, it will be found to come to rest at a point C which is very nearly on the straight line BA_3.

Now drive in a nail at a point A_1 vertically below A, the nail jutting out sufficiently to intercept the string. Start the sphere from the same point B as before; it will describe the arc BD and will then move on an arc DC_1 about A_1 as centre. The point C_1 at which it comes to rest will be found to be very nearly on the horizontal straight line. Reverse the operation, starting the sphere from C_1, and it will be found to describe the path C_1DB.

Repeat the experiment, driving in nails successively at A_2 and A_3. In each case the same result will be obtained, viz., that if the sphere started from B it will come to rest at a point very nearly on the horizontal line through B.

If it were not for the resistance of the air, which, though small, is appreciable, the points C_1, C_2, C_3 would be found to be accurately on the straight line BC.

If a light ball be used, instead of the lead one, but of the same size, the resistance of the air has a greater effect, and in this case the amount by which the ball falls short of the line BC will be found to be greater than in the case of the lead ball.

The same results will follow if we drive in the nail at *any* point P of the board within the triangle ABC, so that the string catches on the nail as it swings past.

149. Motion on the outside of a vertical circle. *A particle slides from rest at the highest point down the outside of the arc of a smooth vertical circle; show that it will leave the curve when it has described vertically a distance equal to one third of the radius.*

Let O be the centre, and A the highest point of the circle. Let v be the velocity of the particle when at a point P of the curve, R the pressure of the curve there, and r the radius of the circle. Draw PN perpendicular to the vertical radius OA, and let $AN = h$.

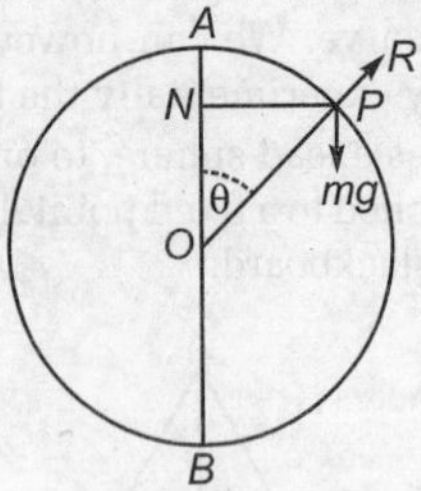

Then $$v^2 = 2g \cdot AN = 2gh.$$

The force along PO is

$$mg \cos \theta - R,$$

where θ is the angle POA.

But the force along PO must, by Art. 135, be $m \cdot \dfrac{v^2}{r}$.

$$\therefore \quad m \frac{v^2}{r} = mg \cos \theta - R.$$

$$\therefore \quad R = m\left[g \cos \theta - \frac{v^2}{r}\right] = m\left[g\,\frac{r-h}{r} - \frac{2gh}{r}\right]$$

$$= mg\,\frac{r-3h}{r}.$$

Now R vanishes, and changes its sign, when, $3h = r$, i.e., when $h = \dfrac{r}{3}$. The particle will then leave the curve, and describe a parabola freely; for, to make it continue on the circle, the pressure R would have to become a tension; but this is impossible since the curve cannot *pull* the particle.

150. Motion in a vertical circle. *A particle, of mass m, is suspended by a string, of length r, from a fixed point and hangs vertically. It is then projected, with velocity u, so that it describes a vertical circle; find the tension and velocity at any point of the subsequent motion, and to find also the condition that it may just make complete revolutions.*

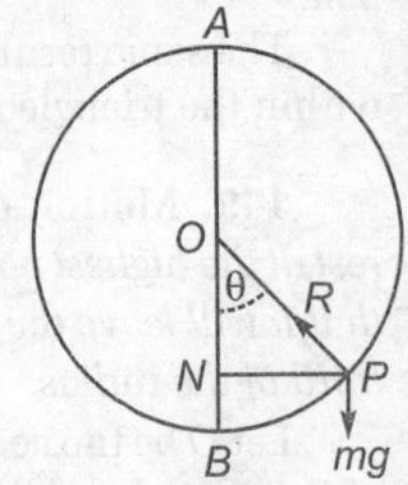

Let O be the point to which the string is attached, and OA the vertical line through O.

Let v be the velocity of the particle at any point P of its path, and T the tension of the string there.

Let PN be drawn perpendicular to OA, let $AN = h$, and let the angle POA be θ.

Then, by Art. 147,

$$v^2 = u^2 - 2gh \qquad \ldots(1).$$

Also, by Art. 135, $m\dfrac{v^2}{r}$ = force at P along the normal, PO, to the path of the particle.

$$\therefore \quad m\frac{v^2}{r} = T - mg\cos\theta = T - mg\frac{r-h}{r},$$

$$\therefore \quad T = m\frac{v^2 + g(r-h)}{r} = m\frac{u^2 + g(r-3h)}{r} \qquad ...(2).$$

These two equations give the velocity of the particle, and the tension of the string, at any point of the path.

The particle will not reach the highest point A if the tension of the string becomes negative; for then, in order that the particle might continue revolving in a circle, the pull of the string would have to change into a push, and this is impossible in the case of a string.

Hence the particle will *just* take complete revolutions if the tension vanishes at the highest point, where $h = 2r$.

This, from (2), is the case if

$$u^2 + g(r - 6r) = 0,$$

i.e., if $\quad u^2 = 5gr.$

Hence, for complete revolutions, u must not be less than $\sqrt{5gr}$.

When $u = \sqrt{5gr}$, the tension at the lowest point, by (2)

$$= m\frac{5gr + rg}{r} = 6mg \text{ dynes.}$$

Hence the string must, at the least, be able to bear a weight equal to six times the weight of the body.

151. Newton's Experimental Law. By using the theorem of Art. 147, we can show how Newton arrived at his law of impact as enunciated in Art. 118.

We suspend two spheres, of small dimensions, by parallel strings OA and $O'B$, whose lengths are so adjusted that when hanging freely the spheres are just in contact with their centres in a horizontal line.

One ball, A, is then drawn back, the string being kept tight, until its centre is at a height AM, (= h), above its original position and is allowed to fall. Its velocity v on hitting the second ball B is $\sqrt{2gh}$.

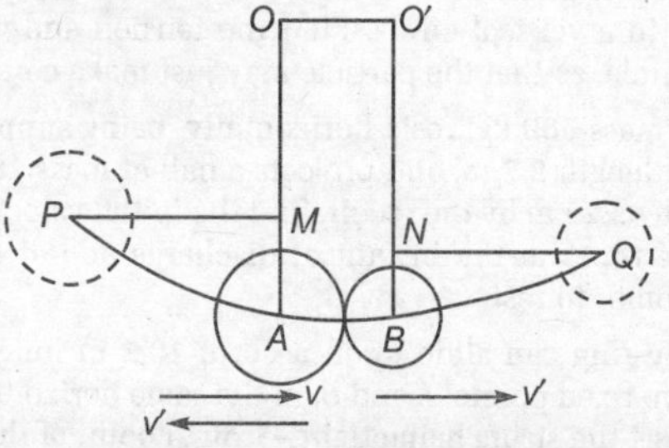

Let v' and v'' be the velocities of the spheres immediately after the impact, and h' and h'' the heights to which they rise before again coming to rest, so that

$$v' = \sqrt{2gh'} \quad \text{and} \quad v'' = \sqrt{2gh''}.$$

The sphere A may either rebound, remain at rest, or follow after B.

Taking the former case the velocity of separation is

$$v' + v'', \text{ i.e., } \sqrt{2g}\,(\sqrt{h'} + \sqrt{h''}).$$

Also the velocity of approach was $\sqrt{2g} \cdot \sqrt{h}$.

We should find that the ratio of $(\sqrt{h'} + \sqrt{h''})$ to $\sqrt{h}$ would be the same whatever be the value of h and the ratio of the mass of A to that of B, and that it would depend simply on the substances of which the masses consist.

We have only considered one of the simpler cases. By carefully arranging the starting points and the instants of starting from rest, both spheres might be drawn aside and allowed to impinge so that at the instant of impact both were at the lowest points of their path. The law enunciated by Newton would be found to be true in all cases.

Examples. XXV.

1. A particle, of mass 2500 gm, hangs at the end of a string, 90 cm long, the other end of which is attached to a fixed point; if it be projected horizontally with a velocity of 750 cm per second, find the velocity of the particle and the tension of the string, when the latter is (1) horizontal, and (2) vertically upwards.
2. In the previous question, find the least velocity of projection that the particle may be able to make complete revolutions, and the least weight that the string must be able to bear.
3. A body, of mass m, is attached to a fixed point O by a string of length 90 cm, it is held with the string horizontal and then let fall; find its velocity when the string becomes vertical, and also the tension of the string then.
4. A smooth hoop, of diameter $122\frac{6}{5}$ cm, is placed in a vertical plane, and a bead slides on the hoop starting from rest at the highest point of the hoop; finds its velocity
   (1) at the lowest point,
   (2) at the end of a horizontal diameter,
   (3) when it has described one-third of the vertical distance to the lowest point,
   (4) when it has described one-third of the actual distance to the lowest point.
5. A heavy particle is attached by a string, 3.04 metres long, to a fixed point, and swung round in a vertical circle. Find the tension and velocity at the lowest point of the circle, so that the particle may just make complete revolutions.
6. A cannon, of mass 600 kg, rests horizontally, being supported by two vertical ropes, each of length 2.7 m, and projects a ball of mass 18 kg; if the cannon be raised through 0.225 m by the recoil, find the initial velocity of the ball, and the tension of the ropes at the instant of discharge and at the instant when the cannot first comes to rest.
7. A small heavy ring can slide upon a cord, 10.2 m long, which has its ends attached to two fixed points. A and B, in the same horizontal line and 9 m apart. The ring starts—the string being tight—from a point of the string distant 1.5 m

from A; show that, when it has described a length of the cord equal to 0.9 m, its velocity will be 3.07 m per second nearly.

8. A particle slides down the arc of a vertical circle; show that its velocity at the lowest point varies as the chord of the arc of descent.

9. A particle runs down the outside of a smooth vertical circle, starting from rest at its highest point; find the latus rectum of the parabola which it describes after leaving the surface.

10. A ball, of mass m, is just disturbed from the top of a smooth vertical circular tube, and runs down the interior of the tube impinging on a ball, of mass $2m$, which is at rest at the bottom of the tube; if the coefficient of restitution be $\frac{1}{3}$, find the height to which each ball will rise in the tube after the impact.

11. Two equal ivory balls are suspended by parallel threads, so that they are in contact, and so that the line joining their centres is horizontal, and 64 cm below the points of attachment of the threads. Determine the coefficient of restitution between the balls of the threads. Determine the coefficient of restitution between the balls when it is found that, by allowing one ball to start from a position when its thread is inclined at 60° to the vertical, it causes the other ball after impact to rise through a vertical distance of 18 cm.

12. A circular arc, subtending 30° at its centre, is fixed in a vertical plane so that its highest point is in the same horizontal plane with its centre, and a smooth particle slides down this curve starting from rest at its highest point. Show that the latus rectum of the parabola, which it describes after leaving the curve, is half the radius of the circular arc.

13. A weightless inextensible string, of length $2l$, is fastened at its extremities to two points A and B in the same horizontal line, at a distance l apart, and supports a body C of mass m, tied to its middle point. If C be projected perpendicular to the plane ACB with double the velocity requisite for it to describe a complete circle, find the greatest and least tension of the strings.
If one portion of the string be cut when C is halfway between its highest and lowest points, find the subsequent motion.

14. A smooth tube, in the form of 7 sides of a regular octagon each of whose sides is a, is placed so that one extreme side is lowest and horizontal and the other extreme side is vertical; an inelastic particle is just placed inside and connected by a string passing through the tube with an equal particle hanging vertically; find the velocity of the particles when the first leaves the tube, the corners of the tube being rounded off so that there is no impact.

15. Show that the effect of the rotation of the earth is to lessen the apparent weight of a body at the equator by $\frac{1}{289}$ of itself, the earth being assumed to be a sphere of radius 6336 km.
Show also that the apparent weight of a train at the equator, which is travelling east at the rate of 1.6 km per minute, is decreased by about 0.004 of itself.

16. A particle slides down a smooth curve, through a vertical height h, and thus acquires sufficient velocity to run completely round the inside of a vertical circle of radius r (as in the centrifugal railway); prove that $2h$ must be greater than $5r$.

17. In the experiment of Art. 151 the spheres are of equal mass and the lengths of the strings attached to them are equal; the first descends through an arc whose

chord is x, and the second ascends through an arc whose chord is y; show that the coefficient of restitution is $\frac{2y - x}{x}$.

18. A small ball is tied to one end of an inelastic string the other end of which is attached to a fixed point O. It is held, with the string tight, at a point which is 0.15 m above O and then let fall; if the length of the string be 0.3 m, find its velocity immediately after the string again becomes tight and the height above O to which it subsequently rises.

19. A particle is projected along the inner surface of smooth vertical circle of radius a, its velocity at the lowest point being $\frac{1}{5}\sqrt{95ga}$; show that it will leave the circle at an angular distance $\cos^{-1}\frac{3}{5}$ from the highest point and that its velocity then is $\frac{1}{5}\sqrt{15ga}$.

20. A bullet of mass 200 grammes is moving with a horizontal velocity of 400 metres per second; it hits the centre of a face of a cube of wood, of mass 20 kilogrammes, which is suspended by a string, and becomes embedded in it. Through what height does the wood move before coming to rest?

21. A box of sand, of mass 907 kg, is suspended by two equal vertical cords each 2.438 metres long and a shot whose mass is 9.07 kg is fired into it in a horizontal direction passing through its centre of gravity and remains embedded; if the centre of gravity of the box recoils through a circular arc the length of whose chord is 183 cm, show that the velocity of the shot was 370 metres per sec.

In general, if m and M be the masses of the bullet and box of sand, l be the length of each vertical cord, and k be the chord of recoil, the velocity of the shot is $\frac{M + m}{m} k \cdot \sqrt{\frac{g}{l}}$.

[We can thus find the velocity of any bullet. We have only to determine experimentally the value of k.]

11

Simple Harmonic Motion, Pendulums

152. Theorem. *If a point Q describe a circle with uniform angular velocity, and if P be always the foot of the perpendicular drawn from Q upon a fixed diameter AOA′ of the circle, show that the acceleration of P is directed towards the centre, O, of the circle and varies as the distance of P from O, and find the velocity of P and its time of describing any space.*

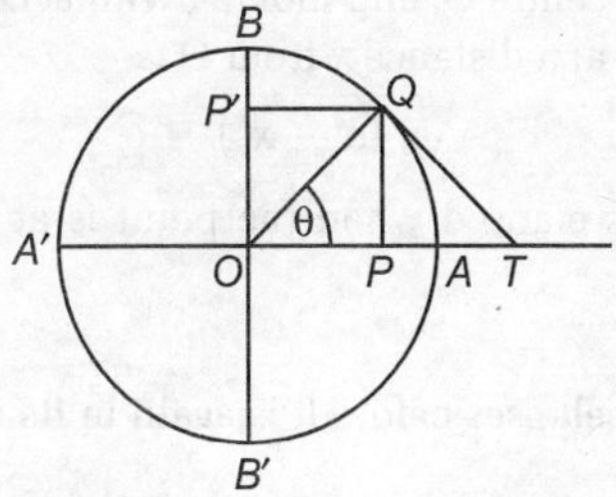

Let a be the radius of the circle, and let the angle QOA be θ. Draw QT the tangent at Q to meet OA in T.

Let ω be the constant angular velocity with which the point Q describes the circle.

Since P is always at the foot of the perpendicular to AA' drawn from Q, its velocity and acceleration are the same as the resolved parts, parallel to AO, of the velocity and acceleration of Q.

By Art. 135, Cor. I., the acceleration of Q is $a\omega^2$ towards O.

Hence the acceleration of P along $PO = a\omega^2 \cos\theta = \omega^2 \cdot OP$, and therefore varies as the distance of P from the centre of the circle.

Also the velocity of P

$$= a\omega \cos QTO = a\omega \sin\theta = \omega . PQ = \omega\sqrt{a^2 - x^2} \qquad ...(1),$$

where OP is x.

This velocity is zero at A and A', and greatest at O.

Also the acceleration vanishes, and changes its sign, as the point P passes through O.

The point P therefore moves from rest at A, has its greatest velocity at O, comes to rest again at A', and then retraces its path to A.

Also the time in which P describes any distance AP

$$= \text{time in which } Q \text{ describes the arc } AQ$$

$$= \frac{\theta}{\omega} = \frac{1}{\omega} \cos^{-1}\left(\frac{x}{a}\right) \qquad ...(2).$$

Hence the time from A to $A' = \frac{1}{\omega} \cos^{-1}(-1) = \frac{\pi}{\omega}$.

Also the time from A to A' and back again to A

$$= \frac{2\pi}{\omega} \qquad ...(3).$$

153. Simple Harmonic Motion. Def. *If a point move in a straight line so that its acceleration is always directed towards, and varies as its distance from, a fixed point in the straight line, the point is said to move with simple harmonic motion.*

The point P in the previous article moves with simple harmonic motion.

From the results (1), (2) and (3) of the previous article we see, by equating ω^2 to μ, that if a point move with simple harmonic motion, starting from rest at a distance a from the fixed centre O, and moving with acceleration μ. OP, then

(1) its velocity when at a distance x from O is

$$\sqrt{\mu\,(a^2 - x^2)},$$

(2) the time that has elapsed when the point is at a distance x from O is $\frac{1}{\sqrt{\mu}} \cos^{-1} \frac{x}{a}$,

and (3) the time that elapses before it is again in its initial position is $\frac{2\pi}{\sqrt{\mu}}$.

The range, OA or OA', of the moving point on either side of the centre O is called the **Amplitude** of the motion.

The time that elapses from any instant till the instant in which the moving point is again moving through the same position with the same velocity and direction is called the **Periodic Time** of the motion.

It will be noted that **the periodic time,** $\frac{2\pi}{\sqrt{\mu}}$, **is independent of the amplitude of the motion.**

154. From the result (2) of the previous article, it follows that, if t be the time the moving point takes to describe the distance from rest at a to the distance x, then

$$x = a \cos(\sqrt{\mu}\, t)$$

From (1) it then follows that the velocity v

$$= \sqrt{\mu\,[a^2 - a^2 \cos^2(\sqrt{\mu}\, t)]}$$

$$= a\sqrt{\mu} \sin(\sqrt{\mu}\, t)$$

154. (a) The results of simple Harmonic Motion of the previous articles can also be derived by use of calculus.

Let x be the distance OP of the particle from O at any time t; and let the acceleration at this distance be μx.

The equation of motion is then

$$\frac{d^2 x}{dt^2} = -\mu x \qquad \text{...(1).}$$

We have a negative sign on the right-hand side because $\frac{d^2 x}{dt^2}$ is the acceleration in the direction of x increasing, i.e., in the direction OP; whilst μx is the acceleration towards O, i.e., in the direction PO.]

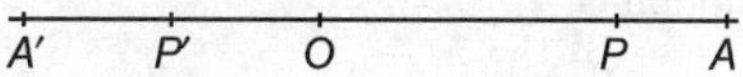

Multiplying by $2\frac{dx}{dt}$ and integrating, we have

$$\left(\frac{dx}{dt}\right)^2 = -\mu x^2 + C.$$

If OA be a, then $\frac{dx}{dt} = 0$, when $x = a$, so that

$$0 = -\mu a^2 + C, \text{ and}$$

$$\therefore \quad \left(\frac{dx}{dt}\right)^2 = \mu\,(a^2 - x^2)$$

$$\therefore \quad \frac{dx}{dt} = -\sqrt{\mu}\,\sqrt{a^2 - x^2} \qquad \text{...(2)}$$

[The negative sign is put on the right-hand side because the velocity is clearly negative so long as OP is positive and P is moving towards O.]

Hence, on integration,

$$t\sqrt{\mu} = -\int \frac{dx}{\sqrt{a^2 - x^2}} = \cos^{-1}\frac{x}{a} + c_1,$$

where $0 = \cos^{-1}\frac{a}{a} + c_1$, i.e., $c_1 = 0$, if the time be measured from the instant when the particle was at A.

$$\therefore \quad x = a\cos\sqrt{\mu}\,t \qquad \text{...(3).}$$

When the particle arrives at O, x is zero; and then, by (2), the velocity $= -a\sqrt{\mu}$. The particle thus passes through O and immediately the acceleration alters its direction and tends to diminish the velocity; also the velocity is destroyed on the left-hand side of O as rapidly as it was produced on the right-hand side; hence the particle comes to rest at a point A' such that OA and OA' are equal. It then retraces its path, passes through O, and again is instantaneously at rest at A. The whole motion of the particle is thus an oscillation from A to A' and back, continually repeated over and over again.

The time from A to O is obtained by putting x equal to zero in (3). This gives $\cos(\sqrt{\mu}\,t) = 0$, i.e., $t = \frac{\pi}{2\sqrt{\mu}}$.

The time from A to A' and back again, i.e., the time of a complete oscillation, is four times this, and therefore $= \frac{2\pi}{\sqrt{\mu}}$.

This result is independent of the distance a, i.e., is independent of the distance from the centre at which the particle started. It depends solely on the quantity which is equal to the acceleration at unit distance from the centre.

154. (b). A particle of mass m moves in a straight line under a force mn^2 (distance) towards a fixed point in the straight line and under a small resistance to its motion equal to $m \cdot \mu$ (velocity); find the motion.

The equation of motion is

$$m \frac{d^2x}{dt^2} = -m \cdot n^2 x - m \cdot \mu \frac{dx}{dt}$$

i.e.,
$$\frac{d^2x}{dt^2} + \mu \frac{dx}{dt} + n^2 x = 0 \qquad \text{...(1).}$$

[This is clearly the equation of motion if the particle is moving so that x is increasing.

If as in the second figure the particle is moving so that x decreases, i.e., towards the left, the frictional resistance is towards the right, and equals $m \cdot \mu v$. But in this case $\frac{dx}{dt}$ is negative, so that the value of v is $-\frac{dx}{dt}$; the frictional resistance is thus $m\mu \left(-\frac{dx}{dt}\right) \to$. The equation of motion is then $m \frac{d^2x}{dt^2} = -mn^2 x + m\mu \left(-\frac{dx}{dt}\right)$, which again becomes (1).

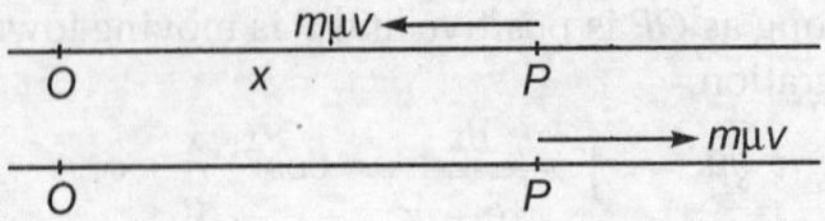

Hence (1) gives the motion for all positions of P to the right of O, irrespective of the direction in which P is moving.

Similarly it can be shown to be the equation of motion for positions of P to the left of O, whatever be the direction in which P is moving.]

To solve (1), put $x = L e^{pt}$, and we have

$$p^2 + \mu p + n^2 = 0,$$

Giving
$$p = -\frac{\mu}{2} \pm i \sqrt{n^2 - \frac{\mu^2}{4}}$$

$$\therefore \quad x = e^{-\frac{\mu}{2}t} \left[L e^{\sqrt{n^2 - \frac{\mu^2}{4}}\, it} + L e^{-\sqrt{n^2 - \frac{\mu^2}{4}}\, it} \right],$$

i.e.,
$$x = Ae^{-\frac{\mu}{2}t} \cos\left[\sqrt{n^2 - \frac{\mu^2}{4}}\, t + B\right] \qquad \text{...(2),}$$

where A and B are arbitrary constants.

If μ be small, then $Ae^{-\frac{\mu}{2}t}$ is a *slowly* varying quantity, so that (2) approximately represents a simple harmonic motion of period $2\pi \div \sqrt{n^2 - \frac{\mu^2}{4}}$, whose amplitude, $Ae^{-\frac{\mu}{2}t}$, is a slowly decreasing quantity. Such a motion is called a *damped* oscillation and μ measures the damping.

This period depends on the square of μ, so that, to the first order of approximation, this small frictional resistance has no effect on the period of the motion. Its effect is chiefly seen in the decreasing amplitude of the motion, which $= A\left(1 - \frac{\mu}{2}t\right)$ when squares of μ are neglected, and therefore depends on the first power of μ.

Such a vibration as the above is called a free vibration. It is the vibration of a particle which moves under the action of no external periodic force.

If μ be not small compared with n, the motion cannot be so simply represented, but for all values of μ, $\angle 2n$, the equation (2) gives the motion.

From (2) we have, on differentiating, that $\dot{x} = 0$ when

$$\tan\left[\sqrt{n^2 - \frac{\mu^2}{4}}\,t + B\right] = -\frac{\mu}{\sqrt{4n^2 - \mu^2}} = \tan\alpha\,(\text{say})\ (3),$$

giving solutions of the form

$$\sqrt{n^2 - \frac{\mu^2}{4}}\,t + B = \alpha,\ \pi + \alpha,\ 2\pi + \alpha, \ldots$$

Hence $\dot{x}$ is zero, that is the velocity vanishes, at the ends of periods of time differing by $\pi \div \sqrt{n^2 - \frac{\mu^2}{4}}$.

The times of oscillation thus still remain constant, though they are greater than when there is no frictional resistance.

If the successive values of t obtained from (3) are $t_1, t_2, t_3, \ldots$ then the corresponding values of (2) are

$$Ae^{-\frac{\mu}{2}t_1}\cos\alpha,\ -At^{-\frac{\mu}{2}t_2}\cos\alpha,\ Ae^{-\frac{\mu}{2}t_3}\cos\alpha, \ldots$$

so that the amplitudes of the oscillations form a decreasing GP whose common ratio

$$= e^{-\frac{\mu}{2}(t_2 - t_1)} = e^{-\mu\frac{\pi}{2} \div \sqrt{n^2 - \frac{\mu^2}{4}}}.$$

If $\mu > 2n$, the form of the solution changes; for now

$$p = -\frac{\mu}{2} \pm \sqrt{\frac{\mu^2}{4} - n^2}$$

and the general solution is

$$x = e^{-\frac{\mu t}{2}} \left[L e^{\sqrt{\left(\frac{\mu^2}{4} - n^2\right)}\, t} + L e^{-\sqrt{\left(\frac{\mu^2}{4} - n^2\right)}\, t} \right]$$

$$= e^{-\frac{\mu t}{2}} A_1 \cos \left[\sqrt{\left(\frac{\mu^2}{4} - n^2\right)} \cdot t + B_1 \right]$$

In this case the motion is no longer oscillatory. If $\mu = 2n$, we have by the rules of Differential Equations

$$x = L e^{-nt} + \underset{\gamma = 0}{L}\; t\, M e^{-(n+\gamma)t}$$

$$= L e^{-nt} + \underset{\gamma = 0}{L}\; t\, M e^{-nt} (1 - \gamma t + \text{squares})$$

$$= L_1 e^{-nt} + M_1 t e^{-nt} = e^{-nt} (L_1 + M_1 t)$$

155. Examples of Simple Harmonic Motion. This motion is of frequent occurrence in Physical and Mechanical problems.

It is the motion of a point of a tuning fork, and of a point in a violin string when the string is plucked sideways. The motion of a pendulum (Art. 158) is simple harmonic when the angle through which it moves is small; so also is that of a mass tied to an elastic string or a spring and allowed to oscillate up and down in a vertical line. The motion of the revolving mass of a Conical Pendulum (Art. 140) as seen from a distant point in its plane is simple harmonic; and also that of Jupiter's satellites when observed from a distant point in their plane.

Generally the motion of all elastic bodies, in which the force brought into play is proportional to the displacement, follows the same law.

The expression Simple Harmonic Motion is often shortened into S.H.M.

156. Ex. 1. *A point moves with simple harmonic motion whose period is 4 seconds; if it starts from rest at a distance* 1.2 m *from the centre of its path, find the tme that elapses before it has described* 0.6 m *and the velocity it has then acquired.*

If the acceleration be μ times the distance, we have $\frac{2\pi}{\sqrt{\mu}} = 4$,

$$\therefore \qquad \mu = \left(\frac{\pi}{2}\right)^2.$$

When the point has described 0.6 m; it is then at a distance of 0.6 m from the centre of its motion.

Hence, by Art. 153 (2), the time that has elapsed

$$= \frac{1}{\sqrt{\mu}} \cos^{-1} \frac{x}{a} = \frac{1}{x/2} \cos^{-4} \left(\frac{0.6}{1.2}\right) = \frac{2}{\pi} \times \frac{\pi}{3} = \frac{2}{3} \text{ second.}$$

Also, by Art. 153 (1), the velocity it has acquired

$$= \sqrt{\mu\,(a^2 - x^2)} = \sqrt{\left(\frac{\pi}{2}\right)^2 (1.2)^2 - (0.6)^2} = \frac{3\pi\sqrt{3}}{10} \text{ m per second.}$$

Ex. 2. *A point starts from rest at a distance of 4.8 m from the centre of its path and moves with simple harmonic motion; if in its initial position the acceleration be 1.2 m/sec. units, find (1) its velocity when at a distance of 2.4 m from the centre and when passing through the centre, and (2) its periodic time.*

(1) Let the acceleration be μ times the distance.

Then $$\mu \times 4.8 = 1.2, \text{ i.e., } \mu = \frac{1}{4}$$

Hence by Art. 153 (1), its velocity when at a distance of 2.4 m from the centre

$$= \sqrt{\frac{1}{4}(4.8^2 - 2.4^2)} = \frac{6\sqrt{3}}{5} \text{ m per second.}$$

Also its velocity when passing through the centre

$$= \sqrt{\frac{1}{4} \cdot 4 \cdot 8^2} = 2.4 \text{ m per second.}$$

(2) Its periodic time $= \dfrac{2\pi}{\sqrt{\mu}} = 4\pi = \text{about } 12\dfrac{4}{7}$ seconds.

Ex. 3. *A light spiral spring, whose unstretched length is l cm and whose modulus of elasticity is the weight of n grammes, is suspended by one end and has a mass of m grammes attached to the other; show that the time of a vertical oscillation of the mass is*

$$2\pi\sqrt{\frac{m}{n} \cdot \frac{l}{g}}$$

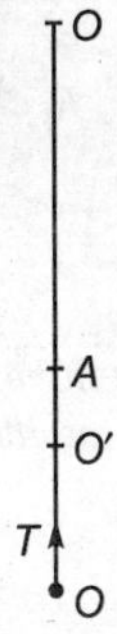

Let O be the fixed end of the spring, OA its position when unstretched. When the particle is at P, where $OP = x$, let T be the tension of the spring. Then, by Hooke's Law,

$$T = \lambda\,\frac{x - l}{l} = ng\,\frac{x - l}{l}.$$

Hence the resultant upward force on $P = T - mg$

$$= ng\,\frac{x - l}{l} - mg = \frac{ng}{l}\left[x - \frac{m + n}{n}\,l\right]$$

Let O' be a point on the vertical through O such that

$$OO' = \frac{m + n}{n}\,l.$$

Hence the resultant upward force on P

$$= \frac{ng}{l}\,[OP - OO'] = \frac{ng}{l} \cdot O'P.$$

Hence the upward acceleration of $P = \dfrac{n}{m}\dfrac{g}{l}\,O'P$, i.e., its motion is simple harmonic about O' as centre, and its time of oscillation, by Art. 153,

$$= 2\pi \div \sqrt{\frac{n}{m}\frac{g}{l}} = 2\pi\sqrt{\frac{ml}{ng}}$$

It will be noted that O' is the point where the mass would hang at rest. For, if it were placed at rest at O', the upward tension would

$$= ng\,\frac{OO' - l}{l} = ng\left[\frac{\frac{m + n}{n}\,l - l}{l}\right] = mg,$$

and would therefore just balance its weight.

Ex. 4. *A particle moving with simple harmonic motion in a straight line has velocities v_1, v_2 at distances x_1, x_2 from the centre of its path. Show that if T be the period of its motion,*

$$T = 2\pi \sqrt{\frac{x_1^2 - x_2^2}{v_2^2 - v_1^2}}.$$

Let x be the distance of the particle from the centre of motion at any time t; and let the acceleration at this distance be μx.

The equation of motion is then

$$\frac{d^2 x}{dt^2} = -\mu x \qquad ...(1).$$

Integrating (1), we get,

$$\left(\frac{dx}{dt}\right)^2 = \mu\,(a^2 - x^2), \qquad ...(2),$$

where a is the amplitude.

Thus we have

$$v_1^2 = \mu\,(a^2 - x_1^2)$$

and

$$v_2^2 = \mu\,(a^2 - x_2^2)$$

$\therefore$

$$n_2^2 - v_1^2 = \mu\,(x_1^2 - x_2^2).$$

Hence the periodic time is

$$T = \frac{2\pi}{\sqrt{\mu}} = 2\pi \sqrt{\frac{x_1^2 - x_2^2}{v_2^2 - v_1^2}}.$$

Ex. 5. *In a S.H.M. the distances of a particle from the middle point of its path at three consecutive seconds and observed to be x, y, z. Show that the time of complete oscillation is*

$$\frac{2\pi}{\cos^{-1}\left(\frac{x + 2}{2y}\right)}.$$

Let x be the distance of the particle from the centre of motion at any time t.

The equation of motion is

$$\frac{d^2 x}{dt^2} = -\mu x \qquad ...(1)$$

The solution of (1) is

$$x = a \cos(\sqrt{\mu}\, t + c) \qquad ...(2)$$

So we have

$$y = a \cos(\sqrt{\mu}\,(t + 1) + c) \qquad ...(3)$$

and

$$z = a \cos(\sqrt{\mu}\,(t + 2) + c) \qquad ...(4)$$

$\therefore$

$$x + z = 2a \cos(\sqrt{\mu}\,(t + 1) + c) \cos \sqrt{\mu}$$

or

$$x + z = 2y \cos \sqrt{\mu}$$

$$\therefore \qquad \sqrt{\mu} = \cos^{-1}\frac{x+z}{2y}$$

Hence the time of a complete oscillation is

$$\frac{2\pi}{\sqrt{\mu}} = \frac{2\pi}{\cos^{-1}\frac{x+z}{2y}}.$$

Examples. XXVI.

1. A particle moves in a straight line with simple harmonic motion find the time of an oscillation from rest to rest when
(1) the acceleration at a distance 60 cm is 120 cm/sec. units;
(2) the acceleration at a distance 7.5 cm is 270 cm/sec. units;
(3) the acceleration at a distance 30 cm is $30\pi^2$/sec. units.
2. In each of the cases in the previous example, find the velocity when the point is passing through the centre of its path, the amplitudes of the motion being respectively 60 cm, 7.5 cm, and 30 cm.
3. A particle moves in a straight line with simple harmonic motion, and its periods of oscillations are (1) 2, (2) $\frac{1}{16}$, and (3) π seconds, respectively; the amplitude of its motion in each case is 30 cm; find the velocity of the particle when moving through the centre of its path.
4. A point, moving with S.H.M., has a velocity of 120 cm per second when passing through the centre of its path, and its period is π seconds; what is its velocity when it has described 30 cm from the position in which its velocity is zero?
5. A point moves with S.H.M.; if, when at distances of 90 and 1200 cm from the centre of its path, its velocities are 240 and 180 cm per second respectively, find its period and its acceleration when at its greatest distance from the centre.
6. A mass of one gramme vibrates through a millimetre on each side of the middle point of its path 256 times per second; assuming its motion to be simple harmonic, show that the maximum force upon the particle is $\frac{1}{10}(512\pi)^2$ dynes.
7. A horizontal shelf moves vertically with S.H.M., whose complete period is one second; find the greatest amplitude in centimetres that it can have, so that objects resting on the shelf may always remain in contact with it.
8. A mass of 5.44 kg is hanging by a light spiral spring which stretches 25.4 mm for each 0.454 kg/wt. of tension. If the upper end of the spring be instantaneously raised 101.6 mm and then held fast, find the amplitude and period of the subsequent motion of the mass.
9. A weight is attached to the lower end of a light spiral spring whose upper end is fixed and is released. If it oscillates in a vertical line through a space of six inches, what is the period of its oscillation?
10. An elastic string, to the middle point of which a particle is attached, is stretched to twice its natural length and placed on a smooth horizontal table, and its ends are then fixed. The particle is then displaced in the direction of the string; find the period of oscillation.

11. A rod AB is in motion so that the end B moves with uniform speed u in a circle whose centre is C, whilst the end A moves in a straight line passing through C. If $AB = BC = a$, and $AC = x$, show that the velocity of A is $u\dfrac{\sqrt{4a^2 - x^2}}{a}$, and that it moves with simple harmonic motion.
[Hence we have a method of obtaining practically a simple harmonic motion. Let CB be a revolving crank and BA a connecting rod, of length equal to CB, attached to a point A, which, as in the case of the piston of a steam engine, is compelled to move in a straight line CA. Then the motion of A is simple harmonic.]

12. A body performing S.H.M. in a straight line OPQ has its velocity zero when at points P and Q whose distances from O and x and y respectively, and has velocity v when half-way between them. Show that the complete period is $\dfrac{\pi\,(y - x)}{V}$.

13. In a S.H.M., if f be the acceleration and v the velocity at any instant, and T is the periodic time, then $f^2T^2 + 4\pi^2v^2$ is constant.

14. A particle of mass m moves on straight line under an attraction mn^2x towards a point O on the line, where x is the distance from O. Show that, if $x = a$ and $\dot{x} = u$ when $t = 0$, then at time t,

$$x = a\cos nt + \frac{u}{n}\sin nt.$$

15. A particle rests in equilibrium under the attraction of two centres of force which attract directly as the distance, their attractions per unit of mass at unit distance being μ and μ'. The particle is displaced towards one of them; show that its motion is oscillatory, of period $\dfrac{2\pi}{\sqrt{\mu + \mu'}}$.

157. *Extension to motion in a curve.*

Suppose that a moving point P is describing a portion, AOA', of a curve of any shape, starting from rest at A and moving so that its tangential acceleration is always along the arc towards O and equal to $\mu \cdot$ arc OP, then the propositions of Art. 153 are true with slight modifications.

For let $O'B$ be a straight line equal in length to the arc OA', and let P' be a point describing it with acceleration $\mu \cdot O'P'$; also let $O'P' =$ arc OP.

Since the acceleration of P' in its path is always the same as that of P, the velocities acquired in the same time are the same, and the times of describing the same distances are the same.

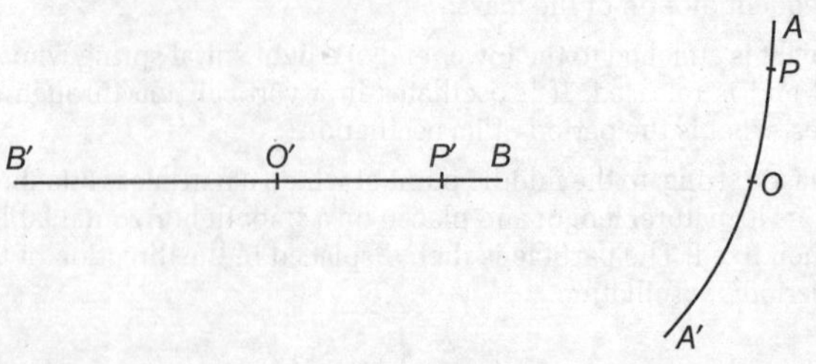

Hence
(1) The velocity of P = the velocity of P'

$$= \sqrt{\mu\,(O'B^2 - O'P'^2)} = \sqrt{\mu\,\{(\text{arc } OA)^2 - (\text{arc } OP)^2\}},$$

(2) The time from A to P = time from B to P'

$$= \frac{1}{\sqrt{\mu}} \cos^{-1}\left(\frac{O'P'}{O'B}\right) = \frac{1}{\sqrt{\mu}} \cos^{-1}\left(\frac{\text{arc } OP}{\text{arc } OA}\right),$$

and (3) The time from A to A' and back again $= \dfrac{2\pi}{\sqrt{\mu}}$.

Pendulums.

158. Simple Pendulum. A particle tied to one end of a string, the other end of which is fixed, and which oscillates in a vertical circle having the fixed point as centre, is called a simple pendulum.

The time of oscillation depends on the angle through which the string swings on each side of the vertical.

If however this angle of oscillation be small, we shall show in the next article that the time of oscillation of the pendulum is approximately constant.

159. Theorem. *If a particle be tied by a string to a fixed point, and allowed to oscillate through a* **small** *angle about the vertical position, show that the time of a complete oscillation is* $2\pi\sqrt{\dfrac{l}{g}}$, *where l is the length of the string.*

Let O be the fixed point, OA a vertical line, AP a portion of the arc described by the particle, and let the angle AOP be θ.

If PT be the tangent at P meeting OA in T, the acceleration of the bob along PT

$$= g \sin\theta$$
$$= g\theta, \text{ approximately, if } \theta \text{ be small}$$
$$= \frac{g}{l} \times \text{arc } AP$$

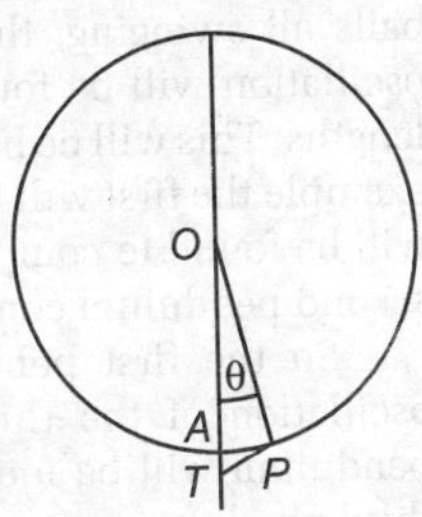

The acceleration along the tangent to the path therefore varies as the actual distance from the lowest point.

It follows that the motion is harmonic and hence, by Art. 157 (3), the time of a complete oscillation is independent of the extent of the oscillation, and equals

$$\frac{2\pi}{\sqrt{\dfrac{g}{l}}}, \quad \text{i.e., } 2\pi\sqrt{\frac{l}{g}}$$

The first discovery of this principle of the time of swinging of a pendulum is said to have been made by Galileo about the year 1582; he observed that the great bronze lamp which hangs from the roof of the cathedral at Pisa seemed to have a uniform time of swing, whatever be the arc through which it moved, and he verified the fact by counting the beats of his pulse.

Ex. *Find the length of a pendulum which will oscillate* 56 *times in* 55 *seconds.*

The time of oscillation is $\frac{55}{56}$ seconds. Hence, if l be the length of the pendulum, we have

$$\frac{55}{56} = \pi\sqrt{\frac{l}{g}} = \frac{22}{7}\sqrt{\frac{l}{9.8}};$$

$$\therefore \qquad \sqrt{\frac{l}{9.8}} = \frac{5}{16}$$

$$\therefore \qquad l = 9.8 \times \frac{25}{256} = \frac{245}{256} \text{ m} = 95.7 \text{cm nearly.}$$

160. Experimental Verification. The important result of the previous article may be easily verified to a fair degree of accuracy. We cannot actually make use of the "particle" and the "massless string" of the mathematical demonstration; but a small sphere, made of brass or other metal, with a hook firmly fastened to it and a light strong silk thread will make a very good approximation.

First, *to show that the time varies as the square root of the length.*

Take several such spheres, and to them attach threads the other ends of which are attached to fixed points; for example by passing the threads through eyes screwed into a fixed horizontal bar, and then tieing their other ends to some convenient support. Adjust the lengths so that the distances measured from the centre of the spheres to the points from which the strings swing are in the ratios of 1, 4, 9,1 6, ... [For example, let the lengths be 6 in., 2 ft, 4 ft 6 in., 8 ft ...] Start the balls all swinging, through small angles, at the same instant. Their times of oscillation will be found to be as 1, 2, 3, 4, ... i.e., as the square roots of their lengths. This will be best seen if the observer sets only two swinging at a time. For example the first will be found to swing in half the time of the second, and hence will be found to complete every second complete swing at the same time as the second pendulum completes its swing.

So the first pendulum will be found to oscillate three times for each oscillation of the third pendulum, and hence every oscillation of the first pendulum will be found to end simultaneously with successive swings of the third pendulum.

Similarly for any other case.

Secondly, *to show that the time of oscillation is independent, approximately, of the material of which the bob is made.*

Take spheres, of the same size approximately, but made of different materials, provided that these materials are not made of very light substances such as cork. As in the first experiment attach them by strings of the same length and set them all swinging together. This may be done by pushing the spheres all sideways to the same extent by means of a board, and then sharply withdrawing the board. The pendulums will then be found to swing in the same time for a large number of oscillations provided the lengths of the strings have been carefully adjusted so as to be equal. After some time the spheres, made of the lighter material, will be found to lag behind the others; this is because the resistance of the air has more effect on the lighter than on the heavier spheres.

Thirdly, *to find the value of g by means of a simple pendulum.*

Take one of the spheres and adjust the length of its string to a convenient distance, say about two feet. Carefully measure the distance from the point of suspension of the silk thread to the centre of the sphere. Set the sphere swinging and find the time T of a complete oscillation. This is best done by observing the time of (say) 40 observations and dividing the result by 40. [An ordinary watch with a seconds hand will give sufficiently accurate results.]

Then in the formula

$$T = 2\pi\sqrt{\frac{l}{g}}$$

of Art. 159, we now know both l and T, so that the value of g

$$= 4\pi^2 \frac{l}{T^2}$$

By the use of a logarithm Table, or by ordinary calculation, we now easily obtain the value of g correct to the second place of decimals in foot-seconds units.

Similarly, if we measure l in centimetres, we shall get the value of g in the C.G.S. system.

161. Seconds Pendulum. A seconds pendulum is one which vibrates from rest to rest (i.e., makes half a *complete* oscillation) in one second.

Hence, if l be its length, we have

$$1 = \pi\sqrt{\frac{l}{g}}.$$

$$\therefore \qquad l = \frac{g}{\pi^2} \text{length units}$$

Since, g varies at different points of the earth's surface, we see that the length of the seconds pendulum is not the same at all points of the earth.

For an approximate value, putting $g = 9.8$ and $\pi = \frac{22}{7}$, we have

$$l = 0.993 \text{ m} = 99.3 \text{ cm}.$$

If we use the F.P.S. system we have, by putting $g = 32.2$, $l = 39.12$ inches.

For the latitude of London more accurate values are 39.13929 ... inches and 99.413 ... centimetres.

Examples. XXVII.

[In the following examples, π may be taken to be $\frac{22}{7}$]

1. If $g = 981$, what is the length of a pendulum vibrating in 2.5 seconds?
2. The time of a complete vibration at a given place of a pendulum 64 metres long is 16 seconds; show that the corresponding value of g is 987 cm/sec. units.
3. A pendulum, 91.41 cm long, is observed to make 700 oscillations in 671 seconds; find approximately the value of g.
4. Given that the length of a seconds pendulum is 99.3 cm, find the lengths of the pendulums which will vibrate in (1) half a second, (2) one quarter of a second, (3) 2 seconds.

5. How many oscillations will a pendulum, of length 53.41 centimetres, make in 242 seconds at a place where g is 981?
6. Show that a pendulum, 1584 metres in length, would oscillate in 39 seconds nearly.
7. A pendulum, of length 94.5 cm, makes 183 beats in three minutes at a certain place; find the acceleration due to gravity there.
8. How many oscillations will a pendulum of length 121.9 cm, make in one day?
9. A pendulum, 137.16 metres long, has been suspended in the Eiffel Tower; prove that it makes a complete oscillation in about 23.57 seconds.

162. The result of Art. 159, although not mathematically accurate, is very approximately so. If the angle α through which the pendulum swings on each side of the vertical be 5°, the result is within one two thousandth part of the accurate result, so that a pendulum which beats seconds for very small oscillations would lose about 40 seconds per day, if made to vibrate through 5° on each side of the vertical.

163. The simple pendulum of which we have spoken is idealistic. In practice, a pendulum consists of a wire whose mass, although small, is not zero and a bob at the end which is not a particle. Whatever be the shape of the pendulum, the simple pendulum which oscillates in the same time as itself is called its **simple equivalent pendulum.**

The discussion of the connection between a rigid body and its simple equivalent pendulum is not within the range of this book. We may, however, mention that a uniform rod, of small section, swings about one end in the same times as a simple pendulum of two-thirds its length.

164. *Acceleration due to gravity.* Newton discovered, as a fundamental law of nature, that every particle attracts every other particle with a force which varies directly as the product of the masses and inversely as the square of the distance between them.

From this fact it can be shown, as in any treatise dealing with Attractions, that a sphere attracts any particle *outside* itself just as if the whole mass of the sphere were collected at its centre, and hence that the acceleration caused by its attraction varies inversely as the square of the distance of the particle from the centre.

Similarly the attraction on a particle *inside* the earth can be shown to vary directly as its distance from the centre of the earth.

Hence, if g_1 be the value of gravity at a height h above the earth's surface, g the value at the surface, and r the earth's radius, then $g_1 : g :: \frac{1}{(r+h)^2} : \frac{1}{r^2}$,

so that
$$g_1 = g\left(\frac{r}{r+h}\right)^2.$$

So, if g_2 be the value at the bottom of a mine of depth d, we have $g_2 = g\,\frac{r-d}{r}$.

The value of g is therefore greater at the earth's surface than either outside or inside the earth.

165. We shall now investigate the effect on the time of oscillation of a simple pendulum due to a *small* change in the value of g, and also the effect due to a *small* change in its length.

If a pendulum, of length l, makes n complete oscillations in a given time, show that

(1) *If g be changed to g + G, the number of oscillations gained is* $\frac{n}{2}\frac{G}{g}$,

(2) *If the pendulum be taken to a height h above the earth's surface, the, number of oscillations lost is* $n\frac{h}{r}$, *where r is the radius of the earth,*

(3) *If it be taken to the bottom of a mine of depth d, the number lost is* $\frac{n}{2}\frac{d}{r}$,

(4) *If its length be changed to l + L, the number lost is* $\frac{n}{2}\frac{L}{l}$.

Let T be the original time of oscillation, T' the new time of oscillation, and n' the new number of oscillations in the given time, so that

$$nT = n'T'$$

(1) In this case $T = 2\pi\sqrt{\frac{l}{g}}$ and $T' = 2\pi\sqrt{\frac{l}{g+G}}$

Hence $\frac{n'}{n} = \frac{T}{T'} = \sqrt{1+\frac{G}{g}} = 1 + \frac{1}{2}\frac{G}{g}$, approximately,

(by Binomial Theorem, squares of $\frac{G}{g}$ being neglected).

Hence, the number of oscillations gained $= n' - n = \frac{n}{2}\frac{G}{g}$.

So, if g becomes g – G, the number lost is $\frac{n}{2}\frac{G}{g}$.

(2) If $g - G$ be the value of gravity at a height h, we have

$$\frac{g-G}{g} = \frac{r^2}{(r+h)^2} = \left(\frac{1+h}{r}\right)^{-2} = 1 - \frac{2h}{r} \text{ approximately.}$$

Therefore, $G = g\frac{2h}{r}$, and hence, as in (1), the number of oscillations lost is $n\frac{h}{r}$.

(3) If $g - G$ be the value at a depth d, we have $g - G : g :: r - dgr$ so that the number of oscillations lost $= \frac{n}{2}\frac{G}{g} = \frac{n}{2}\frac{d}{r}$.

(4) When the length l of the pendulum is changed to $l + L$, we have

$$T = 2\pi\sqrt{\frac{l}{g}} \quad \text{and} \quad T' = 2\pi\sqrt{\frac{l+L}{g}}.$$

$$\frac{n'}{n} = \frac{T}{T'} = \left(1+\frac{L}{l}\right)^{-\frac{1}{2}} = 1 - \frac{1}{2}\frac{L}{l} \text{ approximately}$$

Hence the number of oscillations lost $= n - n' = \frac{n}{2}\frac{L}{l}$.

From this article it follows that the height of a mountain, or the depth of a mine, could be found by finding the number of oscillations lost by a pendulum which beats seconds on the surface of the earth.

166. Ex. 1. *A pendulum, which beats seconds at the surface of the earth, is carried to the top of a mountain 8 km high; find the number of seconds it will lose in a day, assuming the radius of the earth to be 6336 km.*

Let g and g_1 be the acceleration due to gravity at the sea-level and the top of the mountain respectively.

Then
$$g : g_1 :: \frac{1}{6336^2} : \frac{1}{6344^2}$$

$$\therefore \quad \frac{g}{g_1} = \left(\frac{6344}{6336}\right)^2 = \left(\frac{793}{792}\right)^2.$$

Since the pendulum beats seconds at the earth's surface, we have

$$1 = \pi\sqrt{\frac{l}{g}} \qquad ...(1).$$

Also, if T be the time of oscillation at the top of the mountain, we have

$$T = \pi\sqrt{\frac{l}{g_1}} \qquad ...(2).$$

Dividing (2) by (1), we have

$$T = \sqrt{\frac{g}{g_1}} = \frac{793}{792}$$

Hence the number of beats in a day at the top of the mountain

$$= \frac{86400}{T} = 86400 \times \frac{792}{793}$$

$$= 86400 \times \frac{1}{1 + \frac{1}{792}} = 86400\left(1 + \frac{1}{792}\right)^{-1}$$

$$= 86400\left(1 - \frac{1}{792}\right) \text{approximately} = 86400 - 109 \text{ nearly.}$$

Therefore the number of beats lost is 109.

Ex. 2. *A faulty seconds pendulum loses 20 seconds per day; find the required alteration in its length, so that it may keep correct time.*

The pendulum beats 86380 times in 86400 seconds, so that its time of oscillation is $\frac{8640}{8638}$ seconds. Hence, if l be its length,

$$\frac{8640}{8638} = \pi\sqrt{\frac{l}{g}} \qquad ...(1).$$

Let $l + x$ be the true length of the seconds pendulum at the place. Then

$$1 = \pi\sqrt{\frac{l + x}{g}} \qquad ...(2).$$

Subtracting the square of (1) from the square of (2), we have

$$1 - \left(\frac{8640}{8638}\right)^2 = \pi^2 \cdot \frac{x}{g};$$

$$\therefore\ x = -\frac{g}{\pi^2}\left[\left(\frac{8640}{8638}\right)^2 - 1\right]$$

$$= -\frac{g}{\pi^2}\left[\left(1 - \frac{2}{8640}\right)^{-2} - 1\right] = -\frac{980 \times 7^2}{22^2}\left[1 + \frac{4}{8640} - 1\right] \text{ approximately}$$

$$= -\frac{980 \times 49}{484} \cdot \frac{4}{8640} = -\frac{49 \times 49}{121 \times 432} \text{ cm} = 0.046 \text{ cm}$$

Hence the pendulum must be *shortened* by 0.046 cm.

167. *Verification of the law of gravity by means of the moon's motion.* We may show roughly the truth of the law of gravitation, by finding the time that the moon would take to travel round the earth, on the assumption that it is kept in its orbit by means of the earth's attraction.

Let f be the acceleration of the moon due to the earth's attraction; then, since the distance between the centres of the two bodies is roughly 60 times the earth's radius, we have $f : g :: \frac{1}{(60r)^2} : \frac{1}{r^2}$, so that $f = \frac{g}{3600}$.

Let v be the velocity of the moon round the earth so that, by Art. 135,

$$\frac{v^2}{60r} = f = \frac{g}{3600}$$

$$\therefore\qquad v^2 = \frac{gr}{60}.$$

Hence the periodic time of the moon

$$= 2\pi \times 60r \div v = 2\pi \cdot 60 \times \sqrt{\frac{60r}{g}} \text{ seconds.}$$

Taking the radius of the earth to be 4000 miles, and g as 32.2, this time is 27.4 days, and this is approximately the observed time of revolution.

Examples. XXVIII.

1. A pendulum which beats seconds at Greenwich, where $g = 981$, is taken to another place where it loses 20 seconds per day; find the value of g at the latter place.
2. A seconds pendulum which gains 10 seconds per day at one place, loses 10 seconds per day at another; compare the accelerations due to gravity at the two places.
3. Assuming the values of g m foot-second units at the equator and the north pole to be 977.6 and 982.5 respectively, find how many seconds per day would be gained at the north pole by a pendulum which would beat seconds at the equator.
4. A clock with a seconds pendulum loses 9 seconds per day; find roughly the required alteration in the length of the pendulum.
5. A clock gains give seconds per day; show how it may be made to keep correct time.

6. If a pendulum oscillating seconds be lengthened by its hundredth part, find the number of oscillations it will lose in a day.
7. A simple seconds pendulum is lengthened by 0.127 cm; find the number of seconds it will lose in 24 hours.
8. A simple pendulum performs 21 complete vibrations in 44 seconds; on shortening its length by 47.6875 centimetres it performs 21 complete vibrations in 33 seconds; find the value of g.
9. A simple seconds pendulum consists of a heavy ball suspended by a long and very fine iron wire; if the pendulum be correct at a temperature 0°C, find how many seconds it will gain, or lose, in 24 hours at a temperature of 20°C, given that the iron expands by 0.000233 of its length owing to this rise of temperature.
10. If a seconds pendulum loses 10 seconds per day at the bottom of a mine, find the depth of the mine and the number of seconds that the pendulum would lose when halfway down the mine.
11. A clock, which at the surface of the earth gains 10 seconds a day, loses 10 seconds a day when taken down a mine; compare the accelerations due to gravity at the top and bottom of the mine and finds its depths.
12. If a seconds pendulum be carried to the top of a mountain 805 metres high, how many seconds will it lose per day, assuming the earth's centre to be 6440 km from the foot of the mountain, and by how much must it be shortened so that it may beat seconds at the summit of the mountain?
13. Show that the height of a hill at the summit of which a second pendulum loses n beats in 24 hours is $\frac{220n}{3}$ metres.
14. A balloon ascends with a constant acceleration and reaches a height of 274 metres in one minute. Show that a pendulum clock, which has a seconds pendulum and is carried in the balloon, will gain at the rate of about 28 seconds per hour.
15. A cage-lift is descending with unit acceleration; show that a pendulum clock, which has a seconds pendulum and is carried with it, will lose at the rate of about 56 seconds per hour.
16. Show that a seconds pendulum would, if carried to the moon, oscillate in $2\frac{1}{4}$ seconds, assuming the mass of the earth to be 81 times that of the moon, and that the radius of the earth is 4 times that of the moon.
17. A railway train is moving uniformly in a circular curve at the rate of 97 km per hour, and in one of the carriages a seconds pendulum is observed to beat 121 times in 2 minutes. Show that the radius of the curve is about 402 metres.
18. A particle would take a time t to move down a straight tube from the surface of the earth (supposed to be a homogeneous sphere) to its centre; if gravity were to remain constant from the surface to the centre, it would take a time t'; show that

$$t : t' :: \pi : 2\sqrt{2}$$

19. A simple pendulum swings under gravity in such a manner that, when the string is vertical, the force which it exerts on the bob is twice its weight show that the greatest inclination of the string to the vertical is $\frac{\pi}{3}$.
20. A mass is hung on the end of a string 243.8 cm long and swings to and fro through a distance of 76.2 mm. Find approximately; the periodic time of the swing, the accelerations at the ends of the swing, and the velocity at the middle.

12 Units and Dimensions

168. WHEN we wish to state the magnitude of any concrete quantity we express it in terms of some unit of the same kind as itself, and we have to state,

(1) what is the unit we are employing, and

(2) what is the ratio of the quantity we are considering to that unit.

This latter ratio is called the *measure* of the quantity in terms of the unit. Thus, if we wish to express the height of a man, we may say that it is six feet. Here a foot is the unit and six is the measure. We might as well have said that he is 2 yards, or 72 inches high.

The measure will vary according to the unit we employ. The measure of any quantity multiplied into the unit employed is always the same (e.g., 2 yards = 6 feet = 72 inches).

Hence, if K and k' be the measures of a physical quantity when the units used are denoted by $[K]$ and $[K']$, we have

$$k\,[K] = k'\,[K'],$$

and hence
$$[K] : [K'] :: \frac{1}{k} : \frac{1}{k'},$$

So that, by the definition of variation, we have $[K] \propto \frac{1}{k'}$, i.e., *the unit in terms of which any quantity is measured varies inversely as the measure and conversely.*

169. A straight line possesses length only, and no breadth or thickness, and hence is said to be of one dimension in length.

An area possesses both length and breadth, but no thickness, and is said to be of two dimensions in length. The unit of area usually employed is that whose length and breadth are respectively equal to the unit of length. Hence if we have two different units of length in the ratio $\lambda : 1$, the two corresponding units of area are in the ratio $\lambda^2 : 1$, so that, if $[A]$ denote the unit of area and $[L]$ the unit of length, then

$$[A] \propto [L]^2$$

For example, 100 cm make 1 metre, but 10000 (i.e., 100^2) square cm make one square metre.

A volume possesses length, breadth and thickness and is said to be of three dimensions in length. The unit is that volume whose length, breadth and thickness are each equal to the unit of length. As in the case of areas, it follows that, if $[V]$ denotes the unit of volume, then

$$[V] \propto [L]^3.$$

Since the units of area and volume depend on that of length, they are said to be **derived units,** whilst the unit of length is called a fundamental unit.

Another fundamental unit is the unit of time, usually denoted by $[T]$. A period of time is of one dimension in time.

The third fundamental unit is the unit of mass, denoted by $[M]$. Any mass is said to be of one dimension in mass.

These are the three fundamental units; all other units depend on these three, and are therefore called derived units.

170. In Art. 9 we defined the unit of velocity to be the velocity of a point which describes the unit of length in the unit of time. Hence if the unit of length, or the unit of time, or both, be altered, the unit of velocity will, in general, be altered.

For example, let the units of length and time be changed from a metre and a second to 2 m and 3 seconds. The new unit of velocity is the velocity of a point which describes 2 m in 3 seconds, i.e., which describes $\frac{2}{3}$ m in one second, i.e., is equal to $\frac{2}{3}$ rds of the original unit of velocity.

Similarly, since a body is moving with unit acceleration when the change in its velocity per unit of time is equal to the unit of velocity, it follows that the unit of acceleration depends on the units of velocity and time, i.e., it depends ultimately upon the units of length and time.

Again, the unit of force is, by Art. 61, that force which in the unit of mass produces the unit of acceleration. Hence the unit of force is altered when either the unit of mass, or the unit of acceleration, or both, are altered. Hence the unit of force depends ultimately upon the units of length, time, and mass.

171. Theorem. *To show that the unit of velocity varies directly as the unit of length, and inversely as the unit of time.*

In one system let the units of length, time, and velocity be denoted by $[L]$, $[T]$, and $[V]$, and in a second system by $[L']$, $[T']'$, and $[V']$; also let

$$[L'] = m\,[L], \text{ and } [T'] = n\,[T].$$

Then a body is said to be moving with the original unit of velocity

when it describes a length $[L]$ in time $[T]$;

therefore with velocity $m\,[V]$

when it describes a length $m\,[L]$ in time $[T]$;

therefore with velocity $\frac{m}{n}\,[V]$

when it describes a length $m\,[L]$ in time $n\,[T]$;

therefore with velocity $\frac{m}{n}\,[V]$

when it describes a length $[L']$ in time $[T']$.

But it is moving with velocity $[V']$ when it describes a length $[L']$ in time $[T']$.

$$\therefore \qquad [V'] = \frac{m}{n}[V]$$

$$\therefore \qquad [V'] : [V] :: m : n$$

$$:: \frac{[L']}{[L]} : \frac{[T']}{[T]}$$

$$:: \frac{[L']}{[T']} : \frac{[L]}{[T]};$$

hence, by the definition of variation,

$$[V] \propto \frac{[L]}{[T]}, \text{ i.e., } \propto [L]\,[T]^{-1}$$

172. Theorem. *To show that the unit of acceleration varies directly as the unit of length, and inversely as the square of the unit of time.*

Take the units of length and time as before, and let $[F]$ and $[F']$ denote the corresponding units of acceleration.

Then a body is said to be moving with the original unit of acceleration

when a vel. of $[L]$ per $[T]$ is added on per $[T]$;

therefore with acceleration $m\,[F]$

when a vel. of $m\,[L]$ per $[T]$ is added on per $[T]$;

therefore with acceleration $\frac{m}{n}[F]$

when a vel. of $m\,[L]$ per $n\,[T]$ is added on per $[T]$;

therefore with acceleration $\frac{m}{n^2}[F]$

when a vel. of $m\,[L]$ per $n\,[T]$ is added on per $n\,[T]$;

therefore with acceleration $\frac{m}{n^2}[F]$

when a vel. of $[L']$ per $[T']$ is added on per $[T']$.

But now the body is moving with the new unit of acceleration $[F']$.

$$\therefore \qquad [F'] = \frac{m}{n^2}[F]$$

$$\therefore \qquad [F'] : [F] :: m : n^2$$

$$:: \frac{[L']}{[L]} : \frac{[T']^2}{[T]^2}$$

$$:: \frac{[L']}{[T']^2} : \frac{[L]}{[T]^2}$$

Hence, by the definition of variation,

$$[F] \propto \frac{[L]}{[T]^2}, \text{ i.e., } \propto [L]\,[T]^{-2}$$

173. Ex. 1. *If the units of length and time be changed from a metre and a second to* 100 *m and* 50 *seconds respectively, find in what ratio the units of velocity and acceleration are changed.*

The new unit of velocity is a velocity of 100 m per 50 seconds, i.e., a velocity of 2 m per second. Hence the new unit of velocity is twice the original unit of velocity.

Again a body is moving with the new unit of acceleration.

when a velocity of 100 m per 50 seconds is added on per 50 sec.,

i.e., ... 2 m per 1 sec .... per 50 sec.,

i.e., ... $\frac{1}{25}$ m per second .... per sec.

Hence the new unit of acceleration is $\frac{1}{25}$th of the original unit of acceleration.

Otherwise thus : Taking the same notation as in Arts. 171 and 172, we have

$$[L] = 100\,[L], \text{ and } [T'] = 50\,[T].$$

$$\therefore \quad \frac{[V']}{[V]} = \frac{[L']\,[T']^{-1}}{[L]\,[T]^{-1}} = 100 \times [50]^{-1} = \frac{100}{50} = 2,$$

$$\text{and} \quad \frac{[F']}{[F]} = \frac{[L']\,[T']^{-2}}{[L]\,[T]^{-2}} = 100 \times (50)^{-2} = \frac{100}{2500} = \frac{1}{25},$$

so that the new units of velocity and acceleration are respectively double and one twenty-fifth of the original units.

Ex. 2. *Find the measure of the acceleration due to gravity in the yard-minute system, assuming its value in the foot-second system to be* 32.2.

In a falling body a velocity of 32.2 ft per sec. is added on per sec.,

∴ .... 60×32.2 ft per minute is added on per sec.,

∴ .... $60^2 \times 32.2$ ft per minute is added on per min.,

∴ .... $\frac{60^2}{3} \times 32.2$ yd. per minute is added on per minute,

$$\therefore \quad \text{the required measure} = \frac{60^2 \times 32.2}{3} = 38640.$$

This may be more concisely put as follows :

Let x be the new measure; then

$$x \times [F'] = 32.2 \times [F],$$

$$\therefore \quad x = 32.2 \times \frac{[F]}{[F']} = 32.2 \times \frac{[L]\,[T]^{-2}}{[L']\,[T']^{-2}} = 32.2 \times \frac{1}{3 \times (60)^{-2}}$$

$$= 32.2 \times \frac{60^2}{3} = 38640 \text{, as before.}$$

Ex. 3. *If the acceleration of a falling body be taken as the unit of acceleration, and the velocity generated in a falling body in one minute as the unit of velocity, find the units of length and time.*

Using the same notation as in Arts. 171 and 172, the same acceleration is in the two systems represented by

$$9.8\,[F] \quad \text{and} \quad 1 \cdot [F']$$

$$\therefore \quad 1 \cdot [F'] = 9.8\,[F]$$

$$\therefore \quad [L']\,[T']^{-2} = 9.8\,[L]\,[T]^{-2} \qquad \text{...(1).}$$

In m/sec. units the velocity generated in one minute = 60×9.8.

Hence $60 \times 9.8 \cdot [V]$ and $1 \cdot [V']$ represents the same velocity. Hence,

$$1 \cdot [L']\,[T']^{-1} = 60 \times 9.8\,[L]\,[T]^{-1} \qquad \text{...(2).}$$

Dividing the square of equation (2) by (1), we have

$$[L'] = \frac{60^2 \cdot 9.8^2}{9.8}[L] = 60^2 \times 9.8\,\text{m}$$

Hence, from (2),

$$\frac{[T']}{[T]} = \frac{1}{60 \times 9.8}\left[\frac{L'}{L}\right] = \frac{1}{60 \times 9.8} \times 60^2 \times 9.8$$

$$[T'] = 60\,[T] = 60 \text{ seconds} = \text{one minute.}$$

Examples. XXIX.

1. If the unit of length be one metre, and the unit of time one minute, find the units of velocity and acceleration.
2. If the unit of length be one kilometre and the unit of time 4 seconds, find the units of velocity and acceleration.
3. If the unit of velocity be a velocity of 48 km per hour, and the unit of time be one minute, find the units of length and acceleration.
4. If the unit of acceleration be that of a freely falling body, and the unit of time be 5 seconds, show that the unit of velocity is a velocity of 4.9 m per sec.
5. What must be the unit of length, if the acceleration due to gravity be represented by 14, and the unit of time be five seconds?
6. If the unit of velocity be a velocity of 4.83 km per hour, and the unit of time one minute, find the unit of length.
7. If the acceleration of a falling body be the unit of acceleration, and the velocity acquired by it in 5 seconds be the unit of velocity, show that the units of length and time are 243.84 metres and 5 seconds respectively.
8. What is the measure of the acceleration due to gravity
   (1) when a metre and half a second are the units of length and time
   (2) when the units are a km and eleven seconds,
   (3) when the units are 10 metres and 10 minutes respectively?
9. Find the measure in the centimetre-minute system of the acceleration due to gravity, assuming a metre to be 39.37 inches.
10. The acceleration produced by gravity being 32 in ft/sec. units, find its measure when the units are $\frac{1}{10000}$ of an hour and a centimetre, given 1 centimetre = 0.0328 ft.
11. If the area of a 0.04 km^2 field be represented by 100, and the acceleration of a heavy falling particle by $49\frac{2}{3}$, find the unit of time.

174. Dimensions. Def. *When we say that the dimensions of a physical quantity are α, β and γ in length, time, and mass respectively we mean that the unit in terms of which the quantity is measured varies as*

$$[L]^\alpha\ [T]^\beta\ [M]^\gamma$$

Thus the results of Arts. 171 and 172 are expressed by saying that the dimensions of the unit of velocity are 1 in length and –1 in time; while those of the unit of acceleration are 1 in length and –2 in time.

The cases in Arts. 171 and 172 have been fully written out, but the results may be obtained by more simply as in the following article.

175. (1) Velocity. Let v denote the numerical measure of the velocity of a point which undergoes a displacement whose numerical meausre is s, in a time whose numerical measure is t, so that

$$s = vt$$

If $[L]$, $[T]$ and $[V]$ denote the units of length, time, and velocity respectively, we have, as in Art. 168,

$$s \propto \frac{1}{[L]}, t \propto \frac{1}{[T]} \text{ and } v \propto \frac{1}{[V]}.$$

$$\therefore \qquad \frac{1}{[L]} \propto \frac{1}{[V]}\frac{1}{[T]}$$

Hence $$[V] \propto [L]\,[T]^{-1}$$

(2) Acceleration. Let v denote the velocity acquired by a particle moving with acceleration f for time t, so that

$$v = ft$$

If $[F]$ denotes the unit of acceleration, we have

$$f \propto \frac{1}{[F]}$$

$$\therefore \qquad \frac{1}{[V]} \propto \frac{1}{[F]}\frac{1}{[T]}$$

Hence $$[F] \propto [V]\,[T]^{-1} \propto [L]\,[T]^{-2}$$

(3) Density. Let d be the density of a body whose mass is m and volume u, so that $m = du$.

If $[D]$ and $[U]$ denote the units of density and volume, we have

$$d \propto \frac{1}{[D]}; u \propto \frac{1}{[U]}.$$

$$\therefore \qquad \frac{1}{[M]} \propto \frac{1}{[D]\,[U]}$$

$$\therefore \qquad [D] \propto [M]\,[U]^{-1} \propto [M]\,[L]^{-3}.$$

If the body be very thin, so that it may be considered as a surface only, we see similarly that the unit of surface density

$$\propto [M]\,[L]^{-2}.$$

So, if the body be such that its breadth and thickness may be neglected (so that it is a material line only), we have

$$\text{unit of linear density} \propto [M]\,[L]^{-1}.$$

(4) Force. If p be the force that would produce acceleration f in mass m, we have $p = mf$.

Hence, if $[P]$ denotes the unit of force, we have

$$[P] \propto [M]\,[F] \propto [M]\,[L]\,[T]^{-2}.$$

(5) Momentum. If k be the momentum of a mass m moving with velocity v, we have

$$k = mv.$$

Hence, if $[K]$ denotes the unit of momentum,

$$[K] \propto [M]\,[V] \propto [M]\,[L]\,[T]^{-1}$$

(6) Impulse. If i be the impulse of a force p acting for time t, we have

$$i = pt.$$

Hence, if $[I]$ denotes the unit of impulse,

$$[I] \propto [P]\,[T] \propto [M]\,[L]\,[T]^{-1}$$

so that an impulse is of the same dimensions as a momentum.

(7) Kinetic Energy. If e be the kinetic energy of a mass m moving with velocity v, we have

$$e = \frac{1}{2}\,mv^2.$$

Hence, if $[E]$ denotes the unit of kinetic energy,

$$[E] \propto [M]\,[V]^2 \propto [M]\,[L]^2\,[T]^{-2}.$$

(8) Work. If w be the work done when a force p moves its point of application through a distance s, then

$$w = ps.$$

Hence, if $[W]$ denotes the unit of work,

$$[W] \propto [P]\,[L] \propto [M]\,[L]^2\,[T]^{-2}$$

Hence work and kinetic energy are of the same dimensions.

(9) Power or Rate of work. If h be the power at which work w is done in time t, then

$$h = \frac{w}{t} = wt^{-1}.$$

Hence, if $[H]$ denotes the units of power,

$$[H] \propto [W]\,[T]^{-1} \propto [M]\,[L]^2\,[T]^{-3}.$$

(10) Angular velocity. If ω be the angular velocity of a point which moves with velocity v in a circle of radius r, we have

$$\omega = \frac{v}{r} = vr^{-1}, \text{ (Art. 26)}$$

Hence, if $[\Omega]$ denotes the unit of angular velocity, then

$$[\Omega] = [V]\,[L]^{-1} = [T]^{-1}.$$

176. Ex. 1. *If the unit of mass be 50 kg the unit of length one km, and the unit of time one minute, find the unit of force.*

The unit of force is (Art. 82) the force which in unit mass produces unit acceleration,

i.e., which in 56 kg produces an acceleration of 1 km per min.

i.e., in 56 kg .... $\frac{1}{60}$ km per sec. per min., i.e., in 56 kg .... $\frac{1}{60^2}$ km per sec. per sec.

i.e., in 56 kg .... $\frac{1000}{60^2}$ m per sec. per sec.,

i.e., in 1 kg .... $\frac{1000 \times 56}{60^2}$ m per sec. per sec.

Hence the new unit of force $= \frac{1000 \times 56}{60^2}$ newtons

$$= 15\frac{5}{9} \text{ newtons } = \text{wt. of } 1\frac{37}{63} \text{ kg.}$$

Otherwise thus : By Art. 175 (4), we have

$$\frac{[P']}{[P]} = \frac{[M'][L][T']^{-2}}{[M][L][T]^{-2}} = 56 \times 1000 \times 60^{-2}$$

$$= \frac{112 \times 1760.3}{60^2} = 15\frac{5}{3}, \text{as before.}$$

Ex. 2. *The kinetic energy of a body expressed in the foot-pound-second system is 1000; find its value in the metre-gramme-minute system, having given 1 foot = 30.5 cm, and 1 lb. = 450 grammes, approximately.*

Let x be the measure in the new system, so that

$$x\,[E'] = 1000\,[E],$$

i.e.,
$$x\,[M'][L']^2\,[T']^{-2} = 1000\,[M][L]^2\,[T]^{-2}$$

But $[M] = 450\,[M']$, $[L] = 0.305\,[L']$ and $[T] = \frac{1}{60}[T']$

$$\therefore \quad x = 1000 \times 450 \times [0.305^2] \times 60^2$$

$$= 150.700, 500.$$

Ex. 3. *If the unit of velocity be 4 m per second, the unit of acceleration 24 m-second units, and the unit of force 6 newtons, what are the units of mass, length and time?*

Find also the corresponding unit of work.

Find also the corresponding unit of work.

The unit of velocity $[V']$ is equal to 4 $[V]$

$$[L'][T']^{-1} = 4\,[L][T]^{-1} \qquad \text{...(1).}$$

The unit of acceleration $[F']$ is equal to 24 $[F]$

$$\therefore \quad [L'][T']^{-2} = 24\,[L][T]^{-2}. \qquad \text{...(2).}$$

The unit of force $[P']$ is equal to 6 $[P]$.

$$\therefore \quad [M'][L'][T']^{-2} = 6\,[M][L][T]^{-2} \qquad \text{...(3).}$$

Dividing (2) by (1), we have

$$[T']^{-1} = 6\,[T]^{-1}.$$

$$\therefore \quad [T'] = \frac{1}{6}[T] = \frac{1}{6}\text{second.}$$

Dividing the square of (1) by (2), we have

$$[L'] = \frac{4^2}{24}[L] = \frac{2}{3}[L] = \frac{2}{3}\text{ m.}$$

Dividing (3) by (2), we have

$$[M'] = \frac{6}{24}[M] = \frac{1}{4}\text{kg}.$$

Hence the required units of mass, length and time, are.

$$\frac{1}{4}\text{kg}, \ \frac{2}{3}\text{m, and } \frac{1}{6}\text{sec.}$$

Also by Art. 175 (8), we have

$$\frac{[W']}{[W]} = \frac{[M'][L']^2[T']^{-2}}{[M][L]^2[T]^{-2}} = \frac{1}{4} \times \left(\frac{2}{3}\right)^2 \times \left(\frac{1}{6}\right)^{-2}$$

$$\therefore \quad [W'] = \frac{2^2 \times 6^2}{4 \times 3^2}[W] = 4 \text{ metre-newton.}$$

Examples. XXX.

1. If 60 cm be the unit of length, 3 seconds the unit of time, and 50 kg the unit of mass, find the unit of force.
2. If the units of mass, length and time be 10 gm, 10 cm, and 10 seconds respectively, find the units of force and work.
3. If the unit of length be 61 cm, what must be the unit of time in order that 0.454 kg/wt. may be the unit of force, the unit of mass being 0.454 kg?
4. If the unit of mass be 50 kg, the unit of force the weight of one metric ton, and the unit of length one km, show that the unit of time is $\frac{5\sqrt{10}}{7}$ seconds.
5. If the unit of velocity be a velocity of 1.609 km per minute, the unit of acceleration be the acceleration with which this velocity would be acquired in 5 minutes, and the unit of force be equal to the weight of 508 kg, find the units of length, time, and mass.
6. If 50.8 kg be the unit of mass, a minute the unit of time, and the unit of force the weight of 0.45 kg, find the unit of length.
7. If the unit of force be equal to the weight of 30 g, the unit of time be one minute, and a velocity of 20 m per second be denoted by 8, find the units of length and mass.
8. If 5.025 metres be the unit of length, a velocity of 91.4 cm per second the unit of velocity and 82800 dynes the unit of force, what is the unit of mass?
9. Taking as a rough approximation 1 foot = 30.5cm, 1 lb. = 453 grammes, and the acceleration of a falling body = 32 ft/sec. units, show that
   (i) 1 Poundal = 13816 Dynes,
   (ii) 1 Foot-Poundal = 421403 Ergs,
   (iii) 1 Erg = 7.416×10^{-8} Foot-Pounds,
   (iv) 1 Horse-Power = 7.416×10^{9} Ergs per sec.
10. In two different systems of units an acceleration is represented by the same number, whilst a velocity is represented by numbers in the ratio 1 : 3; compare the units of length and time.

    If further the momentum of a body be represented by numbers in the ratio 5 : 2, compare the units of mass.

11. If the units of length, velocity and force be each doubled, show that the units of time and mass will be unaltered, and that of energy increased in the ratio 1 : 4.

12. If the unit of time be one hour, and the units of mass and force be the mass of 50.8 kg and the weight of 0.454 kg respectively, find the units of work and momentum in absolute units.

13. Find a system of units such that the momentum and kinetic energy of a mass of 4 kg, moving with a velocity of 5 m per second, may each be numerically equal to unity, and such that the unit of force may be the weight of one kg.

14. If the unit of acceleration be that of a body falling freely, the unit of velocity the velocity acquired by the body in 5 seconds from rest; and the unit of momentum that of one kg after falling for 10 seconds, find the units of length, time, and mass.

15. If the unit of work be that done in lifting 50.8 kg through 2.743 metres, the unit of momentum that of a mass of 121.9 cm which has fallen vertically 0.454 kg under gravity and the unit of acceleration three times that produced by gravity, find the units of length, time, and mass.

16. Find the units of length, time and mass supposing that when a force equal to the weight of a gramme acts on the mass of 16 grammes the acceleration produced is the unit of acceleration, that the work done in the first four seconds is the unit of work, and that the force is doing work at unit rate when the body is moving at the rate of 93 cm per second.

17. The velocity of a train running at the rate of 97 km per hour is denoted by 8, the resistance the train experiences and which is equal to the weight of 735 kg is denoted by 10, and the number of units of work done by the engine per mile by 10. Find the units of length, time and mass.

18. In a certain system of absolute units the acceleration produced by gravity in a body falling freely is denoted by 3, the kinetic energy of a 272.1 kg shot moving with velocity 488 metres per second is denoted by 100, and its momentum by 10; find the units of length, time, and mass.

19. If the kinetic energy of a train, whose mass is 100 metric tons and whose velocity is 45 km per hour, be denoted by 11, whilst the impulse of the force required to bring it to rest is denoted by 5, and 40 kilowatts by 15, find the units of length, time and mass, and show that the acceleration due to gravity is denoted by $110\frac{1}{4}$, assuming its measure in m-second units to be 9.8.

20. If the unit of force be the weight of one kilogramme, what must be the unit of mass so that the equation $P = mf$ may still be true?

Verification of formulae by means of counting the dimensions

177. Many formulae and results may be tested by means of the dimensions of the quantities involved. Suppose we have an equation between any number of physical quantities. Then the sum of the dimensions in each term of one side of the equation in length, time and mass respectively must be equal to the corresponding sums on the other side of the equation. For suppose that the dimensions in length of one side of the equation differed from the corresponding dimensions on the other side of the equation; then, on altering the unit of length, the two members of the equation would be altered in different ratios and would be no longer equal; this however would be clearly absurd; for two quantities which are equal must have the same measures whatever (the same) unit is used. For example, if two sums of money are the same, their measures must be the same whether we express the amounts in pounds, shillings, or pence.

Again, suppose an equation gives us as a result that 3 feet = 10 seconds; this would be clearly incorrect.

So such an equation as

$$3v^2 = 5mu^2 + 2fs,$$

must be incorrect; for two of the terms are of no dimensions in mass, and the third term, $5mu^2$, is of one dimension in mass. This latter term is therefore the one that is probably incorrect.

Consider again the possibility of the equation

$$Pvs^2 + 8mf^2s - 10v^3f = 0,$$

where the symbols have the meanings we have used throughout this book. Let us set down the dimensions only; they are, for the several terms,

$$[M]\frac{[L]}{[T]^2}\cdot\frac{[L]}{[T]}\cdot[L]^2,\ [M]\cdot\left\{\frac{L}{[T]^2}\right\}^2[L],\ \left\{\frac{[L]}{[T]}\right\}^2\frac{[L]}{[T]^2},$$

i.e., $$[M]\frac{[L]^4}{[T]^3},\ [M]\frac{[L]^3}{[T]^4},\ \frac{[L]^4}{[T]^5}$$

The equation is thus hopelessly incorrect; for the terms have neither the same dimensions in mass, nor in length nor in time.

So again if, in solving a question where we want the work done, we get an answer of the form

$$\text{Work} = MPv + 3Mvf,$$

this is clearly incorrect. For, by Art. 175, the dimensions of a Work are

$$[M]\frac{[L]^2}{[T]^2}.$$

Also the dimensions of MPv are

$$[M]\cdot\frac{[M][L]}{[T]^2}\cdot\frac{[L]}{[T]},\ \text{i.e., } [M]^2\frac{[L]^2}{[T]^3},$$

which is of wrong dimensions in both mass and time.

Also, the dimensions of $3Mvf$ are

$$[M]\cdot\frac{[L]}{[T]}\cdot\frac{[L]}{[T]^2},\ \text{i.e., } \frac{M[L]^2}{[T]^3},$$

which is of the wrong dimensions in time.

178. Much information may be often easily obtained by considering the dimensions of the quantities involved. Thus the time of oscillation of a simple pendulum (which consists of a mass m tied by means of a light string of length l to a fixed point) may be easily shown to vary as $\sqrt{\frac{l}{g}}$. For, assuming the time of oscillation to be independent of the arc of oscillation, the only quantities that can appear in the answer are *m*, *l* and *g*. Let us assume the time of oscillation to vary as $m^{\alpha} l^{\beta} g^{\gamma}$.

The dimensions of this quantity expressed in the usual way are

$$[M]^{\alpha}\,[L]^{\beta}\left\{\frac{[L]}{[T]^2}\right\}^{\gamma},$$

or
$$[M]^{\alpha}\,[L]^{\beta+\gamma}\,[T]^{-2\gamma}.$$

Now the answer is necessarily of one dimension in time, and of none in mass, or length. Hence we have

$$\alpha = 0, \beta + \gamma = 0, \text{ and } -2\gamma = 1$$

$$\therefore \quad \gamma = -\frac{1}{2} \text{ and } \beta = \frac{1}{2},$$

and the time of oscillation therefore $\propto \sqrt{\frac{l}{g}}$. [Art. 159.]

Table of Dimensions and Values of Fundamental Quantities

	Dimensions in		
Physical Quantity	*Mass*	*Length*	*Time*
Volume density	1	−3	
Surface density	1	−2	
Line density	1	−1	
Velocity		1	−1
Acceleration		1	−2
Force	1	1	−2
Momentum	1	1	−1
Impulse	1	1	−1
Kinetic energy	1	2	−2
Power or Rate of work	1	2	−3
Angular velocity			−1

Value of "g".

Place	*Ft/sec. units*	*Cm/sec. units*
The equator	32.091	978.10
Latitude 45°	32.17	980.61
Paris	32.183	980.94
London	32.191	981.17
North Pole	32.252	983.11

Length of the seconds pendulum at London

= 39.139 inches = 99.413 centimetres.

1 centimetre = 0.39370 inches = 0.032809 feet.

1 foot = 30.4797 centimetres.

1 gramme = 15.432 grains = 0.0022046 lb.

1 lb. = 453.59 grammes.

1 dyne = weight of $\frac{1}{981}$ gramme approx.

1 poundal = 13825 dynes.

1 foot-pondal = 421390 ergs.

13

Vectors

1. PURE numbers and physical quantities which do not require direction in space for their complete specification are called *scalar quantities,* or simply *scalars.* Examples of such quantities are mass, temperature, length and energy.

A *vector quantity* or simply a *vector,* is a quantity which needs for its complete specification both magnitude and direction. Examples of such quantities are velocity, momentum and force.

A vector may be represented graphically by an arrow drawn between two points. The length between these points denotes the magnitude of the vector quantity. We shall represent vectors by letters in bold face type and scalars in light face italics.

Vectors may be *localised* or *free.* A localised vector is one which is confined to a definite line. In some cases it is necessary to consider a vector to be localised. For instance, while calculating the moment of a force, the line of action of the force is relevant. A vector is said to be free when it is completely specified by its magnitude and direction. Thus it can be drawn in any convenient position.

2. Addition and subtraction of vectors.

From definition it follows that a vector behaves in the same manner as the rectilinear displacement of a point. So vector addition is reduced to a composition of linear displacements.

Let us consider two vectors **A** and **B** is shown in Fig. 1. The vector **C** is obtained by moving a point along **A** and then along **B.** It is called the sum of the vectors **A** and **B** and is written as **C** = **A** + **B.**

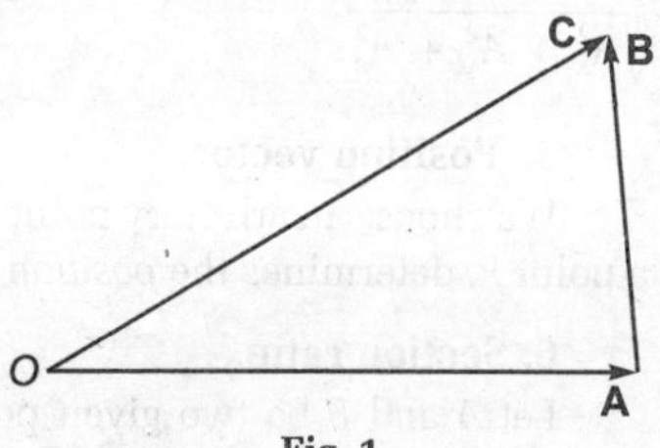

Fig. 1

From the nature of definition of vector addition it is evident that

$$\mathbf{A} + \mathbf{B} = \mathbf{B} + \mathbf{A}$$

and hence we conclude that vector addition is commutative.

For the addition of several vectors **A, B** and **C,** we first find the sum of **A** and **B** and then that of **A** + **B** and **C.** The result is easily seen to be the same as first finding the sum of **B** and **C** and then that of **B** + **C** and **A.** Thus we show that vector addition is associative.

The difference of two vectors **A** and **B,** which is written as **A** – **B,** is obtained by adding–**B** to **A** as shown in Fig. 2.

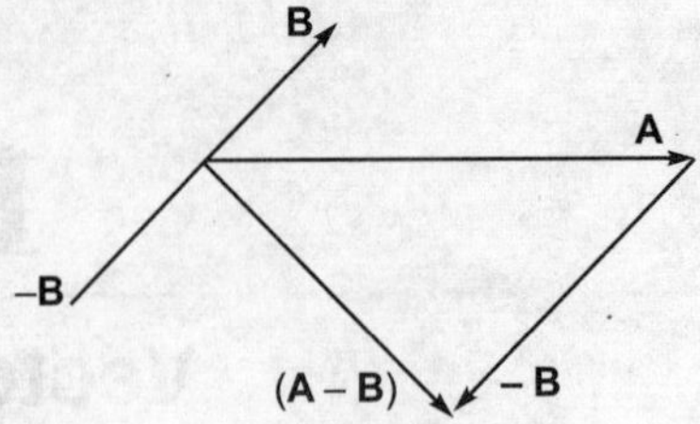

Fig. 2

3. Mutiplication of a vector by a scalar.

Let us consider the product of a vector **A** by a scalar n and which we write as $n\mathbf{A}$. The result of such multiplication yields a vector whose magnitude is the product of the magnitudes of n and **A** and has the direction of **A** or opposite to it, according as n is positive or negative.

4. Unit vectors and components of a vector.

A vector having unit magnitude is called a *unit vector.* A set of important unit vectors is that which has the directions of a right-handed cartesian co-ordinate system as shown in Fig. 3. The vectors **i, j, k** are unit vectors having the directions of x, y and z-axis respectively.

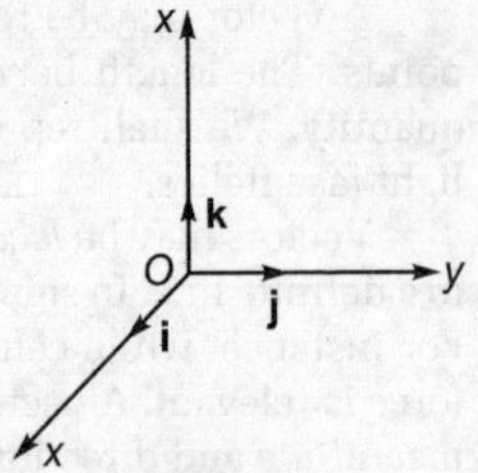

Fig. 3

We can use these unit vectors to write a vector in terms of its components along the axes of co-ordinates. So we write

$$\mathbf{A} = \mathbf{i}A_x + \mathbf{j}A_y + \mathbf{k}A_z$$

where A_x, A_y and A_z are the projections of A on the axis x, y, z respectively.

It can be seen from a diagram that the magnitude of the vector A is $\sqrt{A_x^2 + A_y^2 + A_z^2}$.

5. Position vector.

We choose an arbitrary point O as origin. Then the vector directed from O to a point P, determines the *position vector* of P with reference to the origin O.

6. Section ratio.

Let A and B be two given points whose position vectors with reference to O as origin are **a** and **b** respectively. Let R be a point on AB, dividing it in the ratio $m : n$. The position vector of R is denoted by **r**.

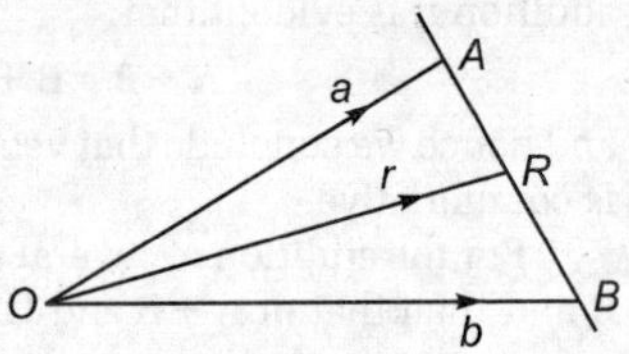

Fig. 4

Since $\dfrac{AB}{RB} = \dfrac{m}{n}$

We have $n\vec{AB} = m\vec{RB}$, (the arrow mark indicates vector)

i.e., $$n(\mathbf{r} - \mathbf{a}) = m(\mathbf{b} - \mathbf{r})$$

$$\therefore \qquad \mathbf{r} = \frac{m\mathbf{b} + n\mathbf{a}}{m + n}$$

N.B. When R is on AB produced, $\frac{m}{n}$ is negative.

7. Scalar product of two vectors.

The *scalar product* of two vectors **a** and **b** is defined as $ab \cos \theta$, where a and b are the magnitudes of **a** and **b** and θ is the angle included between **a** and **b**. It is denoted as $\mathbf{a} \cdot \mathbf{b}$.

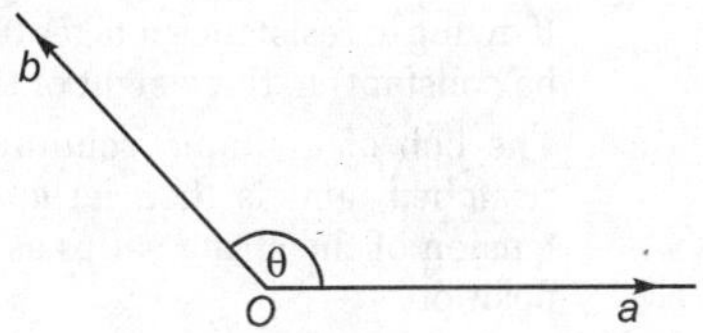

Fig. 5

From the definition it follows that $a \cdot b = b \cdot a$ and thus we see that scalar product of two vectors is commutative.

8. Vector product of two vectors.

The *vector product* of two vectors **a** and **b** is defined by a vector whose magnitude is equal to the product of the magnitudes of **a** and **b** with sine of the angle between them, and is perpendicular to **a** and **b**. It is denoted as $\mathbf{a} \times \mathbf{b}$. The direction of this vector is given by the motion of a right-handed screw rotating from **a** to **b**.

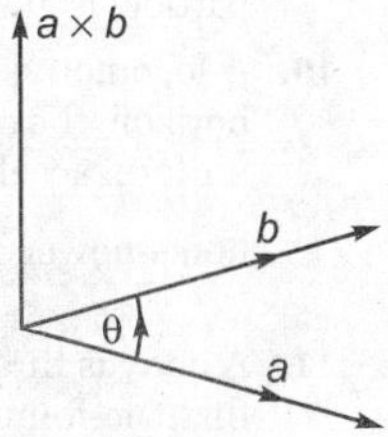

Fig. 6

It easily follows from the definition of $\mathbf{a} \times \mathbf{b}$ that

$$\mathbf{b} \times \mathbf{a} = -\,\mathbf{a} \times \mathbf{b}$$

This means that the vector product of two vectors is not commutative.

Miscellaneous Examples.

1. A particle falls freely from the top of a tower, and during the last second of its motion it falls $\frac{5}{8}$ths of the whole height; what is the height of the tower?
2. A man ascends the Eiffel Tower to a certain height and drops a stone. He then ascends another 130.5 m and drops another stone. The latter takes half a second longer than the former to reach the ground. Neglecting the resistance of the air, find the elevation of the man when he dropped the first stone and the time it took to drop.
3. A bullet moving with a velocity of 360 m per sec. has this velocity reduced to one-half after penetrating 2.4 cm into a target. Assuming the resistance to be uniform, how far will it penetrate before its velocity is destroyed?
4. Two scale-pans, each of mass 200 g are connected by a light inextensible string which passes over a smooth pulley. If a mass of 150 g be placed in one pan and one of 250 g in the other, find the pressures of the masses on the scale-pans.
5. Two equal masses, attached by an inextensible weightless thread which passes over a light pulley, hang in equilibrium. Show that the tension of the thread is unaltered when $\frac{1}{n}$th of its mass is added to one, and $\frac{1}{n+2}$th of its mass removed from the other.

6. A weightless string, of length a, with masses m and $3m$ attached to its ends is placed on a smooth horizontal table perpendicular to an edge with the mass m just over the edge. If the height of the table above the inelastic floor be also a, show that the mass $3m$ will strike the floor at a distance a from the mass m.
7. A particle falling under gravity describes 24.5 m in a certain second; how long will it take to describe the next 24.5 m, the resistance of the air being neglected?

   If owing to resistance it takes 0.9 sec., find the ratio of the resistance (assumed to be constant) to the weight of the particle.
8. The bob of a simple pendulum is held so that the string is horizontal and stretched, and is then let go. Show that during the subsequent motion the tension of the string varies as the vertical distance of the bob below its initial position.
9. A particle hanging vertically from a fixed point by means of a string of length r is projected horizontally with velocity $\sqrt{6gr}$. Show that the tension of the string when the particle is at the end of a horizontal diameter is to its tension, when the particle is at the highest point as 4 : 1.
10. A locomotive engine draws a load of m kg up an incline of inclination α to the horizon, the coefficient of friction being μ. If starting from rest and moving with uniform acceleration, it acquires a velocity v in t seconds, show that the average horse-power at which the engine has worked is $\frac{mv}{1100}\left[\frac{v}{gt} + \mu \cos \alpha + \sin \alpha\right]$.
11. A body is thrown up in a lift with a velocity u relative to the lift and the time of flight is found to be t. Show that the lift is moving up with an acceleration $\frac{2u - tg}{t}$.
12. The smoke from a steamer which is sailing due north extends in the direction E.S.E., whilst that from another sailing with the same velocity due south extends in the direction N.N.E.; show that the wind blows in the direction N.E. with a velocity equal to that of the steamer.
13. A horse gallops round a circus, whose radius is 20 m, with a velocity of 24 km per hour; show that the least value of the coefficient of friction between his hoofs and the ground is about 0.24.
14. A slip-carriage was detached from a train and brought to rest in n minutes during which time it described a distance of s metres. Assuming the retardation to be uniform, find the velocity with which the train was moving when the carriage was slipped.
15. A ship sailing south-east sees another ship, which is steaming as the same rate as itself, and which always appears to be in a direction due east and to be always coming nearer. Find the direction of the motion of the second vessel.
16. A perfectly elastic particle is projected with velocity of at an elevation θ. A smooth plane passes through the point of projection and is inclined at an angle a to the horizon. Show that the particle will return to the point of projection provided $\cos \alpha \cot (\theta - \alpha)$ is an integer.
17. A particle moves from rest in a straight line with alternate acceleration and retardation of magnitudes f and f' during equal intervals of time t; at the end of $2n$ such intervals prove that the space it has described is $\frac{nt^2}{2}[(2n + 1) f - (2n - 1) f']$.

18. A particle is placed upon a rough horizontal plate (coefficient of friction μ) at a distance a from a vertical axis about which the plate can rotate; find the greatest number of revolutions per minute which the plate can make without the particle moving relatively to the plate.

19. A cannon ball has a range R on a horizontal plane. If h and h' are the greatest heights in the two paths for which this is possible, prove that $R = 4\sqrt{hh'}$.

20. Find the greatest angle through which a person can oscillate on a swing, the ropes of which can just support twice the person's weight when at rest.

21. Two masses, m and m', are connected by a string of given length passing through a small smooth ring which turns freely about a vertical axis. The particle m' is made to rotate with angular velocity ω in a horizontal circle, so that the particle m remains at rest hanging freely from the ring. Show that the distance of m' from the ring is $\dfrac{mg}{m'\omega^2}$.

22. Two inelastic balls of equal size, but of masses m and m', lie in contact on a smooth table. The former receives a blow in a direction through its centre making an angle α with the line of centres. Show that the kinetic energy of the balls is

$$\frac{m'(m + m' \sin^2 \alpha)}{m(m' + m \sin^2 \alpha)}$$

of what it would have been if the balls had been interchanged and m' had received the blow.

23. A heavy particle projected with velocity u strikes at an angle of 45° an inclined plane of angle β which passes through the point of projection. Show that the vertical height of the point struck above the point of projection is

$$\frac{u^2}{g} \frac{1 + \cot \beta}{2 + 2 \cot \beta + \cot^2 \beta}.$$

24. An elastic body is projected from a given point with a given velocity V and after hitting a vertical wall returns to the point from which it started. Show that the distance of the point from the wall must be less than $\dfrac{e}{1+e}\dfrac{V^2}{g}$, where e is the coefficient of restitution.

25. Two particles of masses m and m', are moving in parallel straight lines at a distance a apart with given velocities v and v'; the particles are connected by a string of such a length that at the instant when it becomes taut it is inclined at an angle α to the two parallel straight lines; assuming that $v > v'$, show that the impulsive tension on the string at the instant it tightens is

$$\frac{mm'}{m + m'}(v - v') \cos \alpha.$$

26. A smooth wedge, of mass M, is placed on a horizontal plane and a particle, of mass m, slides down its slant face which is inclined at an angle α to the horizon. Show that the acceleration of m relative to the plane face is

$$\frac{M + m}{M + m \sin^2 \alpha} \cdot g \sin \alpha.$$

27. A particle is placed on the face of a smooth wedge which can slide on a horizontal table; find how the wedge must be moved in order that the particle may neither ascend nor descend. Also find the pressure between the particle and the wedge.

28. A particle, of mass m_1, is fastened to one end of a string, and one of mass m_2 to the middle point, the other end of the string being fastened to a fixed point on a smooth horizontal table. The particles are then projected so that the two portions of the string are always in the same straight line and so that the particles describe horizontal circles; show that the tension of the two portions of the string are as

$$2m_1 + m_2 : 2m_1.$$

29. At one end of a light string passing over a small fixed pulley a weight of 3 kg is suspended and a light pulley is suspended at the other end. Over this pulley another light string passes with weights of 2 kg and 1 kg suspended at its ends. The whole system is let go from a position of rest; find the pressure on the fixed pulley while the system is moving and also the acceleration of the greatest weight.

30. In a system of three movable weightless pulleys in which all the strings are attached to a beam, the highest string after passing over a fixed pulley has a mass of 3 kg attached to it, and the lowest pulley has a mass of 28 kg hung on to it. Show that the larger mass will descend with an acceleration of $\frac{g}{55}$.

31. Two straight railways converge to a level crossing at an angle α, and two trains are moving towards the crossing with velocities u and v. If a and b are the initial distances of the trains from the crossing, show that their least distance apart will be

$$\frac{(av - bu)\sin\alpha}{\sqrt{u^2 + v^2 - 2uv\cos\alpha}}.$$

32. If the distance between two moving points at any time be a, if V be their relative velocity, and if u and v be the components of V respectively in and perpendicular to the direction of a, show that their distance when they are nearest to one another is $\frac{av}{V}$, and that the time that elapses before they arrive at their nearest distance is $\frac{au}{V^2}$.

33. Two particles, of masses M and $M + m$, are connected by a light string and placed near one another on a smooth table; on the string slides a light smooth pulley, supporting a mass M, which is placed just over the edge of the table; find the resulting acceleration of the pulley.

34. In the system of pulleys where each string is attached to the bar which supports the weight, if there be two movable pulleys of negligible mass and the power be quadrupled, show that the weight will ascend with acceleration $\frac{3g}{29}$.

35. A string, one end of which is fixed, has slung on it a mass of 3 kg and then passes over a smooth pulley and has a mass of 1 kg attached to its other end; show that

the larger mass descends with acceleration $\frac{g}{7}$ and that the tension of the string is $1\frac{2}{7}$ kg wt.

36. A cyclist, riding at a speed V, overtakes a pedestrian who can move at a speed not greater than v, the two travelling along parallel tracks at a distance d apart. Show that if the cyclist rings his bell when at a distance less than $\frac{V}{v}d$, we may safely maintain his speed and keep to his course regardless of the behaviour of the pedestrian.

37. A boy throws a stone into the air with velocity V at an elevation α; after an interval of time $\frac{2VV' \sin(\alpha - \alpha')}{g\,[V \cos \alpha + V' \cos \alpha']}$ he throws another with velocity V' at an elevation α'; show that the second stone will strike the first.

38. A shot, of mass m, penetrates a thickness t of a fixed plate of mass M; if M be free to move, and the resistance be supposed uniform, show that the thickness penetrated is $\frac{M}{M+m}t$.

39. A string sustains a mass P at one end, then passes over a fixed pulley, then under a movable pulley to which a mass R is attached, and then over a fixed pulley and is attached to a mass Q at its other end. Assuming the masses of the string and pulleys to be negligible, and that the parts of the string not in contact with the pulleys are vertical, find the acceleration of R and the tension of the string.

40. A wedge of mass M can slide on a smooth horizontal plane, and the wedge has a face inclined at an angle α to the horizontal. Initially the wedge is at rest and a particle of mass m is projected directly up the inclined face. If the particle rises to a height h above the point of projection, show that the velocity of projection is

$$\left\{2gh\,\frac{M+m}{M+m\sin^2\alpha}\right\}^{1/3}.$$

41. A particle is at rest on a rough plane (coefficient of friction μ) inclined to the horizon at an angle α. The plane is moved horizontally with a constant acceleration f in a direction away from the particle; prove that the particle will remain at rest relative to the plane if

$$f < \frac{\mu g \cos\alpha - g \sin\alpha}{\cos\alpha + \mu \sin\alpha}.$$

42. A regular hexagon stands with one side on the ground and a particle is projected so as just to graze its four upper vertices. Show that the velocity of the particle on reaching the ground is to its least velocity as $\sqrt{31}$ to $\sqrt{3}$.

43. In order to raise a weight which is half as much again as his own a man fastens a rope to it and passes the rope over a smooth pulley; he then climbs up the rope with an acceleration relative to the rope of $\frac{6g}{7}$. Show that the weight rises with acceleration $\frac{g}{7}$, and find the tension of the rope.

44. A wedge of mass M and angle α can move freely on a smooth horizontal plane; a smooth sphere of mass m strikes it in a direction perpendicular to its inclined face and rebounds. Show that the ratio of the velocities of the sphere just before and just after the impact is

$$M + m \sin^2 \alpha : eM - m \sin^2 \alpha,$$

where e is the coefficient of restitution.

45. Over a smooth light pulley is passed a string supporting at one end a weight of mass 4 kg and at the other a pulley of mass 1 kg. A string with masses 2 kg and 3 kg attached to its ends passes over the second pulley; show that the acceleration of the 4 kg mass is $\frac{9g}{49}$.

46. A string, of natural length a, is stretched on a smooth table between two fixed points at a distance na apart and a particle of mass m is attached to the middle point of the string; the particle is then displaced towards one of the fixed points through a distance not succeeding $\frac{n-1}{2}a$ and then liberated; show that it will perform oscillations in a period which is independent of n and of the distance through which it is displaced.

47. If the unit of kinetic energy be that of 5 kg which has fallen 50 m from rest, the unit of momentum the momentum thus generated and the unit of length the distance through which the particle has fallen, find the unit of time.

48. A particle P moves in a circle, of which OA is a diameter, and OY is drawn perpendicular to the tangent at P. Show that the velocity of Y relative to P is equal to the velocity of P.

49. Two men, of masses M and $M + m$, start simultaneously from the ground and climb with uniform vertical accelerations up the free ends of a weightless inextensible rope which passes over a smooth pulley at a height h from the ground. If the lighter of the two men reaches the pulley in t sec., show that the heavier cannot get nearer to it than $\frac{m}{M+m}\left[\frac{gt^2}{2} + h\right]$.

50. A train, of mass M, is travelling with uniform velocity on a level line; the last carriage, whose mass is m, becomes uncoupled and the driver discovers it after travelling a distance l and shuts off steam. Show that when both parts come to rest the distance between them is $\frac{M}{M-m}l$, if the resistance to motion be uniform and proportional to the weight, and the pull of the engine be constant.

51. A small smooth pulley of mass M is lying on a smooth table; a light string passes round the pulley and has masses m and m' attached to its ends, the two portions of the string being perpendicular to the edge of the table and passing over it to that the masses hangs vertically; show that the acceleration of the pulley is

$$\frac{4mm'}{M(m+m') + 4mm'}g.$$

52. Show that, if the effect of a horizontal wind on a projectile be an acceleration f in the direction of the wind and the effect of the resistance of the air be neglected, the latus-rectum of the path of a particle projected with velocity v at an angle α to the horizon in the same vertical plane as the direction of the wind is

$$\frac{2v^2 (g \cos \alpha + f \sin \alpha)^2}{(f^2 + g^2)^{3/2}}.$$

53. A particle lies on a smooth horizontal table at the foot of a smooth wedge of angle α and height h, and the wedge is made to move along the table with constant acceleration f. If $f > g \tan \alpha$, prove that the particle will ascend the plane. Show also that if the wedge moves in this way for time t, and then moves with constant velocity equal to that gained, the particle will just reach the top if

$$t^2 = \frac{2gh \sec \alpha}{f\,(f \cos \alpha - g \sin \alpha)}.$$

54. Weights of 10 kg and 2 kg hanging by vertical strings balance on a wheel and axle. If a mass of 1 kg be added to the smaller weight, find the acceleration with which it will begin to descend, and the tension of each rope, neglecting the mass of the wheel and axle.

55. In the differential wheel-and-axle c is the radius of the wheel, and a and b the radii of the two parts of the axle. A weight P attached to the wheel-rope just keeps the system in equilibrium; if P be doubled, prove that it descends with acceleration

$$g \times \frac{2c}{a - b + 4c}$$

the mass of the wheel and axle being neglected.

56. A perfectly elastic particle is projected with a velocity v in a vertical plane through a line of greatest slope of an inclined plane of elevation α; if after striking the plane it rebounds vertically, show that it will return to the point of projection at the end of time

$$\frac{6v}{g\,[1 + 8 \sin^2 \alpha]^{1/2}}$$

57. Two pulleys, each of mass m, are connected by a string hanging over a smooth fixed pulley; a string with masses $2m$ and $3m$ at its ends is hung over one pulley, and one with masses m and $4m$ over the other. If the system is free to move, show that the acceleration of either pulley is $\frac{4g}{25}$.

58. A rough vertical circle, carrying a bead, turns in its own plane about its centre with uniform angular velocity greater than

$$\sqrt{\frac{g}{a}}\left[1 + \frac{1}{\mu^2}\right]^{1/4}$$

where a is the radius and μ is the coefficient of friction. Show that the bead will never slip.

59. A particle is projected along the inside of a vertical hoop from its lowest point with such a velocity that it leaves the hoop and returns to the point of projection again. Find the velocity of projection and determine where the particle leaves the hoop.

60. A particle which hangs from a fixed point by a string of length a is projected horizontally from the position of equilibrium with a velocity due to a height $a + b$. If $2b < 3a$, show that the string will be loose for a time t given by the equation

$$27ga^2t^2 = 32\,b\,(9a^2 - 4b^2)$$

61. A heavy particle is attached to one end of an elastic string, the other end of which is fixed. The modulus of elasticity of the string is equal to the weight of the particle. The string is drawn vertically down till it is four times its natural length, and then is let go. Show that the particle will return to this point in time

$$\sqrt{\frac{a}{g}}\left[2\sqrt{3}+\frac{4\pi}{3}\right]$$

where a is the unstretched length of the string.

62. Two men, A and B, each of mass m, sit in loops at the ends of a light flexible rope passing over a smooth pulley, A being h feet higher than B. In B's hands is placed a ball, of mass $\frac{m}{10}$, which he instantly throws up to A, so that it just reaches him. Prove that by the time A has caught the ball he has moved up through the distance $\frac{9}{19}h$, and that will cease ascending when he has ascended a total height of $\frac{59}{361}h$.

63. A smooth ring, of mass M, is threaded on a string whose ends are then placed over two smooth fixed pulleys with masses m and m' tied on to them respectively, the various portions of the string being vertical. The system being free to move, show that the ring will remain at rest if

$$\frac{4}{M}=\frac{1}{m}+\frac{1}{m'}.$$

64. A particle, of mass m, is placed on the face of a smooth wedge, of mass M, which moves along a smooth horizontal table being pulled horizontally by a string which, after passing over a smooth pulley carries a mass M' hanging vertically, the motions being all in a vertical plane passing through a line of greatest slope. Show that the acceleration of m relative to the wedge is

$$\frac{(M+M'+m)\sin a+M'\cos a}{M+M'+m\sin^2 a}g,$$

where a is the inclination of the face. Find also the pressure of m on the wedge.

65. A smooth wedge is free to move on a horizontal place in the direction of the projection of the lines of greatest slope and is held whilst a particle is projected up its face in a direction inclined to the lines of greatest slope, and is then immediately released. Show that the track of the particle on the plane is a parabola.

66. A perfectly elastic ball is thrown from the foot of a plane inclined at an angle a to the horizon. If after striking the plane at a distance l from the point of projection it rebounds and retraces its former path, show that the velocity of projection is

$$\sqrt{\frac{gl(1+3\sin^2 a)}{2\sin a}}.$$

67. A heavy mass M, which can slide along a straight horizontal bar is attached to a fixed point at a distance c from the bar by a spiral spring of natural length a less than c such that a mass m hung on to it will stretch it by a length l; show that the time of a small oscillation of M along the bar, when it is slightly disturbed, will be

$$2\pi\left\{\frac{Mec}{mg(c-a)}\right\}^{1/2}.$$

68. A railway carriage is travelling on a curve of radius r with velocity v; if h be the height of the centre of inertia of the carriage above the rails (which are at the same horizontal level) and $2a$ be the distance between them, show that the carriage will upset if

$$v > \sqrt{\frac{gra}{h}}.$$

69. A wedge of mass M rests with a rough face in contact with horizontal table and with another face which is smooth inclined at an angle α to the table. The angle of friction between the wedge and the table is ε. A particle of mass m slides down the smooth face. Find the condition that the wedge may move; and prove that, if it moves, its acceleration is

$$\frac{m \cos \alpha \sin (\alpha - \varepsilon) - M \sin \varepsilon}{M \cos \varepsilon + m \sin \alpha \sin (\alpha - \varepsilon)} g.$$

70. A window is supported by two cords passing over pulleys in the frame-work of the window (which it loosely fits), the other ends of the cords being attached to weights each equal to half the weight of the window. One cord breaks and the window descends with acceleration f. Show that $f = g \dfrac{a - b\mu}{3a + b\mu}$, where μ is the coefficient of friction, and a is the height and b the breadth of the window.

71. A weight of 300 kg is lifted by a vertical force with varies continually as the weight is raised according to the following table:

Height in metres above the ground:	0,	1,	2,	3,	4,	5,	6.
Lifting force in kgf :	450,	320,	270,	410,	480,	610,	900

Find at the time when it is 5.5 m from the ground (i) the potential energy stored in the mass, (ii) the kinetic energy of the mass, (iii) the work done by the force.

72. A mass of 10 kg is attached to the ground by a spring which requires a pull of 10 kg weight to stretch it 2.5 cm. The mass is lifted by force which continually varies with the height as in the following table:

x in cm :	0,	2,	4,	6,	10,	12
Force in kgf:	22,	36.2,	44.5,	52,	51.8,	48

Estimate the kinetic and potential energies of the mass when it has been lifted 4 cm and 6 cm respectively and estimate the velocity, when it has been lifted 12 cm.

73. An engine pumps water through a hose, and the water leaves the hose with a velocity v; show that the rate at which the engine is working varies as v^2.

74. The weight supported by the driving wheels of a locomotive engine is 24 metric tons and the coefficient of friction between the wheels and the rails is $\frac{1}{2}$; if the engine be 4.9×10^5 watts show that the maximum velocity which the train can have, so that the wheels do not slip, 90 km per hour.

75. A railway train, of mass M, goes from rest at one station to rest at a second station, a distance l, in t seconds; the friction of the rails, etc., causes a resistance of R kgf, and for a portion of the distance the engine exerts a constant pull equal to P kgf. Show that

$$P = \frac{R^2gt^2}{Rgt^2 - 2Ml},$$

and the P acts for a time

$$t - \frac{2Ml}{Rgt}.$$

76. A cyclist and his machine together are of mass M kg; if he rides, without pedalling, down an incline of 1 in m with a uniform speed of v m per sec., show that to go yp an incline of 1 in n at the same rate he must work at a rate equal to

$$M\left[\frac{1}{m} + \frac{1}{n}\right] v \text{ watts},$$

77. A cyclist rides at the rate of 18 kms per hour on the level and 8 km per hour up an incline of 1 in 40. The resistance to his motion other than the due to the incline being supposed constant, find this resistance, and also his greatest velocity down an incline of 1 in 100, if the weight of the rider and his machine be 90 kg, and if the always works at a constant H.P.

78. Find the velocity acquired by a block of wood, of mass M kg which is free to recoil when it is struck by a bullet of mass m kg moving with velocity v in a direction passing through its centre of gravity.
If the bullet be embedded a m, show thatt the resistance of the wood to the bullet supposed uniform is

$$\frac{Mm}{M + m}\frac{v^2}{2ga} \text{ kgf},$$

and that the time of penetration is $\frac{2a}{v}$ sec, during which time the block will move $\frac{m}{M + m}a$ metre.

Answers

I (Pages 9–11)

4. 100 metres. 5. 120°.

7. At an angle $\cos^{-1}\left(-\frac{3}{5}\right)$, i.e., 126° 52′ with the current; perpendicular to the current so that his resultant direction makes an angle $\tan^{-1}\frac{5}{3}$, i.e., 59°2′, with the current.

8. $4\sqrt{3}$ km per hour; 12 km per hour.

9. At an angle of 150° with *AB* produced; it will strike *X* at right angles at the end of fifteen minutes.

10. At an angle of $\cos^{-1}\left(-\frac{3}{5}\right)$ with the direction of the car's motion.

11. $\sqrt{29}$ (= 5.38 . . .) at an angle of elevation of $\tan^{-1}\frac{2}{5}$ (21°48′) with a horizontal line which is inclined at $\tan^{-1}\frac{4}{3}$ (= 53°8′) north of east.

12. $(\sqrt{3}-1)u$; $(\sqrt{6}-\sqrt{2})\frac{u}{2}$. 13. 60°.

14. 14 at an angle $\cos^{-1}\frac{13}{14}$ (= 21°47′) with the greatest velocity.

II (Pages 14–17)

1. $\sqrt{181}$ metres per sec. at an angle $\tan^{-1}\left(-\frac{9}{10}\right)$ with the direction of the train's motion.

2. 20 km per hour at an angle $\tan^{-1}\frac{3}{4}$ (= 36°52′) west of north.

3. 15 km per hour north-east.

4. 10 km per hour towards the south-east.

5. 39 km per hour in a direction $\cos^{-1}\frac{5}{13}$ (= 67°23′) north of east.

6. 52.4 km per hour.

7. $2\sqrt{2}$ km per hour at 45° to the vertical.

8. $7\sqrt{5-2\sqrt{2}}$ (= 10.31) km per hour. Draw *OA*(= 14) towards the east and *OB*(= 7) towards the south-east and complete the parallelogram *OABC*. Then *OC* is the required direction.

10. 5.455 sec. 13. 24 minutes; 6 km.

14. $2\frac{1}{12}$ ft per sec. at $\tan^{-1}\frac{3}{4}$ (= 36°52′) with *BA*; 3 feet at the end of $1\frac{23}{25}$ seconds.

16. $4\sqrt{2}$ km per hour towards the south-east.

17. Towards the east. **18.** $3v$ and v.

III (Pages 18–20)

1. $\frac{20\pi}{3}$ radians per sec. **2.** 8π radians per sec; $12\frac{4}{7}$ metres per sec.

3. $\frac{\pi}{300}$ cm per sec.; $\frac{\pi}{1800}$ radians per sec. **4.** 1 : 20 : 360.

5. $2\frac{1}{7}$ miles per hour. **6.** $\frac{D-d}{D}V$. **8.** $\frac{3a\pi}{u}$.

10. $60\sqrt{3}$ (= 103.9) km per hour at ± 30° to the horizon.

11. $\frac{200}{9}$ radians per sec.; 36 km per hour.

12. $\frac{50}{3}$ radians per sec.; 36 km per hour.

13. 32 km per hour; 16 km per hour at ± 60° to the horizon; $16\sqrt{3}$ km per hour a ± 30° to the horizon.

IV (Pages 21–22)

2. km per hour in a direction $\tan^{-1}\frac{4}{3}$ north of west.

3. 5 metres per sec. at 120° with its original velocity.

4. $20\sqrt{2-\sqrt{2}}$ (= 15.31) metres per sec., towards N.N.W.

5. 4 metres per sec., at 120° with its original direction.

V (Pages 31–34)

1. (1) 17 cm per sec., $47\frac{1}{2}$ cm.; (2) 0; $24\frac{1}{2}$ cm. (3) $-\frac{55}{13}$; $1\frac{7}{11}$ sec.

(4) 3 ft per sec; 6 sec.

2. 40 cm per sec.; 400 cm **3.** 10 min.

4. 40 cm-sec. units. **5.** 10 sec.; 150 cm.

6. In 50 sec.; 25 metres. **7.** 540 cm-sec. units.

8. 300 cm per sec.; –6 cm-sec. unit.

9. 570 cm per sec.; 90 cm-sec. units; 1805 cm.

10. 5 sec.; 3.75 metres. **11.** 16 cm-sec. units; 30 cm per sec.

12. 900 cm per sec.; –60 cm-sec. units **13.** 10 metres.

14. $\frac{1}{3}$, $\frac{\sqrt{2}-1}{3}$, and $\frac{\sqrt{3}-\sqrt{2}}{3}$ sec., respectively.

15. In 2 sec. at 400 cm from O. **16.** Yes.

17. Its displacement is $\sqrt{61 + 42\sqrt{2}}$ (= 10.97) cm at an angle $\tan^{-1}\dfrac{2+\sqrt{2}}{3}$ (= 48°42′) north of east.

18. 10 sec. or 30 sec. **20.** $36\frac{1}{4}$ miles per hour.

21. 323.5 m; in the 4th sec.; 24 m/sec.^{2} **22.** 372.5 m; $\frac{3}{5}$ m/sec. **32.** $\sqrt{\frac{\mu}{c}}$.

VI (Pages 38–39)

1. 872 cm; $\frac{8}{3}$ sec. and 2 sec. **2.** (i) In $\frac{4}{9}$ sec.; (ii) in $1\frac{1}{3}$ sec.

3. In 2 and 6 sec.; 5886 cm.

4. (1) 49050 cm; (2) $\frac{\sqrt{6}}{3}$ sec.; (3) 1962 cm per sec. upwards.

5. 13243.5 cm. **6.** 44 sec. **7.** $\frac{2\sqrt{3}}{3}$ sec. or $\frac{10\sqrt{3}}{3}$ sec.

8. 545 cm per sec.; $\frac{4}{9}$ sec. **9.** 10.2 sec.

10. 218 metres; $6\frac{2}{3}$ sec. **11.** 980 cm-sec. units.

12. $20723\frac{5}{8}$ cm; $6\frac{1}{2}$ sec. **13.** $3065\frac{5}{8}$ cm. **14.** $12262\frac{1}{2}$ cm

15. $4410\frac{1}{2}$ cm **16.** 7848 cm per sec.; 31392 cm.

17. $t = 5$; 1962 cm per sec. **18.** 240.1 m. **19.** 1120 ft per sec.

20. 150 metres.

VII (Page 40)

1. 8829 cm; 6 sec. **2.** 654 cm per sec.; $3\frac{1}{8}$ sec. **3.** 30°. **4.** 1 : 4

5. (1) –27.84 m; –18.72 m per sec.; (2) 66.24 m; 28.32 m per sec.

6. 30°. **7.** $\cos^{-1}\frac{1}{4}$, i.e., 75°31.

VIII (Pages 43–46)

1. 39240 cm. **2.** 1 sec.; $1\frac{1}{2}$ sec. **3.** 3924 cm per sec.; 1962 cm per sec.

4. The first will have fallen through one-quarter of the height of the tower.

5. $\frac{3h}{8}$. **6.** $\sqrt{gh}$, $\sqrt{gh}$, and 0, where h is the height of the plane.

7. At the end of time $\frac{1}{g}\left(u + \frac{1}{2}gt\right)$ from the starting of the first particle and at a height of $\frac{1}{2g}\left(u^2 - \frac{1}{4}g^2t^2\right)$.

8. 15 sec. **9.** 2940 cm. **10.** $6008\frac{5}{8}$ cm; 3433.5 cm per sec.

11. The parts are 981, 2943, and 4905 cm; 3 sec.

19. $\sqrt{\frac{2h}{g}}$ cosec α sec β. **20.** $\sqrt{fs\left(3 - \frac{1}{n}\right)}$.

24. $14\frac{2}{3}$ cm-sec. units; $29\frac{1}{3}$ cm-sec. units; 63 km 360 metres per hour.

25. 95 km 40 metres per hour; 44 sec.; 580 metres 80 cm; 8 sec.

28. $\frac{32}{23}$ m-sec. units; 40 m per sec.

29. 0.0745 m-sec. units; 0.311 m-sec. unis; 2 hr. $3\frac{1}{10}$ min.

IX (Pages 52–54)

4. (1) $\frac{1}{2}$, (2) $\frac{g}{2}$, (3) $\frac{g}{200}$ cm/sec^2. **5.** 27×10^5 dynes; (2) $\frac{3 \times 10^5}{109}$ gm wt or gf.

6. 1200 gm wt. **7.** 2.5 N. **8.** $1471\frac{1}{2}$ cm-sec. units; $22072\frac{1}{2}$ cm.

9. 14 : 981; 140 cm per sec. **10.** 4 sec.; 1308 cm per sec.

11. 2 min. 12 sec. **12.** 20 sec **14.** 529 m, 74 cm.

15. $363\frac{1}{3}$ cm per sec.; $181\frac{2}{3}$ cm; 21800 cm.

16. 49.05 kilograms. **17.** $81\frac{3}{4}$ kg. **18.** 5.4 kg

19. 3.5 kg wt.; 107.5 kg wt. **20.** They are equal.

21. 55 kg wt. **24.** 4000 cm per sec.

X (Pages 62–64)

1. $\frac{g}{5}$; $7\frac{1}{5}$ kg wt.

2. (1) $122\frac{5}{8}$ cm-sec. units; (2) $7\frac{7}{8}$ kg wt. ; (3) $613\frac{1}{8}$ cm per sec.; (4) $1532\frac{13}{18}$ cm.

3. (1) 327 cm per sec.; (2) 654 cm persec.; (3) 19620 cm and –15696 cm respectively.

4. 4.41 … metres; 495 grammes' wt. **6.** By 2 kg wt.

7. $\frac{2P}{3}$. **8.** $\frac{m}{2}$. **9.** $490\frac{1}{2}$ cm.

10. (1) $\frac{g}{10}$; (2) $\sqrt{5}$ sec.; (3) $\frac{981\sqrt{5}}{10}$ cm per sec. **11.** 2 sec.

12. (1) $61\frac{5}{16}$ cm-sec. units; (2) $2\frac{13}{16}$ kg wt.; (3) $183\frac{15}{16}$ cm per sec.; (4) $275\frac{29}{33}$ cm.

13. $\frac{3-2\sqrt{2}}{7}g$; $\frac{5}{4}(\sqrt{2}+1)$ sec. **14.** $1226\frac{1}{4}$ cm **15.** $361\frac{7}{8}$ g

16. $312\frac{1}{2}$ gm **17.** 9.58 kg and 7.04 kg **18.** $2\frac{1}{2}$ and $3\frac{1}{3}$ kg wt.; $\frac{g}{6}$.

19. 9.05 metres

XI (Pages 66–68)

1. $\frac{11}{23}g$; 0.3 **2.** 40.6 ft per sec.; 96 feet. **2.** 0.1

4. $\frac{\sqrt{2}}{2}$ sec.; $\frac{981\sqrt{2}}{4}$ cm per sec. **5.** $\frac{1}{2}\sqrt{5}$ sec.; $\frac{981\sqrt{5}}{10}$ cm per sec.

6. $20\sqrt{3g}$ cm per sec.; $20\sqrt{15g}$ cm per sec.

8. The larger mass descends with acceleration $\frac{2\sqrt{3}-3}{9}g$.

9. The particles do not move. **10.** 55504.5 cm approx. **11.** 605 : 18.

12. (i) 5 min. 39.8 sec. (nearly); (ii) 2836 m

13. 1 min, $42\frac{2}{3}$ sec.; $2258\frac{2}{3}$ feet.

14. 5.825 metric tonnes. **15.** 1 mile 1408 yds.

16. 1120 metres. **17.** 125.4 metres.

18. 5.34 metric tonnes wt.; 1 in 77 about; 1 in 50.

XII (Pages 72–75)

1. Zero **2.** (i) 10 kg wt.; (ii) $10\frac{100}{327}$ kg wt.

3. $66\frac{2}{3}$ kg wt.; $33\frac{1}{3}$ kg wt. **4.** $\frac{g}{8}$. **5.** $63064\frac{3}{7}$ cm.

6. 297 grammes' wt.; 270 and 264 grammes' wt.

7. $\frac{g}{4}$, $112\frac{1}{2}$ gf; 90 gf; 75 gf. **8.** 170.7 metric ton's wt.

9. 44.2 kg wt. nearly. **10.** 3000 kgf. **13.** 10 hang vertically.

14. 3 : 5. **16.** $26\frac{2}{3}$ metres. **18.** 7 metric tonnes.

21. 2 : 1 **22.** 11.7 … sec. **23.** $\frac{3WP}{W+4P}$.

24. m goes up with acc. $\frac{3g}{13}$; M goes down with acc. $\frac{g}{13}$.

26. $M = \frac{4mm'}{m+m'}$; the acc. is $\frac{m-m'}{m+m'}g$

27. $\frac{8}{23}$ ft. sec. units.

29. 97.5 metres; 45.1 km per hour.

XIII (Pages 78–79)

1. $4\frac{2}{27}$ metres per sec.

4. 120 cm per sec.

5. 600 cm per sec.

6. 2.68 m.

7. $15\frac{5}{16}$ metric ton's wt.

8. 436.2 meters per sec. nearly.

XIV (Pages 81–82)

1. 196000 watts

2. 171500 watts

3. $8166\frac{2}{3}$ watts

4. 6.5 kg per metric ton

5. 94.6

6. 191.1

7. 5,390,000 J; 2994 watts

8. 93.15

9. 291.4 metric tons

10. 209.2 ... tons' wt.

XV (Page 86)

1. (i) 24059025×10^2 units, (ii) $\frac{1}{6} \times 24059025 \times 10^3$ units,

(iii) 0, units of kinetic energy.

2. 15625.

3. 125×10^9.

4. 625×10^{10}; 3125×10^8.

5. 437.5 metre kg.

6. 1 : 2; 15 : 1; 4140000 and 8280000 dynes; 182.9 and 6.1 metres.

XVI (Pages 88–91)

3. 1344×10^7 units of impulse; 120 cm,

4. 21.8 cm; $\frac{1}{14}\sqrt{10}(= 0.226)$ sec.; $\frac{3}{4}$

5. 7.997 cm per sec.; 40775 grammes' wt. nearly.

6. 5.28 metric tonnes wt.

7. The masses move with a velocity of $735\frac{3}{4}$ cm per sec.

8. 327 cm per sec.; $327\sqrt{2}$ cm per sec.

11. $\frac{u}{g}$, where u is the common velocity.

12. $\frac{m}{M+m}$.

13. $\frac{35}{18}$ m; 4 sec. (nearly)

14. The velocities become ultimately equal.

16. 0.172 : 1 approx.

17. 14 m per sec.; 1,960,00 J

18. 10.4 metric tons; 37,037,037 J. **19.** 11.64 metric tonnes.

21. 3520 ft. lb. **22.** $10\frac{10}{39}$ **23.** $\frac{50Rng}{3E}$

24. 1.276 kgf (nearly); 9.354 kgf (nearly)

26. 5 kg m/s every sec.; 5 N; 0.45 kW.

27. 30.37 kgf (nearly).

XVII (Pages 98–99)

1. (1) $490\frac{1}{2}$ cm; 2 sec.; $1962\sqrt{3}$ cm.

(2) $2299\frac{7}{32}$ cm.; 4.33 sec.; $\frac{24525\sqrt{3}}{8}$ cm;

(3) $\frac{8829(2\sqrt{2}+\sqrt{6})}{4}$ cm; 5.795 sec.; $4414\frac{1}{2}$ cm;

(4) $6897\frac{21}{32}$ cm; $7\frac{1}{2}$ sec.; $36787\frac{1}{2}$ cm.

2. (1) 981 cm; (2) 8829 cm; (3) 24525 cm.

3. 2609.58 ... metres; 652.39 ... metres.

4. 4.04 sec.; 20 metres. **6.** $2452\frac{1}{2}$ cm per sec. **7.** $2h$; $2\sqrt{gh}$.

8. 80.5 km per hour at $\tan^{-1}\frac{6}{11}$ (= 28°36′) to the horizon.

9. (1) $\frac{981\sqrt{17}}{2}$ cm per sec. at $\tan^{-1} 4$ (–75°58′) with the horizon.

(2) $\frac{981\sqrt{37}}{2}$ cm per sec. at $\tan^{-1} 6$(= 80°32′) with the horizon.

10. $52974\sqrt{3}$ cm. **11.** 13 sec.; 102024 cm.

13. $1962\sqrt{2}$ cm per sec. at 45° to the horizon.

14. 175 m per sec.; 105 per sec.; 503.4 ft per sec.

15. $1:\sqrt{3}; 1:1$ **17.** (1) 45°; (2) 30°. **18.** 15° or 75°.

XVIII (Page 103)

1. 2 km 299 m $21\frac{7}{3}$ cm; 21.7 sec.

2. At a distance $\frac{V^2}{48}(\sqrt{3}-1)$; $\frac{V^2}{48}$.

3. $2616(\sqrt{3}-1)$ cm; $\frac{2}{3}(3\sqrt{2}-\sqrt{6})$, i.e., 1.2 sec. nearly; 2616 cm.

4. (i) 4905 metres; (ii) 34.335 km.

5. 6631 m and 21.6 sec. nearly; $1306\frac{2}{3}$ m and 20.7 sec. nearly; 1089 m and nearly 22.4 sec.; 1019.2 m nearly 24 sec.

6. $4905(2-\sqrt{2})$ metres; $4905(2+\sqrt{2})$ metres.

8. 84.95 metres; 441.4 metres.

XIX (Pages 106–109)

1. A circle of about 147.15 km radius.

2. About $\tan^{-1}\frac{1}{10}$ (i.e., 5°43′) to the horizon.

3. 99.1 cm; 2.8 m. **4.** 2310 cm

5. In $\frac{1}{20}$th sec. at a point whose horizontal and vertical distances from the first gun are 14.29 … and 8.24 m.

8. 30°. **14.** $2\sqrt{\frac{2h}{g}}\cos\alpha$.

15. The rifle must be pointed at the balloon; the bullet will strike the body when it has fallen 4.9 m.

18. 1.022 kg **19.** 1.66 m; 8.37 m **20.** 83 m; 98.75 m; 68.6 m.

21. $\frac{u}{g}(\sin\alpha \pm \cos\alpha)$ sec., where u is the velocity, and α the angle of projection.

23. 1962 cm per sec.

XX (Pages 113–114)

1. 243 cm.

6. $2\sqrt{13}$ (= 7.2) metres per sec. at $\tan^{-1}\frac{\sqrt{3}}{6}$ (= 16°6′) with the plane.

8. (1) $\frac{7\sqrt{42}}{4}$ (= 11.48) m per sec. at $\tan^{-1}\frac{3\sqrt{3}}{4}$ (52°25′) with the plane.

(2) $\frac{35\sqrt{2}}{4}$ (= 12.38) m per sec. at $\tan^{-1}\frac{3}{4}$ (= 36°52′) with the plane;

(3) $\frac{7\sqrt{57}}{4}$ (= 13.21) m per sec. at $\tan^{-1}\frac{\sqrt{3}}{4}$ (= 23°25′) with the plane.

XXI (Pages 118–120)

1. $4\frac{5}{14}$ and $4\frac{5}{7}$ metres per sec. **2.** $3\frac{2}{3}$ and $5\frac{11}{12}$ metres per sec.

3. The first remains at rest; the second turns back with a velocity of 6 metres per sec.

8. $\frac{1}{2}$

9. (i) The masses are as 3 : 1; (ii) the velocities are as 1 : 2.

11. 5.66 . . . and 2.5 sec.

17. $5\sqrt{5}u(= u \times 11.180\ldots)$ at $\tan^{-1}\frac{1}{2}(= 26°34')$, and $\sqrt{205}u\ (= u \times 14.318\ldots)$ at $\tan^{-1}\frac{3}{14}(= 12°6')$ with the line of centres.

XXII (Pages 124–126)

3. $1839\frac{3}{8}$ cm; 3.464 sec.

4. 8 sec.; $7848\sqrt{3}$ cm.

6. At a distance h from the foot of the tower.

9. At a point distant $\frac{1}{18}$th of the circumference from the starting point.

16. $4el \sin^2 \alpha \cos \alpha$

17. $2\sqrt{3}\ ne(1 + e)$ ft.

19. Draw BN perpendicular to the vertical plane, and produce to C so that $BN = e.\,CN$; the required direction is then AC.

XXIII (Pages 131–132)

1. 1080 gm wt.

2. 38.18

3. 95.45.

5. 981 cm per sec.

6. About 13.4.

7. 1.0245 metric tonnes wt.

8. 2.46 metric tonnes wt.

XXIV (Pages 136–138)

1. 4 kg wt.; $327\frac{\sqrt{6}}{2}$ cm per sec.

4. 2.1 m per sec

6. 11.9 cm

7. 7.4 cm.

8. 15.03 cm.

10. $60\sqrt{\frac{g}{\pi^2}}$ = about 59.75 m/s^2

13. 371 : 369 : 370.

16. $m(g - 4\pi^2n^2b)$; $\frac{1}{2\pi}\sqrt{\frac{g}{b}}$.

18. $\sqrt{2gc}$.

19. $mv^2 : m'v'^2$

20. $\frac{1}{2\pi}\sqrt{\frac{mg}{m'(c - a)}}$.

21. It must be reduced to one quarter of its original value.

22. $1 : \sqrt{2}$; $\frac{\pi}{2}\sqrt{2}$ sec.

23. $\sqrt{\frac{\lambda}{m}\frac{r(r - a)}{a}}$.

25. (1) 0.56 metric tonne's wt. on the inner rail approx.;
(2) 0.78 metric tonne's wt. on the outer rail approx.

XXV (Pages 144–146)

1. (1) 621.2 cm per sec.; 1072×10^4 dynes wt.;
(2) 457.5 cm per sec.; 33625×10^2 dynes wt.

2. 6.64 m per sec.; 15 kg wt. **3.** 420.2 cm per sec.; $3mg$.

4. (1) $490\frac{1}{2}$ cm per sec.; (2) $\frac{981\sqrt{2}}{4}$ cm per sec.; (3) $\frac{327\sqrt{3}}{2}$ cm per sec.; (4) $245\frac{1}{4}$ cm per sec.

5. 6 times the wt. of the particle; 12.192 m per sec.

6. 70 m per sec.; wt. of 350 kg; wt. of 275 kg.

9. $\frac{16}{21}$ of the radius of the circle.

10. $\frac{d}{81}$ and $\frac{16d}{81}$, where d is the diameter of the circle.

11. $e = \frac{1}{2}$. **13.** $7\sqrt{3}m$ lb. wt.; $5\sqrt{3}m$ lb. wt.

14. $\frac{1}{2}\sqrt{ga(28 - 2\sqrt{2})}$ **18.** 2.1 m per sec.; 7.5 cm. **20.** 80 cm nearly.

XXVI (Pages 155–156)

1. (1) $\frac{1}{2}\pi\sqrt{2}$ sec.; (2) $\frac{\pi}{6}$ sec.; (3) 1 sec. **2.** $60\sqrt{2}$, 45, and 30π cm per sec.

3. (1) 30π; (2) 960π and (3) 60 cm per sec.

4. $6\sqrt{10}$ cm per sec. **5.** π sec.; 600 cm sec. units.

7. 25 centimetres nearly. **8.** 101.6 mm; 1.11 sec.

9. $\frac{\pi}{8}\sqrt{2}$ sec. = 0.56 sec.

10. $\pi\sqrt{\frac{am}{\lambda}}$, where a is the unstretched length of the string, λ its modulus of elasticity, and m the mass of the particle.

XXVII (Pages 159–160)

1. 620.9 cm. **3.** 982.62 **4.** (1) 24.8 cm; (2) 6.2 cm; (3) 396.8 cm

5. 330 **7.** 902.3 cm/sec.^{2} **8.** 77756 nearly.

XXVIII (Pages 163–164)

1. 980.54 cm/sec.^{2} **2.** 1.00046 : 1. **3.** About 215.

4. It must be shortened by 0.02 cm.

5. It must be lengthened by 0.0114 cm.

6. 432. **7.** 55. **8.** 981.

9. It loses about 10 sec. **10.** 1490 m; 5 sec. **11.** 1.0005 : 1; 3.061 km.

12. 10.8 sec.; about 0.254 mm. **20.** π sec.; $\frac{g}{64}$; 76.2 mm per sec.

XXIX (Page 169)

1. $\frac{5}{3}$ cm per sec.; $\frac{1}{36}$ cm sec. units.

2. 250 metres per sec.; 6250 cm-sec. units.

3. 500 m; $\frac{5}{36}$ m/sec.^{2} 5. 17.5 m 6. 80.5 metres

8. (1) $\frac{49}{20}$, (2) 1.1858, (3) 352800. 9. 3511303 10. $126\frac{16}{41}$ 11. 10 sec.

XXX (Pages 173–174)

1. $3\frac{1}{3}$ N. 2. 1 dyne; 10 cm-dynes. 3. $\frac{1}{4}$ sec.

5. 8050 m; 300 sec.; 55.4 metric tonnes. 6. 314 metres.

7. 150 m; 1.176 kg. 8. 4.99 kg. 10. 1 : 9; 1 : 3; 2 : 15.

12. $\frac{4}{7} \times 120^4$; 115200 13. $5\frac{5}{49}$ m; $2\frac{2}{49}$ sec.; 8 kg.

14. 245 m; 5 sec.; 2 kg. 15. 12900 m; 21 sec.; 3.6 grammes.

16. 18.21… metres; 5.45 sec.; 4.30… grammes.

17. 1.609 km; 8 minutes; 101.3 metric tonnes.

18. 183 m; $7\frac{1}{2}$ sec.; 545 kg.

19. $756\frac{4911}{4744}$ m; $2\frac{467}{104}$ min. 88 metric tonnes. 20. g kg.

Miscellaneous Examples (Pages 179–188)

1. 4414.5 cm. 2. 176.4 m; 6 sec. nearly. 3. 0.8 cm.

4. $218\frac{3}{4}$ gf.; $168\frac{3}{4}$ gf. 7. 0.74… sec.; 217 : 162 14. $\frac{s}{30n}$.

15. South-west. 18. $\frac{30}{\pi}\sqrt{\frac{\mu g}{a}}$.

20. 60° on each side of the vertical.

27. With an acceleration $g \tan \alpha$ toward the side on which the particle is; sec. a times the weight of the particle.

29. $5\frac{11}{14}$ kgf; $\frac{g}{17}$. 33. $\frac{2M + m}{6M + 5m} g$.

39. $g\left(\frac{1}{P} + \frac{1}{Q} - \frac{4}{R}\right) \div \left(\frac{1}{P} + \frac{1}{Q} + \frac{4}{R}\right)$; $4g \div \left(\frac{1}{P} + \frac{1}{Q} + \frac{4}{R}\right)$

43. $\frac{12}{7}$ times the weight of the man.

47. $\frac{5}{7}\sqrt{5}$ sec.

54. $\frac{5g}{17}$; $2\frac{2}{17}$ kgf; $10\frac{10}{17}$ kgf.

59. $\sqrt{\frac{7ag}{2}}$; at a point where the radius makes an angle of 30 with the horizon.

64. $mg \cos\alpha \dfrac{M + M' - M' \tan\alpha}{M + M' + m\sin^2\alpha}$.

69. The coefficient of friction must be $< \dfrac{m\cos\alpha\sin\alpha}{M + m\cos^2\alpha}$

71. to be deduced using the graph.

72. to be deduced using the graph.

77. 1.8 kg; 10 km per hour.